Human-Earth System Dynamics

Rongxing Guo

Human-Earth System Dynamics

Implications to Civilizations

 Springer

Rongxing Guo
Capital University of Economics
   and Business
Beijing
China

2018 High Talent Program of Beijing Municipal Government Capital University of Economics and Business, Information School, Beijing, China.

ISBN 978-981-13-0546-7   ISBN 978-981-13-0547-4   (eBook)
https://doi.org/10.1007/978-981-13-0547-4

Library of Congress Control Number: 2018941225

Printed on acid-free paper

This Springer imprint is published by the registered company Springer Nature Singapore Pte Ltd. part of Springer Nature
The registered company address is: 152 Beach Road, #21-01/04 Gateway East, Singapore 189721, Singapore

To my new colleagues at the Capital University of Economics and Business, Beijing

Acknowledgements

This book is part of a larger research project supported by the National Science Foundation of China (NSFC) entitled "A Study of China's Industrial Agglomeration: Evolution and the Cultivation of New Driving Forces" (No. 71733001).

Many organizations and individuals have provided generous help while the book was prepared. Specifically, the 2018 High Talent Program of Beijing Municipal Government has enabled me to conduct this research without too many loads of teaching and other academic commitments. I particularly thank Professor Eui-Gak Hwang (Seoul), Professor Xinjian Li (Tokyo), Dr. Francis Lankester (Durham), Dr. Xiaoxuan Lu (Hong Kong), Dr. Matthew Piscitelli (Chicago), Professor Vicky Xiubao Yu (Shanghai), Professor Kaizhong Yang (Beijing), and Professor Zhang Yongze (Beijing)—without their generous assistance and advice, this book would not have been finished, at least not in the present appearance. I must mention my son—his disputing and quarreling with me about everything in his 20s has inspired me with an in-depth, genetic inquiry into the nonlinear behaviors of humans and civilizations.

I am especially grateful to Palgrave Macmillan (now part of Springer Nature) for their kind permission of my reuse of the material of my book "An Economic Inquiry into the Nonlinear Behaviors of Nations" (I have made the usual citations in the text). The content included in the beginning of Chap. 4 is based on a story whose authorship is unknown. The image in Fig. 6.1 is created by Robert A. Rohde —thanks go to the Global Warming Art for its permissions for my use of this image in this book. In addition, I have also adopted the images available at the Wikimedia Commons—an online repository of free-use images (License: CC-BY-SA 3.0)—in Figs. 2.3, 4.1c, 4.2, and 7.1. While every effort has been made to ensure copyright compliance, but if any have been inadvertently overlooked, I will be pleased to make the necessary arrangements at the earliest opportunity.

I have also benefited from many other well-received scholars and authors throughout the world, whose viewpoints on humans, civilizations, and nations have been adopted or cited (all being for review purposes) throughout this book.

They include Robert L. Carneiro, Napoleon Alphonseau Chagnon, Jared Diamond, Yuval Noah Harari, Stephen Lansing, and Charles C. Mann. In addition, the first nourishment for the mind in this book draws on, though my criticism also goes to, the works of the following experts:

- Philip J. Adler (Professor Emeritus at East Carolina University, Greenville, NC);
- Henry Thomas Buckle (1821–1862), an English historian who is remembered for his treating history as an exact science;
- Brian M. Fagan (Professor Emeritus of Anthropology at the University of California, Santa Barbara, CA);
- Marvin Perry (Professor at Baruch College, City University of New York);
- Randall L. Pouwels (Professor of African and Middle Eastern History at the University of Central Arkansas, Conway, AK);
- Chris Scarre (formerly Deputy Director of the McDonald Institute for Archaeological Research, University of Cambridge, now Professor of Archaeology at Durham University, UK); and
- Arnold Joseph Toynbee (1889–1975), British historian, philosopher of history, and author of the 12-volume book entitled *A Study of History*.

Last but not least, the efficient efforts made by Springer Nature, especially those of its Beijing Editorial Office (including Lydia Wang, Li, Leana, and Fiona Wu), have made the publication of this book follow a much smooth process. And thanks are also due to various anonymous reviewers whose useful comments have substantially contributed to the final appearance of this book. Of course, all views and remaining errors in this book are only my own.

Changping and Huairou, Beijing   Rongxing Guo
2018

Contents

List of Figures

List of Tables

Introduction

Existing textbooks and relevant monographs in the subjects of anthropology and history have presented incomplete and sometimes misleading descriptions of how mankind has advanced from the hunter-gatherer society to more complicated cultures. For example, historians have suggested that fertile land and other favorable environmental (geographic) factors have helped Sumerians/Egyptians make a creative leap to the early civilizations along river valleys. However, this is not the real story about civilizations, and many fundamental geographic conditions and cyclic environmental factors that have incentivized humans to develop civilizations have not been presented. Still, anthropologists and historians have highly simplified, if not dismissed, the physical and mental factors of humans that have also influenced the dynamic behaviors of various cultures and civilizations.

Homo sapiens—the species *sapiens* (wise) of the genus *Homo* (man)—have appeared and populated Eurasia, Oceania, and the Americas. However, human and cultural evolutions have followed a complex process with various nonlinear facts. When explaining the rise and fall of the various cultures and civilizations throughout the world, historians have overly emphasized intercontinental and environmental differences. Even if natural and environmental influences on the structure and distribution of world civilizations did exist throughout history, the real stories are not always like what some historians have described in the usual text. The roles that many natural and environmental factors have played during the civilizational era have been quite complicated. These factors can never be simply defined as either "good" *or* "bad"; instead, they are both "good" *and* 'bad.' And their influences on cultures and civilizations each are both "positive" *and* "negative."

It seems that some long-established concepts and theories that relate to history and civilization in existing textbooks are not convincing. For example, the "Fertile Crescent" concept could mislead readers to believe that it was the *good* environment in Mesopotamia that gave birth to the world's first civilization. In addition, existing textbooks have not paid enough attention to human's hard struggles against and creative responses to various challenges and threats. It should be noted that humans have always played, and will continue to play, the most important, if not the only, role in *their* cultural evolutions. All civilizations on Earth are also human civilizations. Without human beings, there would be no civilizations. Therefore, in order to understand the driving forces behind the rise and fall of civilizations, one should first examine the inherent characteristics of humankind per se. Or, at the very least, humans and the environments in which humans have been living should be used as a joint proxy for explaining the whole history of civilizations.

Food surplus or population growth stemming from it might not necessarily lead to cultures and civilizations. Population growth or agglomeration may be helpful to the advancement of civilizations, but it may also destroy, through interethnic conflicts or wars, civilizations. The abundance of materials provided by nature has never been bound to give birth to civilizations. However, necessity is the mother of civilization. In this book, my intent is to bring students and other readers into a world of stories that are either absent from or improperly presented in the usual textbook. They include, for example:

- What were really happening in Africa, the Middle East, and East Asia during the first waves of migration of Homo sapiens?
- What incentivized humans to change their lifestyle and to develop agriculture and other, more complicated cultures and civilizations throughout the world?
- Why were almost all of the world's earliest civilizations based in arid, floods-hit river valleys instead of other, more comfortable environments?
- Why do many indigenous languages in different parts of the world tend to generate vocabularies associated with "wa" or any variant of it? And why do the terms derived from "wa" have same or similar meanings in these languages?
- Why do the European languages each include a large portion of polysyllabic words? Why is Chinese monosyllabic?
- Why have the populations in the Americas, Oceania, and other islands that had been isolated from the Eurasian civilizations during the pre-Columbian era tended to be overweight?
- Why had the New World not been able to create civilizations as powerful as those of the Old World during the pre-Columbian era? Will the New World become a Newer World in the future?
- Why did the Mayans use the so-called Long Count calendar ignoring seasonal changes and not apply the lunar- or solar-based calendars that have been adopted by other civilizations in the Eastern Hemisphere?

Frankly speaking, most, if not all, of the above questions have not been satisfactorily answered (or even not discussed) in the usual text. And, traditional historic approaches are based on either environmental (geographic) or human (behavioral) factors. Instead, this book will try to simultaneously consider both of them in the analysis of the major historic process of human civilization.

This book delves into the factors and mechanisms that may have influenced the dynamic behaviors of civilizations. My narratives and analyses are focused on both environmental (geographic) factors on which traditional historic analyses are based and human (behavioral) factors on which anthropological analyses are usually based. In this book, a few of common ancestral terms are resurrected to help understand the complicated process of human and cultural evolutions throughout the world. Specifically, in almost all indigenous languages throughout the world, "wa" and any variants of it were originally associated with the sound of crying of— and certainly were selected as the common ancestral word with the meanings of "house, home, homeland, motherland, and so on" by—early humans living in different parts of the world.

This book provides many neglected but still crucial environmental and biological clues about the rise and fall of civilizations—ones that have largely resulted from mankind's long-lasting "Win-StayLose-Shift" games throughout the world. The narratives and findings presented at this book are unexpected but reasonable— all of which are what every student of anthropology or history needs to know and does not get in the usual text.

One proposed idea that the early civilizations of the world share some common point of origin has been disproved by most archaeologists. Contacts between Mesopotamia, ancient Egypt, and the Harappa are clearly documented. However, this does not lead us to regard any of them as simply an imitation of the others. Ancient China also had some links with Western Asia, via the steppes of Central Asia. But no archaeological evidence has suggested that the Chinese civilization owes its origin in and substantial contact with any foreign land. There is no evidence for substantial contact between the New and Old Worlds until the arrivals of the Norse in Newfoundland in the late tenth century AD and especially of the Spanish conquistadors in Mexico five centuries later.

Yet both Old World and New World civilizations do have similar agricultural regimes, primitive religions, and urban and state organizations. This has impelled anthropologists and historians to search the common features of human civilizations and the mechanisms behind them.

In this book, unless stated otherwise, wadi is defined as an area on earth that receives freshwater from occasional (seasonable) rainfalls or from any other source (s). This is a wide definition. And, throughout this book, wadis and river valleys will be used interchangeably. More precisely, the term "wadi" refers to valley of any river—permanent or seasonable—as long as it is located in the desert or semidesert climate. Unlike the terms "river" and "river valley," which have different forms in different languages, the term "wadi" remains the same in most, if not all major human languages. When trying to clarify the most important factors contributing to the birth of great civilizations in the world, we will arrange the following arguments or hypotheses:

- That physical weakness may provide incentives (whereas physical advantages may provide disincentives) for humans to develop complex societies from previous simpler ones and
- That favorable environmental and external factors may become disincentives (whereas unfavorable environmental and external factors may become incentives) for humans to advance cultural developments.

While all of the world's greatest indigenous civilizations arose in river valleys, there has not been any systematic explanation for why they did so. It is true that the importance of river water to safeguard an abundant and stable food supply provided an initial wide spectrum economy that triggered the creation of permanent villages. Was this the only condition under which ancient civilizations arose? As a matter of fact, many other geographical environments (such as lakeside, coastal area, and oasis) can also provide an abundant and stable food supply. Then, why did they not give birth to indigenous civilizations that are as strong as those in river valleys?

With regard to the world's indigenous civilizations that arose in river valleys, we will arrange the following arguments or hypotheses:

- That it is cyclical natural disasters (or, more precisely, seasonable river floods) —not other natural factors or disasters—that gave birth to the earliest great civilizations and
- That it is Mesopotamia or Multipotamia—land through which two or more independent rivers run—that served as an ideal hedging mechanism for humans and civilizations to survive and advance.

This book will use both narrative and analytic approaches. More often than not, analytics (focusing on theory and analytical models) and narrative (focusing on data and historical events) each have both advantages and disadvantages in presenting a research project. Historical record provides an ample source of narrative. And narrative matters because it is inherently concerned with causality recognizing that from the historical perspective specific events can yield a multiplicity of equilibria. But narrative alone is insufficient since many questions relate to events that did not take place (or have not yet taken place) or are concerned with the motivations behind why certain behavior or events have not occurred. However, the combination of "analytics" and "narrative" can capture the conviction that data linked to theory are more powerful than either data or theory alone.

Chapter 1
Win-Stay, Lose-Shift: A Survival Rule

Abstract Historians have suggested that human civilization first resulted from comparatively fertile land in Mesopotamia. However, the use of the "Fertile Crescent" may confuse our search of the real factors contributing to the birth of ancient civilizations. In fact, existing college-level textbooks and relevant monographs have presented incomplete and sometimes misleading descriptions of the origin of civilizations. Still, historians and anthropologists have highly simplified, if not dismissed, the initial and environmental conditions under which the world's indigenous civilizations emerged and developed. Indeed, "Win-Stay Lose-Shift" is the survival rule for mankind, and it is always losers who have had incentives to advance the cultures and civilizations throughout the world.

Keywords Human evolution · Civilization · Global history · Wadi (river valley) Zero-sum game

1.1 A Last Tree Climber

In 1974, a skeleton was discovered near the bank of a dry riverbed (called "wadi" in local language) in Hadar—a village in the Awash Valley of the Afar Triangle, Ethiopia. It paints a remarkable picture of early hominids in Africa. Though only a partial skeleton, it is the most well-known hominid skeleton in the world. About 3 million years old, it belongs to Australopithecus afarensis (Latin: "Southern ape from Afar")—an extinct hominid that lived between 3.9 and 2.9 million years ago. A. afarensis is thought to be more closely related to the genus Homo (which includes the modern human species Homo sapiens), whether as a direct ancestor or a close relative of an unknown ancestor, than any other known primate from the same time. "Lucy" was nicknamed after the popular Beatles' song "Lucy in the Sky with Diamonds" that the excavation team, led by palcoanthropologist Donald Johanson of the Cleveland Museum of Natural History, had been listening to on the radio.

Lucy was small, about 1.1 m tall and 27 kg. Her skeleton and teeth show that she had reached maturity, and her species matured young (about 15 or 16 years old—note that the average life expectancy for prehistoric humans was estimated at just 20–35 years). Given her size, predators such as hyenas, jackals, and saber-toothed cats would have posed a threat to Lucy. So, Lucy most likely turned to the trees. Lucy had arms that are slightly longer than those of humans; her arms and legs would have been similar lengths, while humans' legs are longer than their arms. These longer arms and curved hand bones lead us to believe that Lucy would have been an agile tree climber, although some doubt whether she actually used these traits or if they were just evolutionary features left from earlier hominids.

It's possible that Lucy scaled trees only from time to time for safety or that she nested in them every night. According to the nesting habits of chimps, a high place above the ground made her feel safe. She stood up straight, with feet, knees, and hips that are similar to ours. But up close, she had a small head, a brain comparable in size to a chimpanzee's, longer arms and hair covering her body (Cartmill and Smith 2009, p. 151). Bridging the gap between humans and chimps, Lucy had slightly curved fingers and toes, with mobile ankles and shoulders that provided more overhead range of movement. Even with those abilities, she would have been better at walking than climbing.

According to the findings published in the journal *Nature* in 2016, Lucy likely died about 3.2 million years ago after tumbling about 14 m (46 ft) out of a tree. Details may be as follows. She hit the ground, while stretching out her arms to break her fall. John Kappelman, a University of Texas geologist who proposes this hypothesis, called it ironic that the fossil that fueled debate about the role tree-climbing played in human evolution died falling out of one. Perhaps Lucy was asleep or settling in for the night, or perhaps she was spooked by a predator. Maybe she spied some fruit and wanted to forage.[1] Either way, this is what Professor Kappelman believes happened next:

> From 46 feet in the air, Lucy fell out of her tree, fully conscious. She fell toward the ground rapidly at 35 mph and hit feet-first, sending an impact punching through her body that created fractures in her ankles, knees, hip and shoulder. Internal organs were probably punctured by this "hydraulic ram effect." Lucy pitched forward and instinctively put out her arms to break the fall, creating fractures in the bone there as well. It would probably be her final conscious act… She twisted to her right, landing primarily on that side. That twist fractured her neck and tilted her head. Unconscious, broken and bleeding, she lay on the stream bed. If there was water present at the time, it gently moved the body a short distance along, naturally carrying her to a final resting place since members of her own species didn't.[2]

The Afar Triangle (also called "Afar Depression") is a geological depression caused by the Afar Triple Junction, which is part of the Great Rift Valley in East Africa. The region has disclosed fossil specimens of the very earliest hominins; and it is generally thought to be the cradle of all humans. The Depression overlaps the borders of Eritrea, Djibouti and the entire Afar region of Ethiopia; and it contains the lowest point in Africa, Lake Asal, Djibouti, at 155 m below sea level. The Awash River is the main waterflow into the region, but it runs dry during the annual dry season. The northern part of the Afar Depression is also known as the Danakil

---

[1]See Kappelman et al. (2016) for a more detailed assessment.
[2]Cited from Strickland (August 30, 2016).

Depression. The lowlands are affected by heat, drought, and minimal air circulation and contain the hottest places of anywhere on Earth. The Afar Triangle is bordered by the Ethiopian Plateau and escarpment on the west; to the northeast (between it and the Red Sea) by the Danakil block; by the Somalian Plateau and escarpment to the south; and by the Ali-Sabieh block to the south-east.

The Afar Depression is the product of a tectonic triple-rifts junction (the Afar Triple Junction), where the spreading ridges forming the Red Sea and the Gulf of Aden emerge on land and meet the East African Rift (Beyene and Abdelsalam 2005). The Afar Triangle is a cradle source of the earliest hominins. Many important fossil localities exist in the Afar region, including the Middle Awash region and the sites of Hadar (the site of Lucy), Dikika, and Woranso-Mille. These sites have produced specimens of the earliest (fossil) hominins and of human tool culture, as well as many fossils of various flora and fauna. In 1994, near the Awash river in Ethiopia, archaeologists found the then-oldest known human ancestor: A fossilized, almost complete skeleton of a female hominin of 4.4 million years old, which is still more than one million years older than that of Lucy.[3]

Over the course of the past millions of years, regardless of significant climate and environmental variations, most species throughout the world have not experienced any significant changes. For example, the primate lineage is thought to go back at least 65 million years ago (mya), even though the oldest known primates from the fossil record date to about 55 mya, or the Late Paleocene of Africa or the Paleocene–Eocene transition in the northern continents.[4] And the evolutionary patterns have been well described by Charles Darwin in his well-known work "On the Origin of Species by Means of Natural Selection or the Preservation of Favored Races in the Struggle for Life" (Darwin 1859). For example, gray langurs (or Hanuman langurs) are a monkey found in India on the lowlands north of the Godavari and Krishna Rivers and south of the Ganges. They are a social animal, living in groups. Each group is generally dominated by a single male, with many females, though the male must struggle with other males for control of the group. When a male tries to take over a group, there is a violent struggle with the existing male leader. If successful in overthrowing the previous male, infants of the females are then killed (Hrdy 1977). This behavior not only reduces intraspecific competition between the incumbent's offspring and those of other males and increases the parental investment afforded to their own young, but also allows females to become sexually receptive sooner. If a male kills a female's young, she stops lactating and is able to become pregnant again. Similar behavior is also seen in lions, among other species, who also kill young cubs, thereby enabling them to impregnate the females. As males are in a constant struggle to protect their group, those that express infanticidal behavior will contribute a larger portion to future gene pools.

---

[3] See White et al. (2009) for more details.

[4] See Miller et al. (2005) and Williams et al. (2010). Other studies, including molecular clock studies, have estimated the origin of the primate branch to have been in the mid-Cretaceous period, around 85 mya (Lee 1999; and Tavaré et al. 2002).

Have early humans and other species experienced similar evolutionary mechanisms? Maybe they had done so before the civilizational era. Since then, however, humans have entered an era in which intelligence and knowledge play a sweeping role. It is very likely that the mechanism of human evolution of today is quite different from that of millions of years ago when our distant ancestors and other species were not different from each other. Given that all modern humans have the same ancestor in southern Africa, what have incentivized humans to migrate out of Africa and to settle in the rest of the world? In addition, there are both similar and very different geographical and environmental factors in different parts of the world. Then what do these factors matter to the differences of existing human civilizations?

Let us return back to the scene in which humans were struggling for survival in Africa millions of years ago. What was Lucy—a direct ancestor of or a close relative of an unknown ancestor of all modern humans—doing during the last moment of her death? Perhaps humans at that time could not speak any complicated language. But it is very likely that Lucy had already mastered of the simplest language, and that she must have told her partner and/or relatives to immediately abandon their dangerous home in the air and to search a new one.

The earliest humans migrating out of southern Africa must have been losers as compared with those who continued staying in there. Then, why were the winners in southern Africa not able to advance their civilizations as powerful as those that were created by the losers in Eurasia?

1.2   Where Is the Land of Promise?

A civilization can be defined as "any complex society characterized by urban development, social stratification, symbolic communication forms (typically, writing systems), and a perceived separation from and domination over the natural environment by a cultural elite."[5] Historically, civilizations were so-called advanced cultures in contrast to more supposedly primitive or even no cultures. In this broad sense, a civilization contrasts with non-centralized tribal societies, including the cultures of nomadic pastoralists, egalitarian horticultural subsistence Neolithic societies, or hunter-gatherers. According to this logic, a civilized way of life is ultimately linked to conditions coming almost exclusively from intensive agriculture. Sedentary and nomadic communities continued to interact considerably; they were not strictly divided among widely different cultural groups.

For a long history of their existence throughout the world, human beings had lived as hunter-gatherers in small, dispersed places or villages that were, as far as we can tell, completely autonomous. A hunter-gatherer or forager society is one in which most or all food is obtained from wild plants and animals. Not until 5000 BC (or perhaps earlier) did villages begin to aggregate into larger areas. But, once this aggregation process began, it continued at a progressively faster pace, which led,

---

[5]Cited from Boyden (2004, pp. 7–8).

around 4000 BC, to the formation of the first agricultural society in history. In contrast to hunter-gatherers, agriculturists have relied mainly on domesticated species. Then what have driven human beings as hunter-gatherers to become agriculturists? Or, to put it in another way, why did human beings throughout the world decide to abandon their traditional living pattern(s) and to create a more complex or advanced culture (or civilization) thousands of years ago?

The concept "cradle of civilization" is referred to as a place that can incentivize inhabitants to build cities, to create writing systems, to experiment in techniques for making pottery and using metals, to domesticate animals, and to develop complex social structures involving class systems. It is generally believed that civilizations arose independently at several locations in both hemispheres. The term "Fertile Crescent" was popularized by the University of Chicago archaeologist James Henry Breasted (1865–1935) in the 1920s.[6] The Fertile Crescent is a region in western Asia or the Middle East as we now generally call it. It includes Mesopotamia and part of the Levant, which is delimited by the dry climate of the Syrian Desert to the south and the Anatolian highlands to the north. Modern-day countries with significant territory within the Fertile Crescent are Iraq, Jordan, Lebanon, Syria, Israel, and the Palestinian Territories, in addition to the southeastern fringe of Turkey and the western fringe of Iran. Sometimes, the northern portion of the Nile Valley is also included in the Fertile Crescent.

The Fertile Crescent is often considered the cradle of civilization, saw the development of many of the earliest human civilizations, and is the birthplace of writing and the wheel. And why it has been so named is because of its rich soil (as compared with that in the rest of the Middle East and northern Africa). Since its popularization in the 1910s, the term "Fertile Crescent" has been widely adopted by historians and anthropologists. And it is now a must-read in almost all high-school and college classrooms throughout the world. Moreover, the fertility of the crescent-shaped land and the favorable environment there, which are believed to have advantages over those of the surrounding areas, have been assumed to be the major, if not the only, factors contributing to the first civilization in the Eastern Hemisphere. For example, in their college-level textbook *Western Civilization* (10th Edition), Marvin Perry and his colleagues (2012, p. 9) summarize that the following factors could have helped Sumerians/Egyptians make the creative leap to civilization:[7]

- Significance of river valleys to early civilizations

  - Deposit fertile silt on field
  - Provide water for crops
  - Serve as avenues for trade.

---

[6]See, for example, Abt (2011, pp. 193–194, 436) for a more detailed description.

[7]See   http://college.cengage.com/history/west/perry/western_civilization/9e/chapters/chapter1.html (accessed 2016-9-28).

- Human thought and cooperative activity

  - Drain swamps; clear jungles; and build dikes, reservoirs, and canals
  - Construct and maintain irrigation works
  - Formulate and obey rules
  - Develop administrative, engineering, and mathematical skills
  - Keep records and build bureaucracy.

Unfortunately, that the favorable environment of the Fertile Crescent played a sweeping role in the birth of a civilization is a pseudo-proposition. It is true that the first human civilization was born in Mesopotamia or the Fertile Crescent as called by historians. However, the crucial factors contributing to the birth of civilization are not those that have been claimed by many historians and anthropologists. Here, it must be noted that, with regard to humans' contributions to civilizations, most, if not all of what Professor Marvin Perry and his colleagues have suggested above seem to be the consequences (rather than the causes) of a civilization.

More often than not, emphasizing the influences of various favorable natural and environmental factors and conditions cannot help us understand the real driving forces behind cultural evolution and development. It is time to answer if it is soil fertility that led to the birth of civilizations. As a matter of fact, historians' views about the natural and environmental influences on ancient civilizations have varied. For example, unlike Marvin Perry and his colleagues, who have emphasized the *good* environment and its contributions to the Sumerian and Egyptian civilizations, Philip J. Adler and Randall L. Pouwels, in their college-level textbook *World Civilizations* (Seventh Edition), describe the *bad* (catastrophic) events that occurred at the late Ice Age (10,000 years ago) as well as their contributions to the cultural advancement in the Near and Middle East:

> The abundant sources of water and plant foods previously available to humans and animals alike disappeared, forcing Natufians [hunter-gatherers of the Near and Middle East] to congregate in small, semipermanent villages near surviving streams and rivers. Coming after a time when populations had grown dramatically, these catastrophic events forced small groups of these western Asians to adopt more intensive ways of managing their food resources. Basically, this encouraged them to switch from gathering and hunting to planting and domesticating cereals like emmer wheat, einkorn, and barley, which grew in wild forms in their natural environment. Thus, the world's first farming settlements appeared in a section of the Near East called the Levantine Corridor, an arc of land that was endowed with especially high water tables and included much of present-day Turkey, Israel, Syria, and the Euphrates River valley...[8]

It seems that historians have not presented a complete picture about the initial factors (or conditions) promoting humans to give birth to various civilizations. Furthermore, the driving forces behind the dynamic behaviors of humans and civilizations have not been well (sometimes have not been correctly) described in existing textbooks on the subjects of history and civilization. Specifically, had the *good* factors, as suggested by Marvin Perry and his colleagues, or the bad factors, as suggested by

---

[8]Cited from Adler and Pouwels (2014, p. 19).

Philip J. Adler and Randall L. Pouwels, been the only (or major) conditions under which civilizations were created along the Tigris, the Euphrates, and Nile Rivers, why did other large river systems, such as the Amazon, the Yangtze, or the Mississippi—to list but three, not receive great human civilizations?[9]

To be sure, the use of the Fertile Crescent may confuse our search of the real factors contributing to the birth of ancient civilizations. As a matter of fact, the Middle East and North Africa are of mostly dry desert climate. Even the lands in Mesopotamia and along the Nile Valley had (or still have) more disadvantages and risks than many other areas in the rest of the world. Without careful irrigation, the water from the rivers there could not allow the land to produce crops that the farmers need to subsist. Obviously the efficient irrigation there could only be done by experienced agriculturists at that time. Furthermore, Mesopotamia generally lacks in building stones, precious metals and timber—all necessary for the development of civilizations and nations. Regardless of these disadvantageous conditions, Mesopotamia has been known as the cradle of civilization. Therefore, when answering what eventually helped Sumerians to create a complicated social organization (or called civilization) for their own, we must pay attention to both the advantages and the disadvantages and environmental challenges in Mesopotamia. In other worlds, when dealing with the so-called Fertile Crescent, we must keep in mind that there is still a large, infertile desert in the Middle East.

Frankly speaking, when addressing geographical and environmental influences on ancient civilizations in existing textbooks, historians have highly simplified or even dismissed the geological and hydraulic characteristics of the rivers in which existing civilizations were based. While it is still unclear when and how the term was invented, "wadi" should have been a very old—if not the oldest—term that has been used not only by Arabs and Jews but also by many other peoples from the rest of the world since prehistoric times. In some other Indo-European languages, the derivative terms (such as vadi, vado, wade, vadoi) are also used, all referring to as valleys or dry riverbeds or even other geographical terms. For example, in Estonia, there is a village, called Vadi, in Avinurme Parish, Ida-Viru County. Vadi in Gujarati—an Indo-Aryan language evolving from Sanskrit—refers to a farmhouse or a big orchard/garden attached generally with a Hindu temple. Some Latin and Germanic toponyms are derived from ancient Egyptian, Arabic, or Hebrew where wadi is used to mean either a permanent river or a dry valley. For example, Guadalcanal (the principal island in Guadalcanal province of Solomon in the south-western Pacific) is from wadi al-Qanal ("river of refreshment stalls"); Guadalajara (the largest city of the Mexican state of Jalisco in the Western-Pacific area) is known by the Arabic name "wadi al-Hayara" ("river of rocks" or "valley of castles"); and Guadalquivir (the fifth longest river in the Iberian peninsula) derives from "wadi al-Kabir" ("great river").

In South Asia, many place names are called "Wadi" or those with the suffix of "wadi". For example, Wadi is a census town in the Nagpur district in the Indian state of Maharashtra; while in the Gulbarga district in the Indian state of Karnataka,

---

[9]Scholars have defined civilization using various criteria. The use of writing is a common one. Some standard criteria include a class-based society and public buildings.

there is also a census town called Wadi. Sawantwadi (also spelt Savantvadi) was one of the non-salute Maratha princely states during the British Raj (from 1858 to 1947). Now, Sawantwadi is a town in Sindhudurg district of Maharashtra, India. Most Maharashtrians with the surname "Sawant" hail from this town. Appachiwadi is a village in Belgaum district in the southern state of Karnataka, India. Rajwadi is a small hamlet in the village of Nivendi near Ganapatipule in the Ratnagiri district of Maharashtra. In Pakistan, Aplānki Wadi is a town in the Sind region; and "Teri Wadi Wadi Ghoomon" is referred to as Pakistan's Great National Song. As a matter of fact, today's Ravi River—a tributary of the Indus River and the one on which the ancient Indus/Harappan civilization was first based—was known as Iravati (Irawati or Irawadi).

In contrast to the Semitic and Indo-European languages, Chinese belongs to a different phylum. However, the Han-Chinese, with a population of more than one-fifth of the world total, also use "wadi" (though with a writing form differing from those of other languages) to denote "land lower than its surroundings"—similar to the meaning of the Arabic and Indo-European word "wadi." In addition, the pronunciations of the two Chinese characters "wadi," unlike those of most of the others, are almost the same in most Chinese languages or dialects.

It is not accidental that so many indigenous peoples in different parts of the world have used wadi and its various variants in their respective languages. Over the course of the past thousands of years, almost all of the indigenous civilizations were based in the desert or semi-desert places that are fed and damaged by seasonable floods of rivers. Those places were and still are never fertile; but all the natural and hydraulic features there are just those that a wadi possesses. As a matter of fact, "wa" is also a common ancestral word; and it has been widely used in almost all indigenous and even in some secondary languages as such important terms as "house," "home," "homeland," "motherland," and so on. And many wa-derivate terms and names also have meanings similar to them.[10]

Indeed, home and homeland have always been crucial to humans, especially to those who were forced to leave away from their own.

1.3   Winners Stay, Losers Shift

Indeed, human and cultural evolution is a much more complicated process. And the key driving forces behind human and cultural evolutions do not always conform to those included in the Darwinian theory. Indeed, this has been well summarized by Yuval Noah Harari in his book *Sapiens: A Brief History of Humankind*: "Organisms are increasingly shaped by intelligent design rather than the Darwin law of natural selection (Harari 2015, ix). Then, what determines intelligence? How does it relate to the environment in which humans have been living? Of course, these are tough questions. Before trying to answer them, let us first deal with some simpler issues.

---

[10] See Glossary A of Guo (2018).

Compared with human evolution that has lasted for millions of years, civilization has only had a history of thousands of years. Furthermore, humans' evolution and development during the civilizational era have followed a much more complicated mechanism than they did in remote antiquity. Indeed, it is an extremely changing task to explain why it is human beings—not other animals—who created various cultural traditions and civilizations. In addition, many phenomena relating to civilizations have still not been quite clear. For example, of the earliest indigenous civilizations throughout the world, each civilization has different characteristics (in terms of language, writing, and religion, among others) from the others. Then, are there any specific environments or conditions under which the ancient civilizations were born? There must have been different factors or mechanisms that led to the diverse developments of these civilizations there.

Many theories with a racial basis have been thoroughly discredited and thus not dealt with in the usual text. We can also reject the belief that "culture" is an expression of the "genius" of a people, or that it arose through a "historical accident." Such notions make the origin of the culture appear to be something metaphysical or adventitious. In the scientific point of view, the origin of the culture was neither mysterious nor fortuitous. It was not the product of "genius" or the result of chance, but the outcome of a regular and determinate human process. However, ignoring the influences of human behaviors on cultural evolution is also a big mistake. Above all, civilizations are also human-based civilizations. Without humans, there would be no civilizations.

The story of the first peoples of various continents must begin with a global perspective, since it involves some of the most contentious contemporary issues in archaeology worldwide and views that have changed radically in recent decades. It has been generally agreed that the ancestors of the Homo sapiens—the species *sapiens* (wise) of the genus *Homo* (man)—evolved into modern humans around 200,000 years ago in Africa. Their migrations out of Africa occurred some time later. Around 50,000–100,000 years ago modern humans reached the Near East from where they later spread across Eurasia. From the Near East, these populations spread easterly to Asia by 50,000 years ago, and southeasterly to Oceania by 40,000 years ago, when for the first time Homo sapiens reached the territory that had never reached by Homo erectus (meaning "upright man," an extinct species of hominid that lived throughout most of the Pleistocene geological epoch and most recent to 70,000 years ago). Homo sapiens reached Europe around 40,000 years ago and eventually replaced the Neanderthal population living there (see Fig. 1.1).

When the earliest Homo sapiens moved to the Americas and Australia, which is called the last glacial period, sea level was over 100 meters lower than it is now.[11] Therefore, all the major continents (Africa, Asia, Europe, the Americas, and Oceania) were more closely connected via land or ice than they are now. The route and date of migration of the Paleo-Indians (meaning "ancient Indians") to the Americas are disputed. The similarity in the words for sweet potato—an agricultural product that was originally domesticated in the New World—constitutes proof of incidental

---

[11] See Fig. 6.1 of Chapter 6 for more detailed, time-series evidence for the changes of sea level.

Fig. 1.1 A map of the spreading of Homo sapiens throughout the world. *Notes* (1) Figures in boxes are the dates (in thousand years before present) around which Homo sapiens are found to exist. (2) Dotted lines denote that conflicting clues or even two-way spreading exist. *Source* Drawn by author based on Bower (January 27, 2011), Bowler et al. (2003), Croft (2002, p. 261), Dillehay and Ocampo (2015). and Wells and Read (2002, pp. 138–40) and the map of the DNA Testing Center

contact between inhabitants of the Andean region and the South Pacific Islanders that Maori kumara and Easter Island kumara are connected with Quechuan k'umar and Aymara k'umara (Adelaar and Muysken 2004, p. 41). However, it is not certain if the sea-route contact was conducted from the Pacific islands to South America or from South America to the Pacific islands. Nevertheless, it is agreed that, except for a few of populations living in the Amazonia and elsewhere, most Paleo-Indians originated in Central Asia and, after crossing the Beringia land (ice) bridge between eastern Siberia and present-day Alaska around 16,000–13,000 years ago, arrived the Americas around 12,000–10,000 years ago.[12]

In his best-selling book *Sapiens*, the Israeli professor Yuval Noah Harari applied the title "Homo sapiens conquers the globe" (Harari 2015, p. 35) to the human-spreading map (see Fig. 1.1). I am afraid that it is appropriate to use the word "conquer" here. Or, more specifically, the Homo sapiens, even if knowing that their homeland (southern Africa) had not been the best place to live, were really not so ambitious of discovering a newer homeland for themselves. They were not so determined, especially given that they had almost no information about how they would be better off in the new place to which they intended to go. As a matter of fact, in contrast to modern colonists or other later conquerors, earlier humankind, like most of other animals on Earth, has adopted the so-called Win-Stay Lose-Shift strategy in their fighting for survival. This is largely decided by the fact that prehistoric humans

---

[12]See Dillehay (2008, pp. 10–27) and Meltzer (2009) for overviews of issues on initial peopling of the New World.

almost had no information about the new places in which they would eventually settle.

In order to provide evidence that could support the view that humans have adopted the "Win-Stay Lose-Shift" strategy, let us first have a comparison of the adult anthropometric measures between Japan and the UK. Lying at the far extremity of the human world, Japan is an archipelago, which has often been likened to the British Isles. The two island nations have similar economic and environmental conditions with each other; and, above all, the populations of both nations have the same origin (Africa). However, their anthropometric measures are quite different. In the early 2010s, for example, the average adult male and female heights in UK (England) were 177.8 cm (5 ft 10 in) and 164.5 cm (5 ft 5 in), respectively; but in Japan, they were only 170.7 cm (5 ft 7 in) and 158.0 cm (5 ft 2 in), respectively.[13] An average 7-cm (or 3-in) gap is not a small figure. Height, like other phenotypic traits, is determined by a combination of genetics and economic and environmental factors. And since Japan and the UK are not quite different from each other in economic and environmental factors, their difference in adult height can only be explained by genetic factors.[14] In other words, their ancestors might also have different heights before migrating out of Africa. If the result is correct, then what does it imply?

There has been no consistent evidence that explains whether human height has increased or decreased throughout history. However, no matter whichever result is correct, Japan and the UK, given their similar environmental and economic conditions, should have the same or similar trends of human evolution. Therefore, there must be other factors (including the genetic factor) that can explain the Japan–UK difference. It is worth noting that Japan's straight-line distance from the Middle East—perhaps the last stop where all humans (including the Caucasoid and the Mongoloid) migrating out of Africa met—is about 8,800 km (about 5,500 miles), which is more than two times of the UK's (4,100 km or 2,560 miles). The distance difference must explain, at least partially, the adult anthropometric measures between Japan and the UK.

Genetic researchers have found compelling evidence that four out of five (or 80% of) White Europeans can trace their roots to the Near East. And their studies have reported that the majority of British people have forefathers from the Near East (Balaresque et al. 2010). If their results are correct, then we can judge that most Britons, together with their European colleagues, had lived in the Middle East (or, to be more precise, in modern day Iraq and Syria, since the deoxyribonucleic acid, or DNA, samples are collected there) for a long time before migrating out of there later on.

Because the Middle East is the only place connecting the African continent (the earliest origin of humankind) and the rest of the world, all the peoples of the Mon-

---

[13] See http://www.mext.go.jp/component/b_menu/other/__icsFiles/afieldfile/2014/03/28/1345147_1.pdf (accessed 2016-10-18) for Japan's figures and Moody (2013) for the UK's figures.

[14] See, for example, Allen et al. (2010) and Wood et al. (2014) for more detailed descriptions in this regard.

goloid, including the Japanese, should have also stayed at there before their long-distance conquering (to use the term that is applied by Professor Harari) of or retreat (the term I would suggest to use) to the Far East. Now, the problem is that the Mongoloid (including the Japanese), unlike the White Europeans (all belonging to the Caucasoid), do not have any DNA linkage with those in the Middle East. The answer to it might probably be that they were only passers (but did not overstay) there.

Given that there is a fertile crescent in the Middle East and that the journey from it to the Far East was long and dangerous, the Mongoloid must have had a "Great Escape" from the Fertile Crescent. In other words, when or shortly after they arrived in the Middle East, the Mongoloid (including the Japanese people) must have competed or fought with the Caucasoid (including British people), with the former being losers and having to escape and the latter being winners and continuing to stay there. And this result seems to be quite justified since the average height of the East Asians has been relatively shorter than that of the Europeans. Although human height is no longer treated as a factor responsible for winning or losing a war at modern times, it did represent, ceteris paribus, the physical strength of warriors without using weapons. (See Sect. 2.4 in Chapter 2 for a spatial econometric analysis of humans' heights.)

The Mongoloid have short limbs, short noses, flat faces, epicanthic fold, and lower surface. According to Allen's rule, which is an eco-geographical rule posited by Joel Asaph Allen in 1877, the body shapes and proportions of endotherms vary by climatic temperature by either minimizing exposed surface area to minimize heat loss in cold climates or maximizing exposed surface area to maximize heat loss in hot climates.[15] Biologists thus have speculated that the Mongoloid skull type was the result of natural selection, and that, according to Allen's ecological rule, the fat in the eyelids of and the stocky builds of Mongoloids were selected for as adaptations to the cold climate of Central Asia and Siberia (Takasaki et al. 2003; Wade 2006, pp. 119–22). However, they were more likely the result of adaptations of Mongoloid's earlier ancestors to the cold desert (or arid) climate in sub-Saharan Africa or elsewhere—evidence shows that Europeans and Asians were already far from distinct from each other between 45,000 to 7,500 years ago.[16]

The "Win-Stay Lose-Shift" games of humans throughout the world were not one-off; instead, they were repeated games. For example, evidence indicates that the ancestors of the Austronesian peoples spread from the South Chinese mainland to the Taiwan Island about 8,000 years ago, and that it was from this island that seafaring peoples migrated, perhaps about 6,000 years ago, to the entire region encompassed by the Austronesian languages (Gray and Jordan 2000). Early humans might have

---

[15]The rule predicts that endotherms from hot climates usually have ears, tails, limbs, snouts, etc. that are long and thin, whereas equivalent endotherms from cold climates usually have shorter and thicker versions of those body parts—see, for example, Allen (1877), Nudds and Oswald (2007) and Alho et al. (2011).

[16]See Yang and Fu (2018). In addition, the original "Y chromosomal Adam"-DNA sequencing has mutated rarely over 20,000 generations (source: https://www.cambridgedna.com/genealogy-dna-genetic-genealogy.php, accessed 2018-1-21) and some genes only have mutation for every million years (Hahn et al. 2007).

migrated due to many factors such as changing climate and landscape, inadequate food supply and intra-human competition. But it is the "Win-Stay Lose-Shift" principle that has played a key role in the whole process of human and cultural evolutions in the Chinese mainland and beyond.

According to the classic Chinese literature, during the late period of the Shang dynasty (c. 1700—1046 BC), Taibo of Wu—the eldest uncle of King Wen (?—1056 BC) of the Zhou, a dependent state of the Shang—fled from Shang's territory and settled in the area comprising today's southern Jiangsu, northern Zhejiang and Shanghai, bringing along a large section of population and Chinese administrative practices to form the state of Wu there. The state of Wu might have been ruled by a Chinese minority along with the sinified Yue peoples, and the bulk of the population would have remained Yue until later migrations and absorption into the greater Chinese populace, though many likely fled south as well (Henry 2007). From the Zhou dynasty onwards, there were over a dozen of major human migrations from central China (i.e., the Yellow River Valley) to southern China. In each migration wave, newcomers, who had been losers in their homeland, soon became a dominative player in southern China, whereas the natives there now became losers and had to flee to the farther south in due course.

The "Win-Stay Lose-Shift" strategy is a cognitive or behavioral method by which a living being persists to render the same reaction as long as it is being rewarded for doing so, but modifies the reaction whenever it is no longer being rewarded. Precisely, that the strategy has been adopted by humans may not be a consensus. At modern times, especially thanks to the dramatic growth of knowledge and the improvement of communications, there have been other strategies for humans. However, the "Win-Stay Lose-Shift" still has been mankind's prime strategy (see Exercise at the end of this chapter for a scientific description).

Rowan, which is in the same form in almost all European languages, has a long tradition in mythology and folklore. It was thought to be a magical tree in Europe that gives protection against malevolent beings. The tree is also called "wayfarer's tree" or "traveler's tree" because it supposedly prevents those on a journey from getting lost (Eyers 2012, p. 9). Belonging to shrubs or trees in the genus Sorbus of the rose family, the rowans are native throughout the cool temperate regions of the Northern Hemisphere. After having imagined humans' early migrations throughout the world, I could not help making up a story happening at ancient times: A mother was reminding her son, time and again, of keeping the rowan (she gave it to him) before his departure for an unexpected journey.

Nevertheless, according to the "Win-Stay Lose-Shift" theory, it is the losers who have eventually contributed to the change and advancement of cultures and civilizations.

1.4   Losers Become Wadiers

Early intra-human conflicts occurred not just between the Caucasoid and the Mon-goloid in the Middle East 50,000 years ago, but between sub-races in the rest of the world as well. The Mongoloid race can be divided into two varieties or sub-races: the Tunguse or Northern Mongoloid and the Southern Mongoloid. Roughly speaking, some ethnic minorities in northern China and Mongolia are the Northern Mongoloid (with a relatively large size in average), while the vast majority of people (including the Han-Chinese) in southern China and Southeast Asia are the Southern Mongoloid (with a relatively small size in average). The intra-Mongoloid conflicts have almost accompanied the whole history of Asia. And the Han-Chinese have lost most, if not all wars with the Northern Mongoloid.[17] As a result, the Great Wall—running from the west to the east in northern China—had been built by the Chinese to prevent invasions by their northern enemies. The long defeat of the Southern Mongoloid (including the Han-Chinese, all of whom are physically weaker than the Northern Mongoloid) to their northern counterpart, during both prehistoric and historic times, must have had a series of cultural consequences. For example, Chinese language—one that has been used by the Han-Chinese majority in China—is monosyllabic.

To understand the differences between Chinese language and those of the Indo-European and other phylums, we need to investigate the initial conditions under which all these languages were born. With regard to the specific origin of the Mongolic and the associated tribal languages, linguists have traditionally proposed a link to the Tungusic and Turkic language families, including a broader group of Altaic languages. No matter whether they are correct or not, the following are certain that the Southern Mongoloid (including the Han-Chinese) were (and still are) physical weaker than the Northern Mongoloid; that, since the scarcity of necessities had widely existed in the hunter-gatherer society, the weaker Chinese population must have been forced to move away from their old homeland; and that the Chinese have created a different, monosyllabic language.[18] Of course, there are still many other factors that have made the Chinese civilization one of the earliest and most influential civilizations in Asia.

Let us return back to the Japanese case. In Japanese, "Wa" refers to as "Japan, Japanese." Its Chinese character 倭 (meaning "little person; dwarf") is the oldest recorded name of Japan. The custom of writing "Japan" as 倭 ended during the Tang Dynasty (AD 618–907). Japanese scribes coined the name Nihon or Nippon (mean-ing "land of the rising sun") around AD 608–645 and replaced Wa 倭 with a more flattering Wa 和 (meaning "harmony; peace, and balance") around AD 756–757 (Carr 1992). In current Japanese usage, Wa 倭 ("old name for Japan") is replaced by a sound-like character Wa (和). In marked contrast, Wa 和 is a common adjec-

[17]Note that the classification of Northern and Southern Mongoloid only applied to the prehistoric era. In modern times the Han-Chinese, especially those who live in northern China, have been classified as 'Northern Mongoloid'.

[18]See Sect. 4.3 in Chapter 4 for an in-depth discussion about the environmental influences on China's Han language and its various dialects.

tive in compounds like Washoku (Japanese cuisine), Wafuku (Japanese clothing), Washitsu (Japanese-style room), Waka (Japanese-style poetry), and Washi (traditional Japanese paper).

Even though Japan has borrowed many Chinese characters in its language, Japanese and Chinese belong to different language families. Above all, none of the Chinese characters adopted as the names of the Japanese nation can represent the original meaning of the latter. Then, what is the original meaning of "wa" in Japanese? Usually, and compared with humans' creation of languages, giving names for specific nations has a much shorter history. And the term "wa," as will be discussed elsewhere in this book, must be a very old, perhaps the oldest, human language—it should have existed far before the like-sounding Chinese characters were adopted as the name of Japan. In addition, the Japanese term "kawa" (sometimes, "gawa"; all in the Chinese character "川" (or 巛 in its old form) meaning river(s) or plain in Chinese) refers to as river. In Japanese, "ka" is a kana either in hiragana or in katakana, which represents one mora. The shapes of these kana both originate from the Chinese character "jia" (meaning add, additional). Thus, it is very reasonable to believe that the original meanings of Wa (name of Japan) and Kawa (river in Japanese) are not different from each other.

There is still another possibility that the Japanese call their nation "Wa" just follows what the Chinese called China at ancient times (or vice versa). The abbreviated name for China and Chinese nation is now called "Hua" in Mandarin Chinese. Since "hua" is read "wa" and "wo" in Cantonese and Wu (both as China's two earliest languages spoken by Han-Chinese), respectively, it is very likely that the Chinese nation "Hua" was read as "wa" at ancient times. Dating back to the 2nd millennium BC, Chinese characters are now perhaps the oldest writing language that is still being used in the world. Each being logographic and monosyllabic, the Chinese characters were or still are used in the writing of Japanese, Korean, and some other Asian languages.

In the Chinese term "wadi" (meaning "land lower than its surroundings"), the old Chinese character for "wa" (洼) is written as 窪. It is also interesting to note that the latter Chinese character includes the same component as that of a set of Chinese characters that once played or are still playing crucial roles in the Chinese civilization. These Chinese characters include family or home (家, called "jia" in Mandarin Chinese), room (室, called "shi"), treasure (宝, called "bao"), government official (官, called "guan"), palace (宫, called "gong"), wealth (富, called "fu"), and so on. Here, the common component of all these characters is 宀 which is originally written as 宀 (representing a house or home). To this end, and witnessed by their meanings, most of these Chinese characters are related to those that have been either highly regarded by or of vital importance to the Chinese populations in China.

Then, why was the Chinese character "wa" (窪) also created as the one crucial to the ancient Chinese? The only answer seems to be that wadis were playing a crucial role in the Chinese daily life at ancient times. Let us first look at the pictographic meanings of the Chinese character "wa" (窪):

⌒ denotes "house" or "home",
氵 denotes "water" and
圭 denotes "land" or "soil."

Oops! They are all what were (and still are) needed by agriculturalists. And the wadis are particularly ideal for agriculture in desert or semi-desert places.

It is generally recognized that all Native Americans originated in Eurasia. Belonging to the Mongoloid or a sub-group of it, the Native Americans were even unluckier than the Japanese who had been losers as compared with their Eurasian counterparts before leaving the Eurasian continent, and therefore, they had been losers before settling in the Americas. As will be discussed in the next chapter, physically weaker populations usually have more incentives to develop their cultures including languages. Iowa is a state in the north-central USA, bordered by many rivers including the Mississippi River on the east and the Missouri River and the Big Sioux River on the west. The Iowa or Ioway is a Native American Siouan people. Today, they are enrolled in either of two federally recognized tribes, the Iowa Tribe of Oklahoma and the Iowa Tribe of Kansas and Nebraska.

Iowa means "[my/our] beautiful land," suggesting that the syllable "wa" has the meanings similar to those in the Chinese and Japanese languages. Chiwere is a Siouan language originally spoken by the Missouria, Otoe, and Iowa peoples, who originated in the Great Lakes region. Like Japanese in Asia and many other indigenous languages in Africa and Andean South America, Chiwere also frequently use the syllable "wa," and there are several intransitive verbs that take the wa-prefix idiomatically, wherein the prefix has no literal meaning (Whitman 1947). The current Ojibwe term for the Sioux and related groups is Bwaanag (singular Bwaan), meaning "roasters" (Ningewance 2009, p. 81). Presumably, this refers to the style of cooking the Sioux used in the past. The Ojibwe language is also known as Ojibwemowin and is still widely spoken, although the number of fluent speakers has declined sharply. The language belongs to the Algonquian group and is descended from Proto-Algonquian. Ojibwemowin is the fourth-most spoken native language in the USA and Canada, after Navajo, Cree, and Inuktitut.

According to the Ojibwe oral history and from the recordings in birch bark scrolls, the Ojibwe people traded widely across the continent for thousands of years as they migrated, and knew of the canoe routes to move north, west to east, and then south in the Americas (Anthony 2007, p. 102). Early legends indicate that, 500 years ago, the Ojibwa lived near the mouth of the Saint Lawrence River. In about 1660, they migrated westward, guided by a vision of a floating seashell referred to as the sacred miigis. At the Straits of Mackinac, the channel of water connecting Lake Huron and Lake Michigan, the vision ended, and the Anishinabe divided into three groups. One group, the Potawatomi, moved south and settled in the area between Lake Michigan and Lake Huron. A second group, the Odawa (also called Ottawa), moved north of Lake Huron. A third group, the Ojibwa, settled along the eastern shore of Lake Superior. Because of this early association, the Potawatomi, the Odawa, and the Ojibwa were part of a long-term tribal alliance called the "Council of Three Fires," which fought other peoples (Williamson and Roberts 2004, p. 102).

No matter whatever languages are spoken, all human beings are Homo sapiens, have the same ancestor in Africa, and thus inherit the same human gene. Above all, the ancestors of humans throughout the world were in fact not as different from each other as we are today, linguistically and religiously. Lucy is generally recognized as a direct ancestor of or a close relative of an unknown ancestor of all modern humans. Even if it is impossible for us to clarify what was Lucy doing during the last moment of her death. But if Lucy could use the simplest language (or voice), she must be able to pronounce "wa."

It has been generally believed that "ma" and "pa" were among the first words that humans have spoken. These words are the first word-like sounds made by babbling babies (babble words), and parents tend to associate the first sound babies make with themselves and to employ them subsequently as part of their baby-talk lexicon. However, after a further comparison of all the baby-talk lexicon, I began to believe that "wa" should have been the first word that humans spoke. The crosslinguistic similarities of the syllable "wa" should have resulted from the nature of language acquisition.

As of 2016, the surname "Wadi" has been found to have users in at least 76 countries, covering all the five continents (Africa, Asia, Europe, Oceania, and the Americas), with Jordan, Iraq, Sudan, Libya, Myanmar, Syria, Malawi, Grenada, Saudi Arabia, and Kuwait having the highest frequencies.[19] In addition, hundreds of surnames that have been used throughout the world have similarities with the term "wadi." The following surnames only include a small portion of the variants of "wadi":

Waad, Waadhi, Waadi, Wad, Wada, Wadai, Wadd, Waddeii, Waddi, Waddia, Waddie, Wade, Wadei, Wadh, Wadhi, Wadia, Wadiaa, Wadiae, Wadiah, Wadie, Wadih, Wadii, Wadiia, Wadio, Wadioo, Wadiou, Wadiu, Wado, Wadt, Wadu, Wadui, Wadw, Wady, Wadyi, Waed, Waedi, Wahd, Wahdai, Wahdi, Waid, Waidi, Wait, Waod, Watd, Wati, Waud, Waudi, Wawd, Wayd, and Waydi…

As a matter of fact, "wa" was first derived from the sound of crying of humans. Crying is believed to be an outlet or a result of a burst of intense emotional sensations, such as agony, surprise, or joy. This theory is more plausible as it explains why people cry during cheerful events as well as during very painful events. Have not babies been accompanied by their crying? Have not human evolutions and cultural developments experienced both cheerful and painful events? Have not the history of civilizations been also the one including a series of cheerful and painful events of our humans as both winners and losers?

In his book *A Study of History*, Toynbee believed that "Man achieves civilization, not as a result of superior biological endowment or geographical environment, but as a response to a challenge in a situation of special difficulty which rouses him to make a hitherto unprecedented effort" (Toynbee 1987, p. 570). Yes, humans who have created various civilizations throughout the world have experienced numerous painful events as well as tearful cries. It is the crying that occurred frequently in the lives of humans at critical and painful events that induced humans to first create the

---

[19]Source: http://forebears.co.uk/surnames/wadi (accessed 2016-10-31).

syllable "wa" among many other syllables. And many words derived from "wa" have been selected by humans as being most closely related to their properties or even themselves.[20]

Indeed, human beings have adopted the "Win-Stay Lose-Shift" strategy throughout history. However, human nature is only one of the key factors contributing to the birth of ancient civilizations. Other factors, especially the environment, have also mattered. In fact, a "Win-Stay Lose-Shift" strategy is entirely plausible from the socioeconomic point of view.

Over the course of the past thousands of years, cultures and civilizations have experienced dramatic changes throughout the world, especially in places where frequent intercultural contacts and other challenging events relating to human–environment interaction have occurred. However, ample evidence about the origin and evolution of mankind can still be found in many early, indigenous civilizations, which thus enables us to conduct an in-depth, more consistent study of human behaviors in the rest of the book.

1.5 Exercise: How to Win at Rock–Paper–Scissors

In December 2010, researchers at Zhejiang University, China started a joint research project on the Rock–Paper–Scissors game. Professor Zhijian Wang and his colleagues carried out their experiments with 360 university students by dividing them into 60 groups of six players each. In each group, the players conducted 300 rounds of "Rock–Paper–Scissors" game against each other with their actions being recorded.

A zero-sum hand game, rock–paper–scissors is usually played between two people, in which each player simultaneously forms one of three shapes with an outstretched hand. These shapes are "rock" (a simple fist), "paper" (a flat hand), and "scissors" (a fist with the index and middle fingers together forming a "V"). The game has only three possible outcomes: A player who decides to play rock will beat another player who has chosen scissors (rock crushes scissors) but will lose to one who has played paper (paper covers rock); a play of paper will lose to a play of scissors ("scissors cut paper"). If both players choose the same shape, the game is tied and is usually replayed to break the tie. The game is often used as a choosing method in a way similar to coin flipping, drawing straws, or throwing dice. Unlike truly random selection methods, however, rock–paper–scissors can be played with a degree of skill by recognizing and exploiting non-random behavior in opponents.[21]

The research of Professor Wang and his colleagues shows that the strategy of real players looks random on average but actually consists of predictable patterns that a wily opponent could exploit to gain a vital edge. As an incentive, the winners were

---

[20] See Glossary B and C of Guo (2018) for the lists of ethnic groups with wa-prefix and wa-suffix names, respectively.

[21] See Fisher (2008, p. 94) for a more detailed description of the rock–paper–scissors game and its influences on everyday life.

paid in local currency in proportion to the number of their victories. To test how this incentive influenced the strategy, Wang and his colleagues varied the payout for different groups. Their result, published in July 2014 by the *Scientific Reports* and selected as the "Best of 2014: How to Win at Rock-Paper-Scissors" by the *MIT Technology Review* on December 24, 2014, reveals a surprising pattern of behavior:

> On average, the players in all the groups chose each action about a third of the time, which is exactly as expected if their choices were random. But these researchers found that players who win tend to stick with the same action while those who lose tend to switch to the next action in a clockwise direction (that is, from Rock to Paper and to Scissors) and those who tie tend to switch to the next action in a counter-clockwise direction (that is, from Scissors, to Paper, to Rock).[22]

References

Abt J (2011) American Egyptologist: the life of James henry breasted and the creation of his oriental institute. University of Chicago Press, Chicago

Adelaar W, Muysken P (2004) The languages of the andes. Cambridge University Press, Cambridge

Adler PJ, Pouwels RL (2014) World civilizations, 7th edn. Wadsworth Publishing, Boston, MA

Alho JS, Herczeg G, Laugen AT, Rasanen K, Laurila A, Merila J (2011) Allen's rule revisited: Quantitative genetics of extremity length in the common frog along a latitudinal gradient. J Evol Biol 24(1):59–70

Allen HL, Estrada K, Lettre G et al (2010) Hundreds of variants clustered in genomic loci and biological pathways affect human height. Nature 467(7317):832–888

Allen JA (1877) The influence of physical conditions in the genesis of species. Radic Rev 1:108–140

Anthony D (2007). The horse, the wheel and language. Princeton University Press Princeton, NJ

Balaresque P, Bowden GR, Adams SM, Leung H-Y, King TE, Rosser ZH, Goodwin J, Moisan J-P, Richard C, Millward A, Demaine AG, Barbujani G, Previderè C, Wilson IJ, Tyler-Smith C, Jobling MA (2010) A predominantly Neolithic origin for European paternal lineages. PLoS Biol 8:e1000285. https://doi.org/10.1371/journal.pbio.1000285

Beyene A, Abdelsalam MG (2005) Tectonics of the afar depression: a review and synthesis. J Afr Earth Sc 41(1–2):41–59

Bower B (January 27, 2011) Hints of earlier human exit from Africa: stone tools suggest a surprisingly ancient move eastward. Sci News. https://www.sciencenews.org/article/hints-earlier-human-exit-africa. Accessed 5 Oct 2016

Bowler JM, Johnston H, Olley JM, Prescott JR, Roberts RG, Shawcross W, Spooner NA (2003) New ages for human occupation and climatic change at Lake Mungo, Australia. Nature 421:837–840

Boyden SV (2004) The biology of civilization: understanding human culture as a force in nature. University of New South Wales Press, Sydney

Carr M (1992) Wa 倭 Wa 和 Lexicography. Int J Lexicogr 5(1):1–30

Cartmill M, Smith FH (2009) The human lineage. Wiley-Blackwell, Hoboken, NJ

Croft W (2012). Verbs: aspect and causal structure (Oxford Linguistics) Oxford: Oxford University Press

Darwin C (1859) On the origin of species by means of natural selection or the preservation of favored races in the struggle for life, 1st edn. John Murray, London

Dillehay TD (2008) Early population flows in the Western Hemisphere. In: Holloway TH (ed) A companion to latin American history. Blackwell, Malden, MA, pp 10–27

---

[22] See Wang et al. (2014) for more details about this research.

Dillehay TD, Ocampo C (2015) New archaeological evidence for an early human presence at Monte Verde, Chile. PLOS ONE, 10 (November 18), e0141923. https://doi.org/10.1371/journal.pone. 0141923

Eyers J (2012) Don't shoot the Albatross!: nautical myths and superstitions. Adlard Coles Nautical, London

Fisher L (2008) Rock, paper, scissors: game theory in everyday life. Basic Books, New York

Gray RD, Jordan FM (2000) Language trees support the express-train sequence of Austronesian expansion. Nature 405:1052–1055

Guo R (2018) The civilizations revisited: the historians may be wrong, really. University Press, Hong Kong

Hahn MW, Han MV, Han SG (2007) Gene family evolution across 12 Drosophila genomes. PLoS Genet 3(11):e197. https://doi.org/10.1371/journal.pgen.0030197

Harari YN (2015) Sapiens: a brief history of humankind. Harper, New York

Henry E (2007). The submerged history of Yuè. Sino-Platonic Papers, No. 176. http://sino-platonic. org/complete/spp176_history_of_yue.pdf. Accessed 4 Mar 2017

Hrdy SB (1977) Infanticide as a primate reproductive strategy. Am Sci 65(1):40–49

Kappelman J, Ketcham RA, Pearce S, Todd L, Akins W, Colbert MW, Feseha M, Maisano JA, Witzel A (2016) Perimortem fractures in Lucy suggest mortality from fall out of tall tree. Nature 537(7621):503–507

Lee M (1999) Molecular clock calibrations and metazoan divergence dates. J Mol Evol 49(3):385–391

Meltzer D (2009) First Peoples in a new world: colonizing ice age America. University of California Press, Berkeley, CA

Miller ER, Gunnell GF, Martin RD (2005) Deep time and the search for anthropoid origins. Am J Phys Anthropol 128:60–95

Moody A (2013) Adult anthropometric measures, overweight and obesity. www.hscic.gov.uk/ catalogue/PUB13218/HSE2012-Ch10-Adult-BMI.pdf. Accessed 18 Oct 2016

Nudds RL, Oswald SA (2007) An interspecific test of Allen's rule: Evolutionary implications for endothermic species. Evolution 61(12):2839–2848

Ningewance PM (2009) Zagataagan, A Northern Ojibwe Dictionary, Anishinaabemowin Ikidowinan gaa-niibidebii'igadegin dago gaye ewemitigoozhiibii'igaadegin, Ojibwe-English (Vol. 2). Sioux Lookout, ON, Canada: Kwayaciiwin Education Resource Center

Perry M, Chase M, Jacob J, Jacob M, Von Laue TH (2012) Western civilization—ideas, politics, and society (Volume I: To 1789), 10th edn. Wadsworth Publishing, Boston, MA

Strickland A (August 30, 2016) How did Lucy, our early human ancestor, die 3 million years ago? CNN. http://edition.cnn.com/2016/08/29/health/lucy-early-human-ancestor-cause-of-death/index.html. Accessed 22 Oct 2016

Takasaki Y, Loy SF, Juergens HW (2003) Ethnic differences in the relationship between bioelectrical impedance and body size. J Physiol Anthropol Appl Hum Sci 22:233–235

Tavaré S, Marshall CR, Will O, Soligo C, Martin RD (2002) Using the fossil record to estimate the age of the last common ancestor of extant primates. Nature 416(6882):726–729

Toynbee AJ (1987) A study of history, vol I. Oxford University Press, Oxford

Wade N (2006) Before the dawn: recovering the lost history of our ancestors. Penguin Publishing, New York

Wang Z, Bin X, Zhou H-J (2014) Social cycling and conditional responses in the Rock-Paper-Scissors game. Scientific Reports, 4, 5830. http://arxiv.org/format/1404.5199v1. Accessed 22 Jan 2016

Wells S, Read M (2002) The journey of man—a genetic odyssey. Random House, New York

Whitman W (1947) Descriptive grammar of Ioway-Oto. Int J Am Linguist 13(4):233–248

White TD, Asfaw B, Beyene Y, Haile-Selassie Y, Owen Lovejoy C, Suwa G, WoldeGabrie G (2009) Ardipithecus ramidus and the paleobiology of early hominids. Science, 326(5949):75–86

Williams BA, Kay RF, Kirk EC (2010) New perspectives on anthropoid origins. Proc Natl Acad Sci 107(11):4797–4804

Williamson P, Roberts J (2004) First nations peoples, 2nd edn. Emond Montgomery Publications, Toronto

Wood AR, Esko T, Yang J, Vedantam S, Pers TH, Gustafsson S, Goddard ME, Abecasis GR, Chasman DI, Goddard ME, Visscher PM, Hirschhorn JN, Frayling TM (2014) Defining the role of common variation in the genomic and biological architecture of adult human height. Nat Genet 46(11):1173–1186

Yang MA, Fu Q (2018) Insights into modern human prehistory using ancient genomes. Trends in Genetics 34(3):184–196

Chapter 2
Human Thermodynamics and Culture (I)

Abstract Why did humans begin their first cultural change? This could likely happen only after humans—especially those who were the most physically inferior—found that the environment in which they were living had changed or that they could not compete with other, stronger carnivores. During this process, humans began to learn how to use simple tools and to create more complicated cultural traditions. As a result of population growth on the one hand and of the constraints in living spaces and resources available on the other hand, some groups of humans began to migrate out of Africa. Existing archaeological findings suggest that Homo sapiens existed in environmentally and geographically diverse areas. Of course, this has been the result of "natural selection" of human beings and has followed the so-called Win-Stay Lose-Shift principle. However, historians and anthropologists have highly simplified, if not dismissed, the biological factors that may have decided or influenced the dynamic behaviors of humans and civilizations.

Keywords Human evolution · Civilization · Global history
Human thermodynamics · Intelligence quotient (IQ)

2.1 From Lamarck to Darwin

On August 1, 1744, a boy was born in a big, impoverished aristocratic family in a small village in Bazentin, Picardy, northern France. It is Jean-Baptiste Lamarck who would have become a soldier, biologist, academic, and an early proponent of the idea that evolution occurred and proceeded in accordance with natural laws. At that time, male members of the Lamarck family—like those of other French families—traditionally served in the French army. Lamarck's eldest brother was killed in combat at the Siege of Bergen op Zoom, and two other brothers were still in service when Lamarck was in his teenage years. Yielding to the wishes of his father, Lamarck enrolled in a Jesuit college in Amiens in the late 1750s. Unfortunately, when Lamarck was at the age of 16, his father died.[1]

---

[1] In what follows in this section, unless stated otherwise, all biographical information about Jean-Baptiste Lamarck is based on Packard (1901, Chap. I).

As the 11th child of his family, Lamarck had to leave school and to live on his own. He then bought himself a horse and rode through the wooded hills and valleys to join the French army, which was in Germany at the time. Though physically weaker than his colleagues, Lamarck showed great courage on the battlefield in the Pomeranian War with Prussia, and he was even nominated for the lieutenancy. Lamarck's company was left exposed to the direct artillery fire of their enemies and was quickly reduced to just fourteen men—with no officers. One of the men suggested that the puny, seventeen-year-old volunteer should assume command and order a withdrawal from the field; but although Lamarck accepted command, he insisted they remain where they had been posted until relieved.

When their colonel reached the remains of their company, this display of courage and loyalty impressed him so much that Lamarck was promoted to officer on the spot. However, in the following years, Lamarck was not lucky. He sustained an inflammation in the lymphatic glands of the neck, and he was sent to a hospital in Paris where he underwent a complicated operation and continued his treatment for a year. He was awarded a commission and settled at his post in Monaco. It is there that he encountered *Traité des plantes usuelles*, a botany book by James Francis Chomel. With a reduced pension of only 400 francs a year, Lamarck resolved to pursue a profession. He attempted to study medicine and supported himself by working in a bank office. Lamarck studied medicine, but gave it up four years later. He was interested in botany.

After his visits to the Jardin du Roi, he became a student under Bernard de Jussieu—a notable French naturalist. Under Jussieu, Lamarck spent ten years studying French flora. In 1778, he published some of his observations and results in a three-volume work, titled *Flore françoise*. Lamarck's work was respected by many scholars, and it launched him into prominence in French science. Georges-Louis Leclerc, Comte de Buffon (1707–1788), one of the top French scientists of the day, mentored Lamarck and helped him gain membership to the French Academy of Sciences in 1779 and a commission as a Royal Botanist in 1781, in which he traveled to foreign botanical gardens and museums.

Lamarck began as an essentialist who believed species were unchanging; however, after working on the molluscs of the Paris Basin, he grew convinced that transmutation or change in the nature of a species occurred over time. He set out to develop an explanation, and on May 11, 1800, he presented a lecture at the *Muséum national d'histoire naturelle* in which he first outlined his newly developing ideas about evolution. In 1802, Lamarck published *Hydrogéologie* and became one of the first to use the term biology in its modern sense. In that year, he also published *Recherches sur l'Organisation des Corps Vivants*, in which he drew out his theory on evolution.[2]

Lamarck employed several mechanisms as drivers of evolution. He used these mechanisms to explain the two forces he saw as comprising evolution: a force driving animals from simple to complex forms and a force adapting animals to their local

---

[2]See Osborn (1896, pp. 159-60) and Coleman (1977, pp. 1–2). Although Lamarck was not the first thinker to advocate organic evolution, he was the first to develop a truly coherent evolutionary theory (Gould 2002, p. 187).

environments and differentiating them from each other. For example, according to Lamarck, the giraffe's long neck was an "acquired characteristic," developed as generations of ancestral giraffes strove to reach the leaves of tall trees. Lamarck believed that these forces must be explained as a necessary consequence of basic physical principles, favoring a materialistic attitude toward biology.

Lamarck is usually remembered for his belief in the inheritance of acquired characteristics and the use/disuse model by which organisms developed their characteristics. His contribution to evolutionary theory consisted of the first truly cohesive theory of evolution, in which an alchemical complexifying force drove organisms up a ladder of complexity, and a second environmental force adapted them to local environments through use and disuse of characteristics, differentiating them from other organisms (Gould 2002, p. 187).

Lamarck constructed one of the first theoretical frameworks of organic evolution. However, in those times, there was no scientific evidence to prove the concept of evolution. It is in the nineteenth century that Charles Darwin put forth the theory of natural selection that is widely accepted by scientists and the general public. While Lamarck's theory was generally rejected during his lifetime, Stephen Jay Gould—an evolutionary biologist and historian of science and professor at Harvard University and New York University—argues that Lamarck was the "primary evolutionary theorist," in that his ideas, and the way in which he structured his theory set the tone for much of the subsequent thinking in evolutionary biology, through to the present day (Gould 2002, pp. 170–197).

In his book *On the Origin of Species* (3rd–6th editions), Charles Darwin praised:

> [Lamarck] first did the eminent service of arousing attention to the probability of all change in the organic, as well as in the inorganic world, being the result of law, and not of miraculous interposition. Lamarck seems to have been chiefly led to his conclusion on the gradual change of species, by the difficulty of distinguishing species and varieties, by the almost perfect gradation of forms in certain groups, and by the analogy of domestic productions. With respect to the means of modification, he attributed something to the direct action of the physical conditions of life, something to the crossing of already existing forms, and much to use and disuse, that is, to the effects of habit.[3]

During the last decade of his life, Lamarck was blind. When he died in Paris on December 18, 1829, his family was so poor that they had to apply to the Academie for financial assistance and that Lamarck's books and the contents of his home were sold at auction.[4] However, Lamarck was rich in making theories. And all Lamarck did in his life span has provided some evidence that supports the hypothesis that a man who has disadvantages in one aspect may still have other advantages. Above all, his personal experience did show that the success or failure of a man has nothing to do with the initial conditions of his or of his family.

---

[3]Cited from http://biology.ucsd.edu/research/faculty/_example-katie.html. Accessed 2014-11-22.

[4]See http://fineartamerica.com/featured/1-jean-baptiste-lamarck-french-naturalist-science-source.html. Accessed 2014-11-22.

Charles Robert Darwin—a naturalist and geologist, best known for his contributions to evolutionary theory—was born in Shrewsbury, Shropshire, England, on the February 12, 1809.[5] At the age of nine, Darwin entered Anglican Shrewsbury School. Then, he was sent to Edinburgh to study medicine and, in 1825, became an apprentice to his father, a doctor—all which he hated. But in Edinburgh, Darwin met a freed black slave who told him exciting tales of the South American rainforest, including that birds inhabiting different islands had slight difference in their features.

A final attempt at educating Darwin was made in 1827—he was sent to the University of Cambridge. His father enrolled him in a Bachelor of Arts course at Christ's College, Cambridge, to qualify as a clergyman but Charles Robert Darwin preferred riding and shooting to studying. During that period, he loved to collect plants, insects, and geological specimens, guided by his cousin William Darwin Fox, an entomologist. His scientific inclinations were encouraged by his professor, John Stevens Henslow (1796–1861)—a botany expert in Cambridge. Professor Henslow was instrumental, despite heavy paternal opposition, in securing a place for Darwin as a naturalist on the surveying expedition of HMS Beagle to Patagonia from 1831 to 1836.

Puzzled by the geographical distribution of wildlife and fossils he collected on the voyage, Darwin began detailed investigations and in 1838 conceived his theory of natural selection (Desmond and Moore 1991, pp. 263–274). During this five-year expedition, Darwin obtained intimate knowledge of the fauna, flora, and geology of many lands, which equipped him for his later investigations. In the Galápagos islands (eastern Pacific Ocean), he identified varied species of finches that differed in their beak shape and size. This difference in the beak was related to the foods available in that particular region. Contrary to this, he observed only one species of finches in South America. He assumed that the species might have evolved from the species found in South America.

According to him, the original species of finches, after arriving at the islands, were dispersed in varied environmental conditions. In due course of time, the anatomy of the birds was modified naturally as an adaptation to the prevailing conditions. In simpler terms, they were modified for better access to food, thus increasing their survival rate for reproduction. For example, a species that possessed beak was best-suited for consuming thorny plants and had better chances of surviving in the arid areas than others. This particular bird survived and reproduced, while those that could not adapt to the environment died eventually. This modification or adaptive feature might have developed after many generations.

Although he discussed his ideas with several naturalists, he needed time for extensive research and his geological work had priority (van Wyhe 2007). From 1842, he lived at Down House, Downe, Kent, where he addressed himself to the great work of his life—the problem of the origin of species. In 1844, he expanded his observations in some short notes into a sketch of conclusions for his own use. These embodied

---

[5]In what follows in this section, unless stated otherwise, all biographical information about Charles Robert Darwin is based on http://www.ourcivilisation.com/smartboard/shop/darwinc/about.htm (accessed 2014-11-23).

the principle of natural selection, the germ of the Darwinian Theory, but with typical caution he delayed publication of his hypothesis. By 1846, he had published several works on the geological and zoological discoveries of his voyage—works that placed him at once in the front rank of scientists. He was writing up his theory in 1858 when Alfred Russel Wallace sent him an essay which described the same idea, prompting immediate joint publication of both of their theories (Beddall 1968). His great work, *On the Origin of Species by Means of Natural Selection,* was eventually published in 1859. This epoch-making work, which received throughout Europe with the deepest interest, was violently attacked because it did not agree with the account of the creation of man given in the Book of Genesis. But eventually it succeeded in obtaining recognition from almost all biologists.

Darwin's work established evolutionary descent with modification as the dominant scientific explanation of diversification in nature. In 1871, he examined human evolution and sexual selection in *The Descent of Man, and Selection in Relation to Sex,* followed by *The Expression of the Emotions in Man and Animals.* His research on plants was published in a series of books, and in his final book, he examined earthworms and their effect on soil.

Although Charles Darwin was not the sole originator of the evolution hypothesis, nor even the first to apply the conception of descent to plants and animals, he was the first thinker to gain for that theory a wide acceptance among biological experts. By adding to the crude evolutionism of Erasmus Darwin (Charles Darwin's grandfather), Lamarck, and others, his own specific idea of natural selection, Darwin supplied a sufficient cause, which raised it from a hypothesis to a verifiable theory.

In 1882, after a long illness, Darwin died. While Darwin made in his life span many significant contributions to human evolutions, his marriage did not follow the natural laws. In 1839, Darwin married his cousin Emma Wedgwood (1808–1896). They had ten children, of whom three died at or before the age of ten and three had no children.

Charles Darwin had an influential family. His grandfather, Erasmus Darwin (1731–1802), was an English physician. One of the key thinkers of the Midlands Enlightenment, Erasmus Darwin was also a natural philosopher, physiologist, slave-trade abolitionist, inventor, and poet. His poems included much natural history, including a statement of evolution and the relatedness of all forms of life. Charles Darwin's father, Robert Waring Darwin (1766–1848), was a medical doctor. In 1783, Robert Darwin began his studies of medicine at the University of Edinburgh. Then, in 1785, his father sent him to the Leiden University in the Netherlands, and he took his MD there. His Leyden dissertation was impressive and was published in the Philosophical Transactions, but his father may have assisted him in this.[6] Probably because of this dissertation, Robert Darwin was elected a Fellow of the Royal Society in 1788.

---

[6]See Darwin (1888, pp. 8–10) and Desmond and Moore (1991, p. 10) for more detailed evidence.

What I mention here is not intended to play down Robert Darwin's academic contributions. Instead, I would say that Lamarck's theory must have played a certain role in the process of human evolution, at least within Darwin's family. Had Lamarck and all Darwins been alive today, Lamarck would have told them that it was the Lamarckism—not the Darwinism—that characterizes the "inheritance of acquired traits" within the Darwin family, at least from Erasmus Darwin to Charles Darwin.

2.2   Who Have the Last Laugh?

In his theory of evolution, Lamarck explained two forces he saw as comprising evolution: a force that drives animals from simple to complex forms and a force that adapts animals to their local environments and differentiates them from each other. Lamarck stressed two main themes in his biological work. The first related to the fact that the environment gives rise to changes in animals. He cited examples of blindness in moles, the presence of teeth in mammals, and the absence of teeth in birds as evidence of this principle. The second principle concerned that life was structured in an orderly manner and that many different parts of all bodies make it possible for the organic movements of animals (Osborn 1896, p. 160). In brief, Lamarck's theory of evolution includes the following ideas:

1. Use and disuse—Individuals lose characteristics they do not require (or use) and develop characteristics that are useful.
2. Inheritance of acquired traits—Individuals inherit the traits of their ancestors.

In essence, a change in the environment brings about change in "needs" (in French: *besoins*), resulting in change in behavior, bringing change in organ usage and development, bringing change in form over time—and thus the gradual transmutation of the species. For example, Jean-Baptiste Lamarck believed the giraffe's long neck was an "acquired characteristic," developed as generations of ancestral giraffes strove to reach the leaves of tall trees.

By way of contrast, Darwin's concept of evolution is different from Lamarck's theory of organic evolution. In Darwin's theory, he stated that nature only selects those organisms that are best-suited to that particular environmental condition, whereas Lamarck's theory states that it is the environment that brings changes in organisms. Taking the giraffe as an example, Darwin believed that the giraffe's neck arose through natural selection—that ancestral giraffes with long necks thereby had a competitive advantage that better enabled them to reproduce and pass on their genes (Prothero and Schoch 2003, pp. 67–72). Natural selection is an important aspect in the process of evolution. It helps in accumulating and preserving beneficial mutations that increase an organism's chance of survival.

Darwin's theory of evolution is based on key facts and the inferences drawn from them, which is summarized by biologist Ernst Mayr as follows:

- Every species is fertile enough that if all offspring survived to reproduce the population would grow (fact).
- Despite periodic fluctuations, populations remain roughly the same size (fact).
- Resources such as food are limited and are relatively stable over time (fact).
- A struggle for survival ensues (inference).
- Individuals in a population vary significantly from one another (fact).
- Much of this variation is heritable (fact).
- Individuals less suited to the environment are less likely to survive and less likely to reproduce; individuals more suited to the environment are more likely to survive and more likely to reproduce and leave their heritable traits to future generations, which produces the process of natural selection (inference).
- This slowly effected process results in populations changing to adapt to their environments, and ultimately, these variations accumulate over time to form new species (inference).[7]

When Charles Darwin published his theory of evolution by natural selection in *On the Origin of Species*, he continued to give credence to what he called "use and disuse inheritance," but rejected other aspects of Lamarck's theories. Later, Mendelian genetics supplanted the notion of inheritance of acquired traits, eventually leading to the development of the modern evolutionary synthesis and the general abandonment of the Lamarckian theory of evolution in biology. Despite this abandonment, interest in Lamarckism has continued, as studies in the field of epigenetics have highlighted the possible inheritance of behavioral traits acquired by the previous generation.[8]

There have been many different societies throughout human history, with estimates as high as over one million; however, only about two hundred or so different societies survive (Elwell 2013 p. 103). Early cultural (or sociocultural) evolution theories—such as those of Auguste Comte, Herbert Spencer, and Lewis Henry Morgan—developed simultaneously with, but independently of, Charles Darwin's works and were popular from the late nineteenth century to the end of First World War (1914–1919). These nineteenth-century evolution theories claimed that societies start out in a primitive state and gradually become more civilized over time, and equated the culture and technology of Western civilization with progress. Some forms of early cultural evolution theories have led to much criticized theories like social Darwinism and scientific racism, used in the past to justify existing policies of colonialism and slavery and to justify new policies such as eugenics.

---

[7]Cited from Mayr (1982, pp. 479–80).

[8]See, for example, Roth et al. (2009), Arai et al. (2009), Hackett et al. (2013), and Bonduriansky (2012).

In the nineteenth century, there were attempts to explain how culture develops in its evolutionary process. However, it is the neoevolutionary thinkers who brought back evolutionary thought and developed it to be acceptable to contemporary anthropology in the twentieth century. Neoevolutionism emerged in the 1930s and extensively developed in the period following the Second World War and was incorporated into both anthropology and sociology in the 1960s. Neoevolutionism is a social theory that tries to explain the evolution of societies by drawing on Charles Darwin's theory of evolution and discarding some dogmas of the previous social evolutionism. It is concerned with long-term, directional, evolutionary social change and with the regular patterns of development that may be seen in unrelated, widely separated cultures. Before raising my own questions and puzzles, let us first have a brief review of some important neoevolutionists' thoughts: [9]

In 1955, Julian Steward, in his book *Theory of Culture Change: The Methodology of Multilinear Evolution*, created the theory of "multilinear" evolution. He argued that different environments and technologies would require different kinds of adaptations and that as the resource base or technology changed, so too would a culture. In other words, cultures do not change according to some inner logic, but rather in terms of a changing relationship with a changing environment. Cultures therefore would not pass through the same stages in the same order as they changed—rather, they would change in varying ways and directions. He believed that it is possible to create theories analyzing typical common culture, representative of specific eras or regions. As the decisive factors determining the development of given culture, he pointed to technology, economics, political system, ideologies, and religion. All those factors push the evolution of a given society in several directions, hence applying the term "multilinear" to his theory of evolution.

In 1959, Leslie White, in his book *The Evolution of Culture: The Development of Civilization to the Fall of Rome*, attempted to create a theory explaining the entire history of humanity. The most important factor in his theory is technology. He proposes a society's energy consumption as a measure of its advancement. He differentiates between five stages of human development. In the first, people use the energy of their own muscles. In the second, they use the energy of domesticated animals. In the third, they use the energy of plants. In the fourth, they learn to use the energy of natural resources: coal, oil, gas. In the fifth, they harness nuclear energy.

In 1960, Marshall D. Sahlins, in the book *Evolution and Culture* (co-edited by Elman R. Service), divided the evolution of societies into "general" and "specific." General evolution is the tendency of cultural and social systems to increase in complexity, organization, and adaptiveness to environment. However, as the various cultures are not isolated, there is interaction and a diffusion of their qualities (like technological inventions). This leads cultures to develop in different ways (specific evolution), as various elements are introduced to them in different combinations and at different stages of evolution.

---

[9]The following five paragraphs heavily draw on a Wikipedia article "Neoevolutionism," though I have also checked the original references and made several revisions of and corrections to them.

In his *Power and Privilege: A Theory of Social Stratification* (1966) and *Human Societies: An Introduction to Macrosociology* (1970; later editions are co-authored by Patrick Nolan), Gerhard Lenski expands on the works of Leslie White and Lewis Henry Morgan, developing the ecological–evolutionary theory. He views technological progress as the most basic factor in the evolution of societies and cultures. Unlike White, who defined technology as the ability to create and utilize energy, Lenski focuses on information. The more information and knowledge a given society has, the more advanced it is. He, on the basis of advances in the history of communication, distinguishes four stages of human development. In the first stage, information is passed by genes. In the second, when humans gain sentience, they can learn and pass information through by experience. In the third, humans start using signs and develop logic. In the fourth, they can create symbols and develop language and writing.

Talcott Parsons, author of *Societies: Evolutionary and Comparative Perspectives* (1966) and *The System of Modern Societies* (1971), divides evolution into four subprocesses: (1) division, which creates functional subsystems from the main system; (2) adaptation, where those systems evolve into more efficient versions; (3) inclusion of elements previously excluded from the given systems; and (4) generalization of values, increasing the legitimization of the ever more complex system. He then tries to reveal the complexity of the processes which take form between two points of necessity: that the first relates to the culture per se, which is given through the values system of each evolving community and that the other concerns environment, which is reflected in the material realities of the basic production system and in the relative capacity of each industrial–economical level at each window of time.

Neo-Lamarckian versions of evolution were widespread in the late nineteenth century. The idea that living things could to some degree choose the characteristics that would be inherited allowed them to be in charge of their own destiny as opposed to the Darwinian view, which made them puppets at the mercy of the environment. Such ideas were more popular than natural selection in the late nineteenth century as it made it possible for biological evolution to fit into a framework of a divine or naturally willed plan. In addition, supporters of neo-Lamarckism such as George Bernard Shaw and Arthur Koestler claimed that Lamarckism is more humane and optimistic than Darwinism (Moorem 2002, p. 330). According to historian of biology Peter J. Bowler:

> One of the most emotionally compelling arguments used by the neo-Lamarckians of the late nineteenth century was the claim that Darwinism was a mechanistic theory which reduced living things to puppets driven by heredity. The selection theory made life into a game of Russian roulette, where life or death was predetermined by the genes one inherited. The individual could do nothing to mitigate bad heredity. Lamarckism, in contrast, allowed the individual to choose a new habit when faced with an environmental challenge and shape the whole future course of evolution.[10]

The evolution of acquired characteristics has also been shown in human populations who have experienced starvation, resulting in altered gene function in both the

---

[10]Cited from Bowler (2003, p. 367).

starved population and their offspring (Lumey 1995). As reported in MIT's Technology Review in February 2009, "The effects of an animal's environment during adolescence can be passed down to future offspring… The findings provide support for a 200-year-old theory of evolution that has been largely dismissed: Lamarckian evolution, which states that acquired characteristics can be passed on to offspring."[11]

In 2010, further evidence linking food intake to traits inherited by the offspring was shown in a study of rats conducted by several Australian universities. The study strongly suggested that fathers can transfer a propensity for obesity to their daughters as a result of the fathers' food intake, and not their genetics (or specific genes), prior to the conception of the daughter. A "paternal high-fat diet" was shown to cause cell dysfunction in the daughter, which in turn led to obesity for the daughter (Ng et al. 2010).

In their 2012 book titled *An Introduction to Zoology*, Joseph Springer and Dennis Holley wrote:

> Lamarck and his ideas were ridiculed and discredited. In a strange twist of fate, Lamarck may have the last laugh. Epigenetics, an emerging field of genetics, has shown that Lamarck may have been at least partially correct all along. It seems that reversible and heritable changes can occur without a change in DNA sequence (genotype) and that such changes may be induced spontaneously or in response to environmental factors—Lamarck's "acquired traits".[12]

Early theories, including those of Lamarck and Darwin, have provided a lighthouse for us to look into the evolutionary process of species including human beings. While Darwin's theory has been generally approved to be a more scientific approach by which to explain the evolutions of species, it cannot be used to understand the whole evolutionary process of human beings. For example, according to Darwin's theory, individuals less suited to the environment are less likely to survive and less likely to reproduce. However, why have human beings—who are believed to be much more physically inferior to many carnivore animals—survived and eventually become the lord of the world by changing their previous behaviors as well as the environment in which they lived? Even more unbelievable is that it is Andean South America—not other places in the Americas and East Asia—that gave birth to an earlier complex civilization. Moreover, many cultural issues, especially those relating to the nonlinear or cyclic process of human development, also remain unexplained.

Scientists have agreed that the ancestors of the human species Homo sapiens evolved into modern humans (i.e., present-day subspecies Homo sapiens) around 200,000 years ago, in Africa. Migrations out of Africa occurred some time later. Around 125,000 years ago, modern humans reached the Near East from where they later spread across Asia and Europe. From the Near East, these populations spread east to Asia by 50,000 years ago and on to Australia by 40,000 years ago, when for the first time Homo sapiens reached territory never reached by Homo erectus. Homo sapiens reached Europe around 43,000 years ago, eventually replacing the Neanderthal population. The date of migration to North America is disputed, but it is agreed that paleo-Indians have originated from Central Asia, crossing the Beringia

---

[11]Cited from Singer (2009).

[12]Cited from Springer and Holley (2012, p. 94).

land bridge between eastern Siberia and present-day Alaska, and lived throughout the Americas around 16,000–13,000 years ago.[13]

In his seminal 1976 book *The Selfish Gene*, Richard Dawkins, Professor of the Public Understanding of Science at the University of Oxford, wrote that "there are some examples of cultural evolution in birds and monkeys, but... it is our own species that really shows what cultural evolution can do" (Dawkins 1976, p. 190). Indeed, there were not much distinction between human beings at their early stage of evolutions and other species such as birds and monkeys. At modern times, however, human beings are so different from (or, more precisely, superior over) the other species (including many terrific carnivore animals) that they may even be treated by the latter as the superspecies or god—all depending how these are defined. Once known as, in terms of physical behavior, one of the weakest groups among all large carnivore animals, human beings are now able to, using their new sciences and advanced technologies, conquer everything in the world. As a result, not like the other species, human beings now have no enemies—or, more precisely, their only enemy is themselves.

Human beings were much more physically inferior to many carnivore animals. While Darwin's theory has been generally approved to be the most scientific approach by which to explain the evolutions of species, it cannot be used to explain the whole process of human evolutions. For example, according to Darwin, individuals less suited to the environment are less likely to survive and less likely to reproduce. If it is true, then why have human beings—who were believed to be much more physically inferior to many carnivore animals—survived and eventually become the lord of the world by changing the behaviors of their own as well as the environment in which they have lived? In addition, according to Darwin's theory of natural selection, the evolutionary process of species has been decided by those with strong (or advantageous) positions, or in a simpler language, that in a world of only two human groups, if their relations are characterized by a zero-sum game, then the stronger group will dominate the whole world. However, this is only a statically optimized outcome; from a dynamic point of view, there may be different outcomes.

Moreover, many cultural issues, especially those relating to the nonlinear or cyclic process of human development, also remain unexplained. For example, given that all modern humans throughout the world came from Africa and that South America is much farther from Africa than both North America and East Asia, why it is Andean South America that gave birth to an earlier complex civilization?

Hundreds of thousands of years ago, when one or more groups of modern humans left Africa, other groups that remained there might have the first laugh. Yes, nature selected the latter as they were more suited to the environment of the African continent. However, the successors of those who were not selected by nature and had to migrate out of Africa, after generations of struggles against the nature and between

---

[13] Based on Bower (January 27, 2011), Bowler et al. (2003), Croft (2002, p. 261), and Wells and Read (2002, pp. 138–40). Note that earlier human migration out of Africa included Homo erectus, followed by that of Homo antecessor into Europe and by Homo heidelbergensis, who was the likely ancestor of both modern humans and Neanderthals.

themselves, have been living quite well in the rest of the world, at least not worse than their counterparts, or the successors of the earlier winners in Africa.

Who would have the last laugh? Indeed, cultural evolution and development are the most complicated issues. To deal with them, we still need to conduct more theoretical and empirical analyses.

2.3   Strong Man, Weak Man

Humans are physically weaker than many other large carnivores. A glance at the whole process of human history reveals that humans have been losing those physical advantages that their ancestors and older generations once possessed. For example, the Neanderthals, an extinct species of human in the genus Homo that was first discovered in Germany's Neander Valley in 1856, emerged between 100,000 and 200,000 years ago. Cro-Magnon is a common name that has been used to describe the first early modern humans (early Homo sapiens) that lived 20,000–40,000 years ago. The name comes from the location of Abri de Cro-Magnon ("abri" means rock shelter in French) in the hamlet of Les Eyzies in the commune of Les Eyzies-de-Tayac-Sireuil in southwestern France, where the first specimen was found in 1868. Similar specimens were subsequently discovered in other parts of Europe and neighboring areas.

In general, the Neanderthals had heavy eyebrow ridges and long, low skulls and were more muscular and stronger on average, while the Cro-Magnons had higher brows and narrower shoulders and were slightly taller on average (see Fig. 2.1). The Cro-Magnons shared the European landscape with the Neanderthals for some 10,000 years or longer, before the latter disappeared from the fossil record. Scientists have also identified that the Neanderthals were more muscular and therefore much stronger than Cro-Magnons (Stringer and Gamble 1993, p. 23). Neanderthals' superiority, thanks to their physical advantage, was represented by the fact that the Neanderthals—especially those who lived in open, grassland environments—subsisted mostly on meat, while early Homo sapiens regularly ate a relatively higher proportion of plant-based foods.[14]

Studies have shown about 15,000 years of coexistence of Neanderthal and modern humans in France.[15] The nature of the two species' coexistence and the extinction of the Neanderthals have been debated, with the suggestive evidence including peaceful coexistence, competition, interbreeding, assimilation, and genocide (Trinkaus 2007). Using a computer simulation on the disappearance of the Neanderthals, Gilpina et al. (2016) suggest that endogenous factors such as relative culture level—rather

---

[14]The differences in eating habits have been witnessed by the ancient teeth (Zaatari et al. 2016).

[15]See Mellars (2006) and Gravina et al. (2005). In addition, a simulation based on a slight difference in the carrying capacity of the two groups indicates that the two groups would be found together only in a narrow zone, at the front of the Cro-Magnon immigration wave (Currat and Excoffier, 2004).

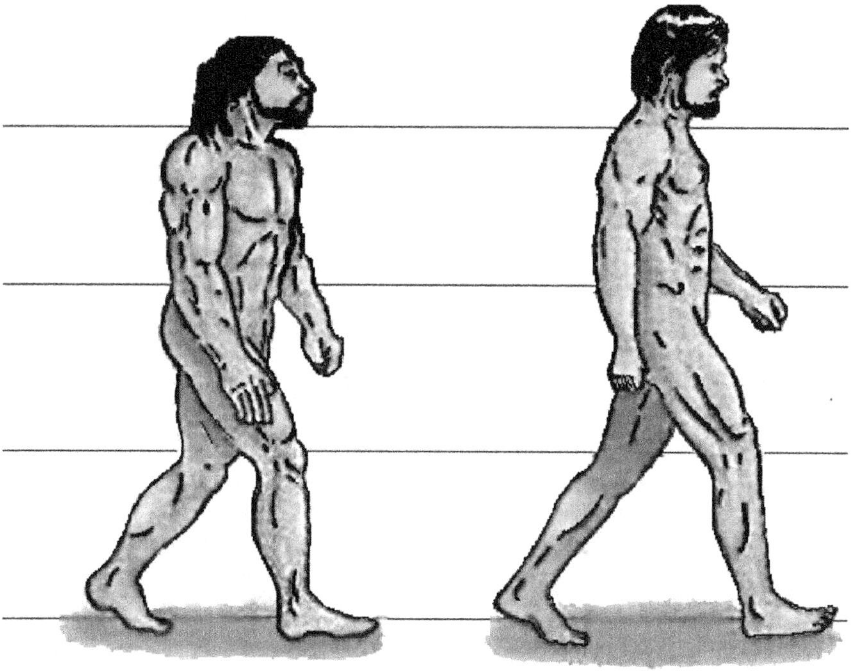

Fig. 2.1 The Neanderthals were replaced by the Cro-Magnons. *Note* Neanderthals (left) had more muscular and were stronger on average, while the Cro-Magnons (right) had narrower shoulders and were slightly taller on average.
Source Drawn by Luc Guo based on Johnson and Edgar (2001, pp. 228 and 244)

than extrinsic factors such as epidemics or climate change—could have caused the eventual exclusion of a comparatively larger (or physical stronger) population by an initially smaller (or physical weaker) one. Nevertheless, no matter whatever had happened, the Neanderthals eventually lost out to their physically weaker cousins: Cro-Magnons.

It seems that the cultural tradition of the Neanderthals was influenced by that of the Cro-Magnons, and not vice versa (D'Errico et al. 1998). Unfortunately, it is now quite difficult, if not impossible, for us to answer whether it was their physical weakness that forced some hunter-gatherers to become agriculturists. Maybe it was the transition from hunter-gatherers to agriculturists that made human beings become more physically weaker than what they had been before. Indeed, this looks like the so-called chicken or egg causality dilemma. But it is likely that, given the fact that the athletes of African descent have always been winners of the sprinting events, the first argument (physical weakness leads to cultural evolution and development) appears to hold the key or at least both are right. Obviously, past human and cultural evolutions conform to the rule of the so-called Win-Stay Lose-Shift game. Think that the earliest humans migrating out of Africa were not physically inferior to those who continued to stay in Africa?

By "human weakness," it means the physical weakness or disadvantages of human beings as compared with their competitors when both of them live in a common environment. Yes, human beings are not strong and fast—our distant ancestors might just act as the tortoise vis-à-vis the hare in the Aesop fable. Otherwise, they would not have learned how to become bipedal. There are many distinct hypotheses as to how and why bipedalism evolved in humans: That bipedalism was favored is because it freed up the hands for reaching food and carrying tools, is because it saved energy during locomotion, and is because it enabled long-distance running and hunting or because it evolved as a strategy for avoiding hyperthermia by reducing the surface exposed to direct sun.[16] No matter whatever is correct, the precondition for this kind of evolution must be that humans had a crying need for that kind of evolution in order to survive.

The history of Africa begins with the emergence of Homo sapiens in East Africa and continues into the present-day's patchwork of diverse nation states. The recorded history of the early African civilization arose in Sudan (i.e., the Kerma culture)—originally as part of the kingdom of Kush predating well-recorded history (Williams 1987, pp. 61–63), and later in ancient Egypt, the Sahel, the Maghreb, and the Horn of Africa. Of course, it is generally recognized that the peoples in northern Africa, including those who had contributed to the well-known ancient Egyptian civilization, directly originated in West Asia, not from Africa per se. Nevertheless, if referred to an earlier stage, all of them, including those in the rest of the world, did have the same Homo sapiens gene that is generally believed to have originated in southern Africa. And, above all, the southern Africans had still done well or even better than other peoples in the rest of the world during the early stage of human evolution.

Archaeological evidence shows that, about 16,000 BC ago, people from the Red Sea hills to the northern Ethiopian Highlands began collecting nuts, grasses, and tubers for food and, by about 13,000 BC to 11,000 BC, wild grains. This spread to West Asia, which domesticated its wild grains, wheat, and barley. A wet climatic phase in Africa turned the Ethiopian Highlands into a mountain forest. Around 7000 BC, the settlers of the Ethiopian highlands domesticated donkeys, and by 4000 BC, domesticated donkeys had spread to Southwest Asia. Cushitic speakers, partially turning away from cattle herding, domesticated teff and finger millet between 5500 BC and 3500 BC.[17] In the steppes and savannahs of the Sahara and Sahel in northern West Africa, the Nilo-Saharan speakers and Mandé peoples started to collect and domesticate wild millet, African rice, and sorghum between 8000 BC and 6000 BC. Between 9000 and 5000 BC, Niger–Congo speakers domesticated the oil palm and raffia palm. Two seed plants, black-eyed peas and voandzeia (African groundnuts), were domesticated, followed by okra and kola nuts. Since most of the plants grew

---

[16]See, for example, Lovejoy (1988) and Hunt (1994).

[17]See, for example, Diamond (1997, pp. 126–7) and Ehret (2002, pp. 64-75, 80-1, 87-8).

in the forest, the Niger–Congo speakers invented polished stone axes for clearing forest.[18]

In fact, just prior to Saharan desertification, the communities that developed south of Egypt, in what is now Sudan, were full participants in the Neolithic Revolution and lived a settled to seminomadic lifestyle, with domesticated plants and animals. For example, the megaliths, found at Nabta Playa in the Nubian Desert, are one of the first known archaeo astronomical devices in the world, predating Stonehenge by some 1,000 years. In addition, it has been suggested that the sociocultural complexity observed at the Nabta Playa basin and expressed by different levels of authority within the society there formed the basis for the structure of both the Neolithic society at Nabta and the Old Kingdom of Egypt.[19]

Then, why did the southern Africans fail to advance their cultures later on? By 5000 BC, Africa entered a dry phase, and the climate of the Sahara region gradually became drier. Did the drier climate impel the pace of cultural development? Not likely. Had it been so, civilizations should have been more seriously affected in northern Africa where the ancient Egyptian civilization was born than in southern Africa. Besides, as will be discussed in Chap. 4, unfriendly geographic and environmental factors had always exerted positive influences on the rise of civilizations. Then, what had eventually prevented southern Africa from developing a powerful civilization?

Darwin's theory of natural selection cannot be used to precisely explain the whole process of human and cultural evolutions (see, e.g., Fig. 2.2). Specifically, compared with many other carnivore animals, humans were less suited to and thus had become losers in Africa and elsewhere. Then, why have they not only survived but also, for the first time in human history, created advanced cultures and civilizations?

Human beings were, and still are, much more physically inferior to many carnivore animals. Even though human beings are now able to, by using their new sciences and advanced technologies, conquer everything in the world, they had been known as, for most of the millions of years long history, the weakest group of all animals with similar sizes. Nevertheless, differences still exist in different human groups, which might be one of the reasons behind the first intra-human competition in sub-Saharan Africa—the cradle of all modern humans (including the Caucasoid, Mongoloid, and Negroid populations). Of course, these human groups' ancestors in Africa might have not had so distinct physical differences as they have today. However, both physically advantageous and advantageous human groups must have existed there as they do now in the rest of the world.

Even though many other factors had also influenced the result of the intra-human competition in sub-Saharan Africa, it is the Negroid's physical advantage that eventually promoted them to become the final winner. Consequently, the Caucasoid and the Mongoloid, as they are called now, had to retreat to the rest of the world. Again, in the Middle East—the only place connecting Africa and the other continents of

---

[18] See Ehret (2002, pp. 82–4). In addition, most of southern Africa was occupied by Pygmy peoples and Khoisan who engaged in hunting and gathering, and some of the oldest rock art was produced by them (pp. 94–5).

[19] Source: https://wikivisually.com/wiki/African_history (accessed 2017-12-29).

Fig. 2.2 Tswana (a South African people) hunting the lion. *Note* In this painting—now a collection in the New York Public Library—the strongest man who has just conducted the first, though not the fatal attack on the lion, has been killed by the latter, while the weakest man is scared and running away.
Source Drawn by Sir William Cornwallis Harris (1841)

the world—the Caucasoid and the Mongoloid must have also competed, quarreled, and fought for a long period of time after their migration out of southern Africa. And the final result is very likely that the Mongoloids were defeated and retreated to Central Asia where the Mongoloids were still quarreling and fighting before the southern Mongoloid (including the Han-Chinese and other Southeast Asian populations) retreated to an even farther place—the Far East (including much of today's China, Japan, Korea, and Southeast Asia).

Among the three relatively distinct groups of Caucasoid, Mongoloid, and Negroid of today, the athletes of the Negroid group have usually performed better than those of the other groups in such sports as in track and field. Nearly all of the sprinters who have beaten the 100-m 10-s barrier are of African descent (see Table 2.1). In 2003, Australia's Patrick Johnson who has Irish and indigenous Australian heritage became the first sub-10-second runner without an African background, and in 2015, Chinese sprinter Su Bingtian made history by becoming the first Asian athlete with the record-tying result of 9.99s. But all these still lagged far behind what the Negroid athletes had achieved. It is believed that biological factors may be largely responsible for the notable success in sprinting events enjoyed by athletes of the Negroid. Chief among these is a preponderance of the Negroid's natural fast-twitch muscle fibers which aid in obtaining higher power and, thus, higher acceleration and speed.

Table 2.1 The world's fastest men from 1968 to 2017

Year	Athlete	Nationality (race)	Time (s)
2017	Christian Coleman	USA (Black)	9.82
2016	Trayvon Bromell	USA (Black)	9.84
2015	Justin Gatlin	USA (Black)	9.74
2014	Justin Gatlin	USA (Black)	9.77
2013	Usain Bolt	Jamaica (Black)	9.77
2012	Usain Bolt	Jamaica (Black)	9.63
2011	Usain Bolt	Jamaica (Black)	9.76
2010	Nesta Carter	Jamaica (Black)	9.78
2010	Tyson Gay	USA (Black)	9.78
2009	Usain Bolt	Jamaica (Black)	9.58
2008	Usain Bolt	Jamaica (Black)	9.69
2007	Asafa Powell	Jamaica (Black)	9.74
2005	Asafa Powell	Jamaica (Black)	9.77
2002	Tim Montgomery	USA (Black)	9.78[a]
1999	Maurice Greene	USA (Black)	9.79
1996	Donovan Bailey	Canada (Black)	9.84
1994	Leroy Burrell	USA (Black)	9.85
1991	Carl Lewis	USA (Black)	9.86
1988	Carl Lewis	USA (Black)	9.92
1983	Calvin Smith	USA (Black)	9.93
1968	Jim Hines	USA (Black)	9.95

Notes Based on various 100-m sprint race in track-and-field competitions. ([a]): doped
Source Author based on miscellaneous news clippings

Ceteris paribus, physically weaker people, in order to survive by themselves, usually have more incentives to create complicated traditions. Though more evidence is still needed, it is very likely that the ancient Sumerians, who created the world's earliest human civilization in Mesopotamia, might be physically weaker or shorter than other hunter-gatherers living there. For example, the statue of Gudea (reign c. 2144–c. 2124 BC, the ninth ruler of the Second Dynasty of Lagash) that is now on display in Louvre, Paris, is much small-sized and gently portrayed as judged by modern norms (see Fig. 2.3).

Nevertheless, the negative correlation between physical output and mental output still roughly exist in the real world (see Fig. 2.4). Here, while I am comparing the major racial groups of the world today, I have no intention of evaluating them from the ethnocentric point of view. In fact, according to the "Win-Stay Lose-Shift" principle as stated in Chap. 1, people living in southern Africa have been superior to those in the rest of the world during most of the past millions of years. Even today, the East Asian, if not the European, athletes in some track-and-field games still feel

Fig. 2.3 Gudea (reign c. 2144–c. 2124 BC), Sumerian ruler of the Second Dynasty of Lagash. *Note* Seating diorite statue, height: 46 cm (1.5 ft); width: 33 cm (1 ft); vertical depth: 22.5 cm (8.8 in). *Source* Musée du Louvre, Atlas database: entry 11975. Wikimedia Commons

themselves inferior to their African counterparts. As a matter of fact, that southern Africa was culturally surpassed by the rest of the world is only a story that has happened within the past thousands of years.

Resulting from a decreasing trend of manual work during the civilizational era, humans have physically weaker than they were before. According to Lamarck's theory of evolution, evolution tends to favor the elimination of traits that are no longer needed. Stemming from the growing cultural complexities that need more mental work than before, humans will only but have less robust muscles. We now have machines, and other tools of our ingenuity, for those tasks. In fact, studies have already shown that we are much weaker than our distant ancestors (Courtiol et al. 2012). And future humans may therefore be more petite than we are today. For similar reasons, future humans may also have weakened immune systems and be more susceptible to pathogens. Modern medical technology and the discovery of

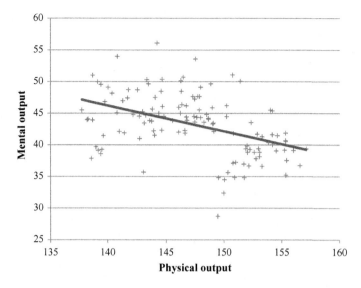

Fig. 2.4 Human thermodynamic law: mental output versus physical output. *Notes* (1) Only nations from the Old World are included. (2) "Physical output" is represented by average female height (AFH) minus an amount that is explained by GNI per capita in Eq. (5.1) and plus an extra 5% of the AFH for the Negroid-dominated nations. (3)"Mental output" is represented by the IQ minus an amount that is explained by GNI per capita in Eq. (5.2) (4) All the original data are shown at Annex A.1 at the end of this book

antibiotics have greatly increased our health and life expectancy, but they also mean our immune systems need to do less work to keep us healthy. Biologically speaking, our immune systems are less necessary than they used to be. Therefore, humans of the future may become more dependent on medical technology and so do they on cultures.

Tool production and use is generally thought to be intimately linked to humans' major changes in cognitive development and morphological features (such as body and brain size). The earliest stone tool-making, which includes the most basic stone toolkits that had been used by early humans, was developed by at least two million years ago (mya). The Oldowan, or spelled Olduwan, is the earliest widespread stone tool archaeological industry in prehistory. Oldowan tools were used by ancient hominids across much of Africa, South Asia, the Middle East, and Europe. This technological industry was followed by the more sophisticated Acheulean industry. The term "Oldowan" was taken by the archaeologist Louis Leakey from the site of Olduvai Gorge in Tanzania, where the first lithic tools were discovered in the 1930s. Previously, only lava and quartz were used to make tools in the Olduvai Gorge, and chert was not used until the period from 1.65 to 1.53 mya (Kimura 2002). This change represents the first instances of technological innovation in human history, wherein our ancestors first began to enhance their biological abilities with the manufacture of stone tools. An important milestone in the following cultural evolution of our ancestors, the technocomplex is characterized by a limited variety of simple artifacts, such as flakes, hammerstones, and cores.

The terms "Oldowan" and "Oldovai" are likely derived from the English word "old" and the Swahili word "wa." Swahili and English are two official languages that have been adopted in Tanzania. Since "wa" is a common (and, perhaps, the oldest) ancestral word and means, in many indigenous languages including Swahili, house, home, and homeland, the original meaning of "Oldowan" and "Oldovai" should be "old home" or "native place." Aren't Oldovai and other places in which the earliest stone toolkits are found the old homeland to all our humans? Our earliest ancestors, in order to survive, had to invent tools and other complicated methods for their own. As a result, they were inclined to name the latter with "wa" or any variant of it—one of the very few syllables they had been able to read. For example, the old Chinese character for axe—one of the earliest stone toolkits and most important weapons of all mankind at ancient times—also denotes "king" that is read as [wang] in Mandarin Chinese but more likely as [wa] or any variant of it in proto-Chinese.[20] Moreover, since the word axe is roughly similarly read in most Indo-European and Afro-Asiatic languages, it must come from a common ancestral word. In this case, and according to the two inferences to be discussed at the end of Sect. 3.2 in Chap. 3, the ancestral word for "axe" should be derived from "was" or any variant of it.

A wand is a thin, handheld stick or rod made of wood, stone, ivory, or metals. In modern language, wands are generally ceremonial and/or have associations with magic, all stemming from the original meaning as a synonym of rod. While the source of the English word "wand" is unclear, it, like all those of other European languages, should originate in the Mesopotamian or the ancient Egyptian civilizations. In ancient Egypt, toilette articles, weapons against possible enemies, and amulets against serpents were usually left in pharaohs' tombs, together with a magic wand. In classical Greco-Roman mythology, the god Hermes/Mercury has a special wand called a caduceus. In Wicca and Ceremonial magic, practitioners use several magical tools including wands for the channeling of energy. The wand is most often used by Neopagans, Shamans, Wiccans, and others in rituals and healing.

Indeed, a stick giving length and leverage is perhaps the earliest and simplest tool of humans. Was-scepter is a symbol that often appeared in relics, art, and hieroglyphics associated with the ancient Egyptian religion. Appearing as a stylized animal head at the top of a long, straight staff with a forked end, the was-scepter was depicted as being carried by gods, pharaohs, and priests. It commonly occurs in the paintings, drawings, and carvings of the Egyptian gods and is often in parallel with emblems such as the ankh. The was-scepter was used as symbols of power or dominion and was associated with the gods (such as Set or Anubis) as well as with the pharaohs in ancient Egypt. This was-scepter was also the symbol of the fourth Upper Egyptian nome—that is, today's Thebes which is called "Waset" in Egyptian. In addition, the personal pronouns for "I" and "me" are called "wo" (likely derived from "wa" in

---

[20]Note that the term for axe is now called as [fu] in Mandarin Chinese. However, it is unlikely that the somewhat twisted syllable "fu" existed in the proto-Chinese language since the ancient Chinese (even some modern Chinese including myself) could not correctly pronounce the letter 'f'.

proto-Chinese) in modern Chinese, which is written as 我 (or 戈 in the original form, representing a massive-killing weapon in ancient China).

Over the course of human evolution, the average volume of human brain has grown from about 600 cm^3 in Homo habilis to about 1,100 cm^3 in Homo erectus and to about 1500 cm^3 in Homo sapiens. Subsequently, there has been a shrinking over the past 28,000 years. The male brain has decreased from 1,500 to 1,350 cm^3, while the female brain has shrunk by the same relative proportion (Schoenemann 2006). In spite of significant changes in social capacity, there has been very little change in brain size from Neanderthals to the present day. However, there have been obvious race differences. A review of the world literature on brain size and intelligent quotient (IQ), by Rushton (2000, pp. 47 and 57), shows that African-descended people (Blacks) average cranial capacities of 1267 cm^3, European-descended people (Whites) 1347 cm^3, and East Asian-descended people (East Asians) 1364 cm^3. These brain size differences, containing millions of brain cells and hundreds of millions of synapses, were hypothesized to underlie the race differences on IQ tests, in which the Blacks average an IQ of 85, the Whites 100, and the East Asians 106 (Rushton and Rushton 2003).

Even though the IQ scores may neglect other important aspects including creativity and social intelligence (Neisser et al. 1996), they somewhat conform to the "Win-Stay Lose-Shift" hypothesis. In other words, losers, after having gotten away from their homeland (Africa), had to change their mind in order to survive; however, winners had no incentive to do so (see Sect. 2.4 for a more detailed analysis). In the average adult human, although the brain represents only 2% of the body weight, it receives 15% of the cardiac output, 20% of total body oxygen consumption, and 25% of total body glucose utilization.[21] If this result is correct, it can be concluded that, ceteris paribus, the larger the brain of a man, the more disadvantages in physical strength he will have. This can partially explain, in terms of average cranial capacity and physical strength, the differences between the African-descended, European-descended, and East Asian-descended peoples.

However, it is not appropriate to say that the growth of a culture or civilization is always positively determined by intelligent humans; sometimes, people with high IQ scores do not have incentives to *collectively* deal with and adapt to various challenges they face.[22] Nevertheless, physical weakness does provide incentives for humans to create cultural complexity by which to survive.

---

[21]Clarke and Sokoloff (1999, p. 644). In addition, the energy consumption for the brain to simply survive is 0.1 calories per minute, while this value can be as high as 1.5 calories per minute during crossword puzzle-solving (Source: https://www.popsci.com/scitech/article/2006-07/mental-workout, accessed 2018-3-1).

[22]See model at the end of Chap. 7 for a more comprehensive description of the conditions under which a civilization is born.

2.4 Spatial Variation of Humans[23]

Discussions about the spatial patterns of variation due to natural selection in humans are always a politically sensitive issue. A classic paper that establishes a reaction–diffusion model for the spread of an advantageous allele and uses it to calculate the speed of the expanding wave of advance would be Fisher (1937), though whose work was pervaded by prejudice against racial groups.[24] In this section, I intend to present some serious, scholarly analyses of the spatial patterns of human variation. It should be noted that the work of eugenicists has often been pervaded by prejudice against racial, ethnic, and disabled groups and thus has been widely disregarded in international communities. Hence, the material, to be presented below, is by no means an endorsement of those views, neither is it a promotion of eugenics in any way—instead, it is purely for scholarly research purposes.

Specifically, in what follows, two empirical tests based on the data of a panel of nations will be conducted so as to statistically prove (or reject, if any) the "Win-Stay, Lose-Shift" hypothesis that has been described in Chap. 1.

(1) A spatial model of physical features of humans

If the "Win-Stay, Lose-Shift" phenomenon existed in early humans' migration process (shown in Fig. 1.1 in Chap. 1), then the physical features of these humans should have the following spatial patterns due to natural selection:

- That people living in or near Ethiopia (the original home to all modern humans) tend to have physical advantages over those living elsewhere and
- That humans living in places farthest from Ethiopia tend to have physical disadvantages over those living elsewhere.

Unfortunately, it is impossible for us to collect the specific information about the earliest humans who were migrating out of Africa. What we can only do now is to demonstrate if the "Win-Stay, Lose-Shift" hypothesis can be proved by the physical features of modern humans. This seems to be somewhat reasonable. Over the course of a significantly long period of time, the genomes of organisms can change significantly in the process called adaptation in which the selection for beneficial mutations can cause a species to evolve into forms better able to survive in their environment (Darwin 1859, p. 1). However, the genetic genes of humans, like those of all other species of the earth, have hardly changed during the past tens of thousands of years or even longer. Evidence shows that the genes of ancient humans who lived in Eurasia were far from distinct from each other between 45,000 and 7,500 years ago (Yang and Fu 2018).[25]

---

[23] This section is based on Guo (2018).

[24] The thoughtful reviews about the effects of population history on spatial patterns of neutral variation in humans would have been conducted by Handley et al. (2007) and Novembre and Di Rienzo (2009).

[25] Furthermore, it has been found that the original "Y-chromosomal Adam"-DNA sequencing has mutated rarely over 20,000 generations (source: https://www.cambridgedna.com/genealogy-dna-genetic-genealogy.php, accessed 2018-1-21) and that some genes only have mutation for every million years (Hahn et al., 2007).

In other words, the existing spatial differences of physical features of humans throughout the world have been the result of the genetic differences of the humans' ancestors in Africa rather than those of the geographical and environmental differences of the world in which they are living. Next, we arrange our test of the spatial patterns of humans' physical features as follows. Assume that the average female height—an indicator for the physical features of humans that are largely decided by humans' genetic genes—is the dependent variable in this research. It is generally believed that the average female height of the Native Americans is shorter than that of the White Europeans in the New World (see, e.g., Fig. 4.3a in Chap. 4). However, since the data on the Native Americans are not available in most, if not all of the nations in the New World, my analysis here is only based on the data from the Old World.

In order to estimate the effects of spatial differences on the physical features of humans, I introduce two dummies:

a. SSA denotes that if a country is in sub-Saharan Africa (if yes, it has a value of 1; otherwise, it has a value of 0).
b. EA denotes that if a country is in East Asia (if yes, it has a value of 1; otherwise, it has a value of 0).

Using the data shown at Annex A.1 and the ordinary least square (OLS) technique, we may conduct a simple regression of average female height (AFH, in natural log form) with respect to the natural log of GNI per capita (GNIPC) and two dummies (SSA and EA):

$$ln\text{AFH} = 4.980 + 0.012 ln\text{GNIPC} + 0.003\text{SSA} - 0.029\text{EA}$$
$$(0.017)\ (0.002)^a \qquad (0.002) \qquad (0.007)^a$$
$$(N = 126, \text{R-squared} = 0.363,\ F = 22.977,\ \text{SE} = 0.022) \qquad (2.1)$$

where N, R-squared, F, and SE represent the number of observations, the squared coefficient of correlation, F-statistic, and the standard error of regression, respectively. The figure within each pair of parentheses below Eq. (2.1) represents the standard error of the estimated coefficient concerned, and superscript "a" denotes that estimates are statistically significant at greater than the 1% confidence level. Obviously, the estimated coefficient on lnGNIPC (0.012), which is statistically significant at the 1% confidence level, shows that the average female height (AFH) is positively related to gross national income per capita (GNIPC). Even though the estimated coefficient on SSA is positive (0.003), it is not statistically significant at the 10% confidence level. Thus, the "Win-Stay" hypothesis—or, specifically, that the average female height of the nations in sub-Saharan Africa is larger than that of the nations in the rest of the Old World—cannot be statistically proved.

However, this does not mean that the Negroid race has (or had) no physical advantage over the other races (such as Caucasoid and Mongoloid) in the Old World. It is very likely that the sub-hypothesis "Win-Stay" may still be proved by other human indicators (see, e.g., Sect. 2.2 in Chap. 2 for the different performances of physical education between the Negroid and other races). Note that statistical significance of regression can be improved in Eq. (2.1) if the AFH variable is modified by a factor favoring the Negroid. Since the Negroid people generally have the preponderance of natural fast-twitch muscle fibers which aid in obtaining higher power, they should have, ceteris paribus, physical advantages over other Eurasian (especially East Asian) peoples. (I leave this to my future research.)

In Eq. (2.1), the estimated coefficient on EA (-0.029), which is statistically significant at the 1% confidence level, does suggest that, ceteris paribus, the average female height (AFH) of East Asia is about 97.14% (i.e., $\exp(-0.029 \times 1) \div \exp(-0.029 \times 0) \approx 0.09714$) that of the rest of the Old World. Obviously, this estimated result is roughly consistent with the differences between Japan and the UK (as discussed in Sect. 1.3 in Chap. 1): that the average adult male height of Japan (170.7 cm) is about 96.01% that of the UK (177.8 cm) and that the average adult female height of Japan (158.0 cm) is about 96.05% that of the UK (164.5 cm).

Since East Asia (or the Far East as the Europeans call it) is farther from Africa than the other places in the Old World and that, in terms of average female height, the East Asians are physically weaker than the Eurasians and the Africans, the sub-hypothesis "Lose-Shift" is statistically proved in the Old World.

(2)   A spatial model of mental features of humans

If the "Win-Stay, Lose-Shift" phenomenon existed in early humans' migration process (shown in Fig. 1.1 in Chap. 1), then the mental features of these humans should have the following spatial patterns due to natural selection:

- That people living in or near Ethiopia (the original home to all modern humans) tend to have mental disadvantages over those living elsewhere and
- That humans living in places farthest from Ethiopia tend to have mental advantages over those living elsewhere.

The above argument could be further transformed into the hypothesis that, facing various challenges and threats, the humans as losers had more incentives to change themselves than those as winners did. An intelligence quotient (IQ) is a total score derived from several standardized tests designed to assess human intelligence. Although basing a concept of intelligence on IQ test scores alone neglects other important aspects (such as creativity and social intelligence) of mental ability (Neisser et al. 1996), IQ is the most thoroughly researched means of measuring intelligence and by far the most widely used in a few of practical settings. For example, Lynn and Vanhanen (2002, pp. 87–158) find that intelligence is a determinant of incomes and related phenomena (educational attainment and socioeconomic status) among individuals, and they further suggest that the intelligence of national populations is likely to be a determinant of per capita incomes among nations.

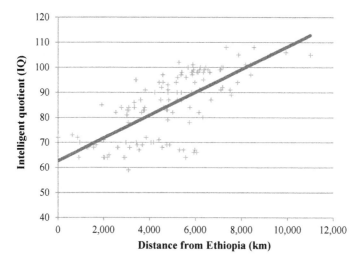

Fig. 2.5 The Old World: IQ increases with respect to the distance from Ethiopia. *Data source* Annex A.1 at the end of this book

Here, my interest is not focused on whether or how the IQ determines income level (or vice versa); instead, I only intend to clarify the spatial mechanism of IQ formation throughout the world. Human genetic scientists have found that, under certain conditions, the spatial patterns of human variation due to natural selection do exist (Novembre and Di Rienzo 2009). My logic for analyzing humans' long-lasting migration throughout the world is as follows:

After having gotten away from their homeland, losers who were usually physically weaker than winners had to change their mind in order to survive, but the winners who were usually physically stronger than the losers had no incentive to do so. However, the spatial pattern of IQ scores with respect to the distance from Ethiopia, even if it exists in the real world, may not exactly be the same as the one shown in Fig. 2.5, since other factors (such as education and income level) also play a role in the formation of IQ. In order to examine the spatial pattern of IQ scores with respect to the distance from Ethiopia, we need to construct a multivariable regression model.

It is generally believed that during the pre-Columbian era, the average level of cultural development in the New World was lower than that in the Old World. However, this does not necessarily suggest that the average human IQ score of the New World was lower than that of the Old World. Since the data on the Native Americans are not available in most, if not all of the nations there, in addition that the real routes of migration of the paleo-Indians (meaning "ancient Indians") to the Americas are disputed (see Fig. 1.1 in Chap. 1) and thus the data on the distance from Ethiopia cannot be calculated, a complete intercontinental comparison is not conducted here. (For a quantitative test of geographical and environmental influences on human evolution in the New World, see Sect. 5.2 in Chap. 5.)

Instead, my analysis of the spatial pattern of IQ scores with respect to the distance
from Ethiopia is only based on the data from the Old World. Using the data shown at
Annex A.1 and the ordinary least square (OLS) technique, we may conduct a simple
regression of IQ (in natural log form) with respect to the natural logs of the distance
from Ethiopia (DFE) and of GNI per capita (GNIPC) in purchasing power parity (the
education variable is excluded here since it is closely correlated with GNIPC):

$$ln\text{IQ} = 3.452 + 0.037 ln\text{DFE} + 0.079 ln\text{GNIPC}$$

$$(0.095) \quad (0.011)^a \quad\quad (0.008)^a$$

$$(N = 126, \text{R-squared} = 0.544, \ F = 72.730, \ \text{SE} = 0.110) \quad\quad (2.2)$$

where N, R-squared, F, and SE represent the number of observations, the squared
coefficient of correlation, F-statistic, and the standard error of regression, respectively. The figure within each pair of parentheses below Eq. (2.2) represents the
standard error of the estimated coefficient concerned, and superscript "a" denotes
that estimates are statistically significant at greater than the 1% confidence. The estimated coefficients on lnDFE and lnGNIPC are 0.037 and 0.079, respectively, both of
which are statistically significant at the 1% confidence level. We may thus believe that
a 1% increase of the distance from Ethiopia and of GNI per capita will increase the
score of intelligent quotient (IQ) by 0.037% and 0.079%, respectively. The particular
importance of the above estimated result suggests that, ceteris paribus, the average
IQ is positively related to the distance from Ethiopia. Therefore, the "Win-Stay,
Lose-Shift" hypothesis is statistically proved in the Old World.

Of course, the above estimated result is still preliminary. First of all, the data on
IQ from 2002 to 2006, shown in the table below, are only roughly calculated by Lynn
and Vanhanen (2006). For instance, as pointed out by Hunt and Wittmann (2008), the
data point for Suriname was based on tests given to Surinamese who had migrated to
the Netherlands and that for Ethiopia was based on the IQ scores of a highly selected
group that had emigrated to Israel and for cultural and historical reasons was hardly
representative of the Ethiopian population.[26]

Secondly, my calculation of a country's distance from Ethiopia (DFE) is only
based on the direct distance between the countries, which may not be that as shown
in the road map of ancient humans' migration out of Africa (see Fig. 1.1 in Chap. 1).

Last but not least, the above estimated result is based on a highly simplified
model. In order to yield a more convincing result, one still needs to construct a more
comprehensive and robust model.

---

[26]See Schönemann (1997) and Mackintosh (2011, pp. 353–4) for more details about existing criticism of the IQ and its measurement.

References

Arai JA, Li S, Hartley DM, Feig LA (2009) Transgenerational rescue of a genetic defect in long-term potentiation and memory formation by Juvenile Enrichment. J Neurosci 29(5):1496–1502

Beddall BG (1968) Wallace, Darwin, and the theory of natural selection. J Hist Biol 1(2):261–323

Bonduriansky R (2012) Rethinking heredity, again. Trends Ecol Evol 27:330–336

Bowler PJ (2003) Evolution: the history of an idea, 3rd edn. University of California Press, Los Angeles, CA

Clarke DD, Sokoloff L (1999) Circulation and energy metabolism of the brain. In: Siegel GJ, Agranoff BW, Albers RW, Fisher SK, Uhler MD (eds) basic neurochemistry: molecular, cellular and medical aspects, 6th edn. Lippincott Williams and Wilkins, Philadelphia, pp 637–670

Coleman WL (1977) Biology in the Nineteenth Century: Problems of form, function, and transformation. Cambridge University Press, Cambridge

Courtiol A, Pettay JE, Jokela M, Rotkirch A, Lummaa V (2012) Natural and sexual selection in a monogamous historical human population. PNAS 109(21):8044–8049

Currat M, Excoffier L (2004) Modern humans did not admix with Neanderthals during their range expansion into Europe. PLoS Biol 2(12):e421

Darwin C (1859) On the origin of species by means of natural selection or the preservation of favored races in the struggle for life, 1st edn. John Murray, London

Darwin C (1888; ed. by Francis Darwin) The life and letters of charles darwin (including an autobiographical chapter). John Murray, London

Dawkins R (1976) The selfish gene. Oxford University Press, Oxford

D'Errico FD, Zilhao J, Julien M, Baffier D, Pelerin J (1998) Neanderthal acculturation in western Europe? A critical review of the evidence and its interpretation. Curr Anthropol 39:S1–S44

Desmond A, Moore J (1991) Darwin. W.W. Norton & Company, New York and London

Diamond J (1997) Guns, germs, and steel: the fates of human societies. W.W. Norton & Company, New York

Ehret C (2002) The civilizations of Africa. University of Virginia, Charlottesville, VA

Elwell FL (2013) Sociocultural systems: principles of structure and change. University of Washington Press, Seattle

Fisher RA (1937) The wave of advance of advantageous genes. Ann Hum Genet 7(4):355–369

Gilpina, W, Feldmanb MW, Aokic K (2016) An ecocultural model predicts Neanderthal extinction through competition with modern humans. PNAS 113(8):2134–2139

Gould SJ (2002) The structure of evolutionary theory. Belknap Press of Harvard University Press, Cambridge, MA

Gravina B, Mellars P, Ramsey C (2005) Radiocarbon dating of interstratified Neanderthal and early modern human occupations at the Châtelperronian type-site. Nature 438(7064):51–56

Guo R (2018) The civilizations revisited: the historians may be wrong, really. University Press, Hong Kong

Hackett JA, Sengupta R, Zylicz JJ, Murakami K, Lee C, Down T, Surani MA (2013) Germline DNA demethylation dynamics and imprint erasure through 5-hydroxymethylcytosine. Science 339(6118):448–452

Hahn MW, Han MV, Han SG (2007) Gene family evolution across 12 Drosophila genomes. PLoS Genet 3(11):e197. https://doi.org/10.1371/journal.pgen.0030197

Handley LJ, Manica A, Goudet J, Balloux F (2007) Going the distance: human population genetics in a clinal world. Trends Genet 23(9):432–439

Hunt E, Wittmann W (2008) National intelligence and prosperity. Intelligence 36(1):1–9

Hunt KD (1994) The evolution of human bipedality: Ecology and functional morphology. J Hum Evol 26(3):183–202

Johnson D, Edgar B (2001) From lucy to language. Casell Paperbacks, London

Kimura YC (2002) Examining time trends in the Oldowan technology at Beds I and II, Olduvai Gorge. J Hum Evol 43(3):291–321

Lenski G, Nolan P (1970) Human societies: an introduction to macrosociology. McGraw Hill, New York

Lovejoy C Owen (1988) Evolution of human walking. Sci Am 259(5):82–89

Lumey LH, Stein AD, Ravelli Anita CJ (1995) Timing of prenatal starvation in women and birth weight in their first and second born offspring: The Dutch famine birth cohort study. Eur J Obstet Gynecol 61(1):23–30

Lynn R, Vanhanen T (2002) IQ and the wealth of nations (Human Evolution, Behavior, and Intelligence Series). Praeger, Westport, CT

Lynn R, Vanhanen T (2006) IQ and global inequality. Washington Summit Publishers, Atlanta, Georgia

Mackintosh NJ (2011) IQ and human intelligence, 2nd edn. Oxford University Press, Oxford

Mayr E (1982) The growth of biological thought: diversity, evolution, and inheritance. Belknap Press of Harvard University Press, Cambridge, MA

Mellars P (2006) A new radiocarbon revolution and the dispersal of modern humans in Eurasia. Nature 439(7079):931–935

Moorem JR (2002) History, humanity and evolution: essays for John C. Cambridge University Pres, Greene. Cambridge

Neisser, U, Boodoo G, Bouchard TJ, Boykin AW, Brody N, Ceci SJ, Halpern DF, Loehlin JC, Perloff R, Sternberg RJ, Urbina S (1996) Intelligence: Knowns and unknowns. Am Psychol 51:77–101

Ng S-F, Lin Ruby CY, Ross Laybutt D, Barres R, Owens JA, Morris MJ (2010) Chronic high-fat diet in fathers programs β-cell dysfunction in female rat offspring. Nature 467(7318):963–966

Novembre J, Di Rienzo A (2009) Spatial patterns of variation due to natural selection in humans. Nat Rev Genet 10:745–755

Osborn HF (1896) From the greeks to darwin: an outline of the development of the evolution idea, 2nd edn. Macmillan, London and New York

Packard, A Spring (1901) Lamarck, the Founder of Evolution: His life and work with translations of his writing on organic evolution. New York: Longmans, Green. http://www.gutenberg.org/ebooks/20556. Accessed 20 Nov 2014

Parsons T (1966) Societies: evolutionary and comparative perspectives. Prentice-Hall, Upper Saddle River, NJ

Parsons T (1971) The system of modern societies (Foundations of Modern Sociology). Prentice-Hall, Upper Saddle River, NJ

Prothero DR, Schoch RM (2003) Horns, tusks, and flippers: the evolution of hoofed mammals. Johns Hopkins University Press, Washington, DC

Roth TL, Lubin FD, Funk AJ, Sweatt JD (2009) Lasting epigenetic influence of early-life adversity on the BDNF gene. Biol Psychiatr 65(9):760–9

Rushton JP (2000) Race, evolution, and behavior: a life history perspective (Second Edition). Charles Darwin Research Institute, Port Huron, MI

Rushton JP, Rushton EW (2003) Brain size, IQ, and racial-group differences: Evidence from musculoskeletal traits. Intell 31(2):139–155

Schoenemann P Thomas (2006) Evolution of the size and functional areas of the human brain. Annu Rev Anthropol 35:379–406

Schönemann PH (1997) On models and muddles of heritability. Genetica 99(2–3):97–108

Singer E (2009) A comeback for Lamarckian evolution? Two new studies show that the effects of a mother's early environment can be passed on to the next generation. MIT Technology Review, February 4. http://www.technologyreview.com/news/411880/a-comeback-for-lamarckian-evolution/. Accessed 26 Oct 2016

Springer J, Holley D (2012) An introduction to zoology: investigating the animal world. Jones and Bartlett Learning, Burlington, MA

Stringer C, Gamble C (1993) In search of the neanderthals: solving the puzzle of human origins. Thames & Hudson, New York

Trinkaus E (2007) European early modern humans and the fate of the Neanderthals. PNAS 104(18):7367–7372 van Wyhe J (2007) Mind the gap: Did Darwin avoid publishing his theory for many years? Notes and Records of the Royal Society 61(2):177–205

Williams C (1987) Destruction of black civilisation. Third World Press, Chicago

Yang MA, Fu Q (2018) Insights into modern human prehistory using ancient genomes. Trends Genet 34(3):184–196. https://doi.org/10.1016/j.tig.2017.11.008

Zaatari SEl, Grine FE, Ungar PS, Hublin J-J (2016) Neandertal versus modern human dietary responses to climatic fluctuations. PLoS One 11(4):e0153277. https://doi.org/10.1371/journal. pone.0153277

Chapter 3
Human Thermodynamics and Culture (II)

Abstract Historians and anthropologists have highly simplified, if not dismissed, the biological factors that may have decided or influenced the dynamic behaviors of humans and civilizations. As a matter of fact, human emigration throughout the world was a response-to-challenge process. Thus, humans coming out of Africa must have been physically inferior to those who continued to stay in or near to their original homes. In all circumstances, physical weakness may provide incentives (whereas physical advantages may provide disincentives) for humans to develop complex societies from previous simpler ones. Not all human and cultural evolutions are consistent with what Darwin called "natural selection." Nevertheless, they all conform to the basic law of human thermodynamics: that humans' mental output and physical output are roughly negatively correlated. As a result, language, religion, and culture as a whole are created by those who are (or who think they are) weak.

Keywords Human evolution · Civilization · Human thermodynamics
Language · Religion

3.1 Why Humans Cry?

Since Darwin's theory of evolution, questions about the origin of language have generated a rapidly growing scientific literature, stretched across a number of disciplines. The diversity of perspectives—from linguistics, anthropology, speech science, genetics, neuroscience, and evolutionary biology—can be bewildering. There have been many theories about the origin of human language. One of the earliest theories sees language as having developed from music, a view already espoused by Jean-Jacques Rousseau, Wilhelm von Humboldt, and Charles Darwin (Fitch 2010, pp. 466–507). However, this is not convincing since it does not explain the inherent factor(s) contributing to the birth of human language or of the music itself. In addition, Linguist and philosopher Noam Chomsky even desperately proposed that:

© Springer Nature Singapore Pte Ltd. 2019
R. Guo, *Human-Earth System Dynamics*,
https://doi.org/10.1007/978-981-13-0547-4_3

To tell a fairy tale about it, it is almost as if there was some higher primate wandering around a long time ago and some random mutation took place, maybe after some strange cosmic ray shower, and it reorganized the brain, implanting a language organ in an otherwise primate brain.[1]

Though cautioning against taking this story too literally, Chomsky insisted that abovementioned tale might be closer to reality than many other fairy tales that are told about evolutionary processes, including language (Chomsky 2000, p. 4). It is obvious that the origin of human language still remains as one of the biggest unsolved puzzles of human history.

Language is what has made us human, and it appears that no communication system of equivalent power exists elsewhere in the animal kingdom. In fact, language originated from humans' crying. It has been known that emotional tears are a universal and uniquely human behavior. Further, shedding tears may influence the mood of the crier and his/her outlook on life primarily as a consequence of fulfillment of the proposed signaling function of tears (Gračanin et al. 2018). Unsurprisingly, over hundreds of years, scholars from different backgrounds have speculated about the origin and functions of human tears. Humans are the only creatures who can cry for emotional reasons. Many distinctions have been offered between humans and the rest of the animal world, which include the anguished tear, and the apprehension that life is tragic, among others. For example, in his book, *Why Humans Like to Cry: Tragedy, Evolution, and the Brain*, Michael Trimble writes:

In the summer of 2008, Gana the gorilla gave birth to a male baby in the Munster Zoo, which three months later died of unknown causes. Images of Gana holding on to the dead infant for several days were widely reported in the newspapers and on the Internet. Someone from the zoo said that such behavior was not uncommon in gorillas, and it was interpreted by another as mourning. This may well have been correct, but what was more interesting was that yet another spokesman implied that the whole of Germany was mourning for her. It was reported in the newspapers that many visitors to the zoo, who came to see Gana and the dead child, were moved to tears – but Gana shed none.[2]

Human voice consists of sounds made by human beings using the vocal folds for laughing, crying, screaming, talking, singing, and so on. The human voice is specifically a part of human sound production in which the vocal folds (vocal cords) are the primary sound source.[3] Language is the ability to acquire and use complex systems of communication, particularly the one for humans to do so, and a language is any specific example of such a system. Then how were different languages created throughout the world? Because language emerged in the early prehistory of mankind, its early development has left no historical traces, and it is believed that no comparable processes can be observed today.

It is generally believed that "ma" and "pa" were among the first words that humans have spoken. The crosslinguistic similarities of these terms are thought to result from the nature of language acquisition. These words are the first word-like sounds made

---

[1] Cited from Chomsky (2000, p. 4).

[2] Cited from Trimble (2012, pp. 1–2).

[3] See, for example, Smith et al. (1975) and Williams and Stevens (1972).

by babbling babies (babble words), and parents tend to associate the first sound babies make with themselves and to employ them subsequently as part of their baby-talk lexicon.[4] Thus, humans' common ancestry should have contributed to the similarities of Mandarin Chinese māma, Swahili mama, Navajo amá, Quechua mama, Polish mama, Romanian mama, and English mama (all denoting "mother") or of Aramaic abba, Mandarin Chinese bàba, Persian baba, and French papa (all denoting "father"). It is reasonable to assume that human languages have experienced much more rapid changes since humans entered complicated societies than they did in their hunter-gatherer lifestyle. And, without good reason, the earliest language(s) was (were) built up from speech sounds that were easiest to produce (bilabials like "m," "p," and "b" and the open vowel "a").

Of course, ma or mama was adopted as a formal concept much earlier than pa or papa, though it is still not clear when the concept of motherhood was first created. Anthropological evidence suggests that patriarchal social structures did not develop until the appearance of agriculture and domestication and other social and technological developments.[5] Some scholars even precisely set about 4000 BC as the beginning of the spread of patriarchy (Kraemer 1991). In the Sumerian King List—an ancient stone tablet originally recorded in the Sumerian language—Gilgamesh is generally seen by scholars as a historical figure, and the father–son relationship between Gilgamesh and Ur-Nungal have been confirmed. Precise dates cannot be given for the lifetime of Gilgamesh, but they are generally agreed to lie between 2800 BC and 2500 BC (Dalley 2000, p. 40). In ancient China, the throne succeeded from fatherhood before the Xia dynasty (c. 2100–c. 1700 BC) has never been mentioned in existing literature. Nevertheless, the patriarchy could have appeared earlier than those dates in both Mesopotamia and China but definitely later than them in some other places of the rest of the world.

It is easy to understand that the word for mother ('ma') came into existence much earlier than that for father ('pa')—even today, babies still pronounce "ma" earlier than they pronounce "ba." However, "wa" is the earliest word that was used by our distant ancestors. It is very likely that "wa" was originally associated with the sound of crying of humans. Given the harsh and depressed living conditions of early humans, wa and its variants must have been used by peoples from various parts of the world to denote the terms that were most critical to them, including "house," "home," "land," "village," or even "motherland." For example, in Japanese, "wa" represents "Japan" and "Japanese." In some Chinese dialects, the traditional names of the Chinese nation "華" (or "华") and of China's first dynasty "夏"—now called "Hua" and "Xia" in Mandarin Chinese, respectively—have the pronunciations similar to "wa" or any variant of it.[6] It is thus very likely that they all were pronounced "wa" in Proto-Chinese as well (see Table 3.1).

---

[4]See, for example, Jakobson (1962, pp. 538–45) and Bancel and de l'Etang (2008, pp. 417–38).

[5]See, for example, Eagly and Wood (1999) and Hughes and Hughes (2001, pp. 118–19).

[6]See Guo (2018, Chap. 5) a more detailed description of the cultural meanings and historical evolutions of the two Chinese characters.

Table 3.1 Changing pronunciations of the names for Chinese nation

Language (dialect)	Approximate date of appearance	Pronunciations for	
		華	夏
Root/Proto-Chinese	Xia-Shang (c. 2100-1046 BC)	[wā][a]	[wā][a]
Wu Chinese	Zhou (1046-221 BC)[b]	[wŏ][c]	[wū] [hō][c]
Cantonese	Qin (221-206 BC)[b]	[wā][c]	[hā][c]
Hakka[d]	Sui-Tang (AD 581-907)[b]	[fā][c]	[hā][c]
Southern Fujian	Song (960-1279)[b]	[huā]	[hā]
Mandarin Chinese	Ming-Qing (1368-1911)	[huá]	[xià]

Notes The pronunciations shown in the last two columns are contemporary in each language or dialect concerned and may not be the same as what they were
[a]Hypothetical, based on the fact that "wa" is the common ancestral language and the two inferences that are stated at the end of Sect. 2.3
[b]Based on the main period during which speakers of the language (dialect) concerned migrated out of central China (i.e., the middle and lower reaches of the Yellow River Valley)
[c]Other, more twisted pronunciations also exit in different areas, but are omitted here since, according to note ([a]), more twisted pronunciations are less likely derived from an older or proto-language
[d]Hakka literally means "guest family" or "guest people" in Chinese
Source Guo (2018)

Indeed, the syllable "wa" can be found more frequently in indigenous languages than in other languages. Still, a large number of terms prefixed and suffixed with "wa" (or "va") have been adopted in almost all existing languages. The earliest humans, not like modern humans, had been only able to make use of a few syllables—such as "ma" (already used to denote "mother"), "pa" or "ba" (already used to denote "father"), and "wa"—in their oral communication. Therefore, they had to frequently use these syllables. For example, Teiwa (also referred to as Tewa) is a non-Austronesian, Papuan language spoken on the Pantar Island in eastern Indonesia. Tiwa (also called Lalung) is a Sino-Tibetan language of Assam in Northeast India. In Indonesia, Java is an island that dominates it politically, economically, and culturally. The name Java or Jawa is derived from the Proto-Austronesian root word "Iawa" that means "[my/our] home" (Hatley 1984, pp. 1–32), while the word "Yawa-dvipa" (here, "dvipa" means island), which is mentioned in India's earliest epic, the Ramayana, is also referred to as the island of Java. In Kichwa (Spanish: Quechua)—an indigenous language of Andean South America—the terms "Qhichwa" (denoting "temperate valley") and "Kichwa" (denoting both "Quechua language" and "Quechua people") are similarly spelled and each include the syllable "wa." It is more interesting to note that in Amharic—an Afro-Asiatic language of the Semitic branch and spoken as a mother tongue by the Amhara people in Ethiopia—if a noun is definite or specified, this is expressed by a suffix, the article, which is -wa, -itwa, or -ätwa for feminine singular nouns.

Frankly speaking, it is quite difficult to clarify when and why oral languages were invented, but it is almost certain that it existed much earlier than written languages did. It is worth noting that, not just Han-Chinese, but many other languages in Asia are monosyllabic. Therefore, we have to pay some attention to the influences of both environmental and human features on the evolution of linguistic styles there. As discussed in the British-Japanese case of Sect. 1.3 in Chap. 1, many peoples of the Mongoloid (especially those of its southern group, including the Han-Chinese) have been physically weaker than those of the Caucasoid. As a result, the Han-Chinese had been more disadvantageous than the Caucasoid before they settled at their current places in the Far East. In addition, even though the Caucasoid had also suffered from various natural disasters and attacks by predators, the still weaker Chinese and many (if not all) other peoples of the Mongoloid must have suffered more seriously in their past history.

Humans inhabited the Tibetan Plateau at least 21,000 years ago. However, this population was largely replaced around 3,000 years ago by Neolithic immigrants from northern China, though there is a partial genetic continuity between the Paleolithic inhabitants and contemporary Tibetan populations (Zhao et al. 2009). Ü-Tsang (or Tsang-Ü) is one of three traditional areas of the Tibetan civilization, the other two being Amdo in the northeast and Kham in the east. Taken together, Ü and Tsang (or Zang) are considered to be the center of Tibet from historical, cultural, political, and economic perspectives. Of this territory, Ü constitutes central Tibet, controlled by the Gelug lineage of Tibetan Buddhism under the early Dalai Lamas, up to Sokla Kyao in the east where it borders to Kham. It includes the Lhasa River valley, where Lhasa (meaning "place of the gods" in Tibetan) is situated, and the Yarlung, and Chonggye valleys to the south of the Tsangpo.

Linguistically, Ü (or Wü) is pronounced [w-yu] in Tibetan, which is believed to have evolved from "wa." The close relations of the Tibetan language (as represented by the Lhasa dialect) with humans' common ancestral language can also be found in the following fact: that many Tibetan personal nouns have the suffix of "-wa" similar to that of "-er" or "-ist" in English. It is still not clear how the evolution of Tibetan language—a branch of the Sino-Tibetan language family—has been related to the high-elevation climate in Tibet, though all human languages have been influenced by the environment. And the meanings of "wa" in Tibetan, like in many other indigenous languages, include house, home, homeland, motherland, kingdom, and even land of the gods. In addition, Namchabarwa (or Namjagbarwa), with meanings of "a spear piercing the sky" and of "thunder is burning like fire" in Tibetan, is the highest of the entire Tibetan Himalaya chain as well as the earth's easternmost peak.

Creativity has kept people alive during harsh conditions, and it has also made certain individuals wealthy. We use creativity in our daily lives as well, such as finding a shortcut to a destination. All this must have been achieved by those who have a demand—demand is the mother of invention. As matter of fact, humans are not the only species that have optimized their linguistic style in order to fit in with their surroundings. Many other mammals may have also created the best languages of their own. Though much simpler than those of human languages, the voices (or languages) of the following animals can be divided into two categories:

- Long syllabic: badgers, big cats (such as tigers, lions, jaguars, and leopards), cattle, dogs, elephants, giraffes, hippopotamuses, oxen, and wolves; and
- Short syllabic: antelopes, chinchillas, deer, guinea pigs, hamsters, hares, mice, moose, pigs/hogs, prairie dogs, rhinoceros, and tapirs.[7]

Note that this kind of classification is not a mandate and that there might still have been a few exceptions. For example, cheetah, also known as the hunting leopard, is a big cat that occurs mainly in eastern and southern Africa and a few parts of Iran. Its short-syllabic voices may have stemmed from the fact that the cheetah will surrender its kill to sturdier carnivores such as lions, leopards, spotted hyena, brown hyena, and wild dogs.[8] The accurate meanings of some voices (or languages) of the above animals have not been quite clear. However, a general law can still be set here: the large animals and predators, given that they are physically stronger than other, small or herbivorous animals living around them, usually utter relaxed, long-syllabic voices. On the other hand, however, the small, herbivorous animals usually face various threats and hence have to use short, and uneasy (alerting?), syllabic voices to hurriedly inform their colleagues of any dangers and threats.

With regard to the human case, the same logic exists. Of course, compared with those physically strong animals and predators (such as elephants, tigers, and lions), who usually utter long-syllabic voices, all human languages can only but be defined as short-syllabic. Nevertheless, human languages do differ from each other. And the reasons why the physically weaker humans have used monosyllabic and highly simplified oral languages must be additionally due to the fact that, given the harsh living conditions under which they were living, they had to invent an efficient and "time-saving" approach to their communications and cooperation (see Sect. 4.3 in Chap. 4 for a more detailed explanation of the environmental influences on language evolution).

Above all, human language has developed from animal communication in primates: either gestural or vocal communication to assist in cooperation (Tomasello 2008, p. 44). It is reasonable to assume that the creation of a language must have been driven by the crying demand of humans who were physically weak. Without demand, there would be no incentives for the creation of complicated languages. How to explain this? Let us consider a scenario that might be found tens of thousands of years ago:

> In a cold winter, three male adults, named Clever, Slyer, and Titan, are looking for food in a vast forestry. As his name suggests, Titan is a strong guy and usually can hunt enough animals – small and large. His hunting method is simple but still works quite well; and he believes that there is no need to change it. He neither needs any help nor wants to help others. But Clever and Slyer have different stories. Each of them is only able to hunt small animals.

---

[7]Note that the differing lengths of animals' necks also influence the types of their voices.

[8]Generally, cheetahs lose around 10–15% of their kills to other predators (Sunquist and Sunquist, 2002, pp. 14–36); sometimes the percentage was found to be as high as 50% (O'Brien and Wildt, 1986).

They have had nothing to eat for a couple of days. Suddenly, a large animal appears at the line of sight; but a successful hunt needs the cooperative work of two male adults. If their hunting is successful, Clever and Slyer could have enough food for a couple of weeks; if they failed, they may die from starvation. Now, Clever and Slyer, both of whom are in hungry, have no other choice but quickly form a union of hunting.

Probably the above story had happened frequently when human beings were still hunter-gatherers. Of course, not all cases ended in cooperation and succeeded in hunting. In case of no cooperation, men and women who were physically weak were unlikely to survive. Still, there was another situation in which men or women were strong enough that they did not need any form of cooperation. In this case, they did not have incentives to develop more complicated linguistic system and, thus, they would not have created any form of civilization for their own. Nevertheless, our distant ancestors were not strong enough. And, with joint participation and cooperation through effective communication and bargaining, they have survived. In most, if not all circumstances, compared with those who were physically strong, people who were physically weak had more incentives to invent languages. As a result, language—an effective tool of interpersonal communication—was gradually developed from primary to advanced forms.

3.2 Law of Language Evolution[9]

Archeological evidence shows that humans' early migration outside the African continent was conducted from tropical and subtropical areas (suitable for early humans to live) to frigid areas (not quite suitable for early humans to live).[10] And humans did not know which place was the best one for their own. As a matter of fact, when humans migrated out of Africa, they finally settled in almost each corner of earth—forestry, coastal area, mountains, and so on—results that were subject to various cooperative and non-cooperative games and wars. And, according to the final results of the "Win-Stay Lose-Shift" game, physically weaker humans must have been settled in places farther away from Africa. For example, one study shows that Peru's Native Americans based at the highlands of the Andes had the average heights of 1.57 m (5'2") and 1.45 m (4'9") for men and women, respectively.[11] However, why did the physically weak Americans not achieve a civilization as powerful as the Eurasian civilizations? It must be noted here that, even though humans' physical weakness tended to incentivize them to create cultural complexity, other factors have also played crucial roles in the rise and fall of ancient civilizations.

A consistent comparison of the Americas and Eurasia cannot be easily conducted since many internal and external factors in there cannot be held fixed. Nevertheless,

---

[9]This section heavily draws on Guo (2018, ch. 1).

[10]See Bower (January 27, 2011), Bowler et al. (2003), Croft (2012, p. 261), and Wells and Read (2002, pp. 138-40) for more detailed analyses of humans' early migration throughout the world.

[11]Source: http://www.worldebooklibrary.com/articles/eng/Incas, accessed 2017-2-11.

since the Native Americans and the Native Africans had remained quite isolated from each other and from those in the rest of the world before the Columbian era, a comparison of them seems to be more appropriate. The case study at the end of this chapter shows that humans' past process of migration throughout the world can explain, to a greater or lesser extent, the diverse developments of the Cherokee and Vai peoples. The Negroid (to which the Vai people belong) had been first winner and thus had no demand of change or invention; by way of contrast, the Mongoloid (to which the Cherokee people belong) had been the long-lasting loser through their way from Africa to the Eurasia and to North America. However, it is their long and difficult journeys that helped the Cherokee people become more creative (at least in the creation of a writing system). Winners stay and losers shift!

During much of the prehistoric period, complicated cultural traditions did not emerge, and language and many other cultural elements only existed at primitive levels. As a result, intercultural differences were very small. Edward Sapir, an American anthropologist, provided an interesting fact, suggesting that certain languages might be related in that they have evolved from a common ancestral language (Sapir 1985, p. 11). In addition, Stephen Anderson, Yale Professor of Linguistics, states: "Researchers on the evolutionary origin of language generally find it plausible to suggest that language was invented only once, and that all modern spoken languages are thus in some way related, even if that relation can no longer be recovered..."[12]

'Wadi' is the Arabic and Hebrew terms traditionally referring to a dry valley. In some instances, it may refer to an ephemeral riverbed that contains water only during times of heavy rain or simply an intermittent stream. The Han-Chinese, with a population of about one-fifth of the world total, now also use "wadi" to denote a similar place ('land lower than its surroundings'). If it is not accidental, then there must be broader implications. Note that word "wadi" is short-syllabic—a style that has been thoroughly adopted in the Han-Chinese and other Southeast Asian language. On average, the short-syllabic speakers are physically weaker than long-syllabic speakers (including, for example, White Europeans). However, in general, the earliest prehistoric human beings, no matter which race they belonged to, must have spoken just like the small, herbivorous animals do (as stated earlier).

What have decided or influenced the formation of languages? As a matter of fact, the short and heartrending scream of "wa" is also very similar to those that apes, gorilla, and several other animals physically similar to humankind produce whenever they meet difficult or dangerous situations. However, it is never similar to those of physically stronger animals and predators (such as elephants, tigers, and lions). Indeed, many comfortable places in which peoples—both natives and newcomers—have been living quite well have never given birth to an indigenous civilization. Prehistoric languages must have been short-syllabic at the early stage of evolutions. And humans' living conditions must have faced various dangerous situations. However, it is these dangerous situations and threats that have provided incentives for humans and their cultures and civilizations to change and advance. (See next chapter for a more detailed analysis.)

---

[12]Cited from Anderson (2012, p. 107).

The above law can also be applied to southern Africa—a place that has raised the Negroid who had been and still are the strongest among all the human races in the world. Frankly, though physically stronger than both the Caucasoid and the Mongoloid, the Negroid are still far weaker than the large predators that had once lived with them in a same piece of forestry or grassland in sub-Saharan Africa. As a result, in southern Africa, the Negroid must have developed their linguistic and other cultural skills according to the same logic as adopted by peoples living elsewhere.

Swahili, also known as Kiswahili, belongs to the Niger–Congo language family and is the first language of the Swahili (Waswahili) people. It is a lingua franca of the African Great Lakes region and other parts of eastern and southeastern Africa, including Tanzania, Kenya, Uganda, Rwanda, Burundi, Mozambique, and the Democratic Republic of the Congo. The closely related Comorian language, spoken in the Comoros Islands, is sometimes considered a dialect. Swahili is used as a lingua franca in much of Southeast Africa and is the most widely spoken language by number of speakers. Estimates of the total number of Swahili speakers vary widely, with the largest number over 150 million (Kimutai et al. 2013). Swahili serves as the official language of three nations: Tanzania, Kenya, and the Democratic Republic of the Congo. Shikomor, the official language in Comoros and also spoken in Mayotte (Shimaore), is related to Swahili. Swahili is also one of the working languages of the African Union and officially recognized as a lingua franca of the East African Community. The name Swahili means "boundary" or "coast", used as an adjective meaning "coastal dwellers." Standard Swahili has a very common semivowel, "wa." It is used to make diphthongs, as in the following: mwaka (year), watu (people), watoto (children), mwahali (places), wavu (net), wali (cooked rice), wazo (thought), maridhawa (abundance), ziwa (lake), bwana (sir), mwavuli (umbrella), kingugwa (spotted hyena), mbwa (dog)…

More evidence can be found to support the hypothesis that existing human languages come from the wa-based ancestral language. "Kwa" means "place" in Zulu—a Bantu language that is most widely spoken in South Africa. Tswana are a Bantu-speaking ethnic group who are native to Southern Africa. Ethnic Tswana have made up the majority of the population of Botswana. The Tswana language also belongs to the Bantu group. According to historical records, three main branches of the Tswana tribe formed during the seventeenth century. Three brothers, Bakwana, Ngwaketse, and Ngwato, broke away from their father, Chief Molope, to establish their own tribes, probably in response to drought and expanding populations in search of pasture and arable land.[13]

Swaziland, officially the Kingdom of Swaziland, is a sovereign state in southern Africa. The country and its people take their names from Mswati II (c. 1820–1868), the nineteenth-century king under whose rule Swazi territory was expanded and unified. At no more than 200 km from north to south and 130 km from east to west, Swaziland is one of the smallest countries in Africa. Despite its size, however, its climate and topography is diverse, ranging from a cool and mountainous highveld (highland) to a hot and dry lowveld (lowland). The population is primarily ethnic

---

[13] Source: https://www.lonelyplanet.com/botswana/history, accessed 2017-11-24.

Swazis whose language is Swazi (or Swati). They established their kingdom in the mid-eighteenth century under the leadership of Ngwane III; and the present boundaries were drawn up in 1881.[14]

Before entering Swaziland, the Swazi settlers, then known as the Ngwane (or bakaNgwane), had settled along the banks of the Pongola River. Prior to that they settled in the area of the Tembe River near present-day Maputo. Continuing conflict with the Ndwandwe people pushed them further north, with Ngwane III establishing his capital at Shiselweni at the foot of the Mhlosheni hills. KaNgwane, named for Ngwane III, is an alternative name for Swaziland. Mswati II extended the area of his country to twice its previous size. Many neighboring clans were incorporated into the kingdom with wide autonomy, often including grants of special ritual and political status. The extent of their autonomy, however, was drastically curtailed by Mswati, who attacked and subdued some of them in the 1850s. With his power, Mswati greatly incorporated more people into his kingdom either through conquest or by giving them refuge. These later arrivals became known to the Swazis as Emafikamuva.[15]

Obviously, many of these African names each include the syllable "wa" or a variant of it. To be certain, "wa" is the common ancestral language of all humans, and other, more twisted syllables did not come into being until later stages when cultures became more complicated.

The earliest human civilization is believed to have been associated with the Euphrates and the Tigris. The ancient Greek name for the Euphrates was borrowed from Old Persian Ufratu, itself from ú-ip-ra-tu-iš in Elamite—an extinct language of Elam (an ancient pre-Iranian civilization centered in the far West and Southwest of what is now modern-day Iran). The Elamite name is ultimately derived from the Sumerian Buranuna, possibly through the Akkadian name. In Akkadian, the river was similarly called Purattu (Woods 2005). It has been suggested that, since Mesopotamia was the center of copper metallurgy during the period, and that the Euphrates was the river by which the copper ore was transported in rafts, the Sumerian *burudu or urudu (meaning "copper") is the origin (Gamkrelidze and Ivanov 1995, p. 616).

However, given the river's importance to the survival of the ancient Sumerians on the one hand, and that the ancient Sumerian culture was highly subject to various deities, on the other, the original meaning of the Euphrates should not be "copper." Think that the history of transporting copper via the Euphrates was much shorter than that the ancient Sumerians' early agricultural activity along this river. It is likely that the ancient Sumerians must have given the Euphrates a name before they knew the importance of copper and that there must be a more auspicious name for the Euphrates. As a matter of fact, "urudu" actually was "wadu," meaning the "goddess of weaving and clothing" (i.e., Uttu) as defined in Sumerian mythology.

The ancient Greek name for the Tigris was borrowed from Old Persian Tigra, itself from Elamite Tigra, itself from Sumerian Idigna. The Middle Persian name for the Tigris was Arvand Rud (literally "swift river"), though it now refers to the confluence of the Euphrates and Tigris (in Arabic: Shatt al-Arab) in the New Persian

---

[14]See, for example, Bonner (1982, pp. 9–27) and Kuper (1997, pp. 9–10).
[15]Based on Bonner (1982, pp. 60, and 85–88).

language. In Kurdish, it is known as Ava Mezin, meaning "the great water." Since the Tigris did not run through southern Mesopotamia (home to the earliest Sumerian civilization), its Sumerian name should have come into existence later than that of the Euphrates. Of course, the exact dates for the Proto-Sumerian names for both the Euphrates and the Tigris are unclear.

Tradition holds that the Arabian desert is the birthplaces of many ancient Mesopotamians. The Arabs were first mentioned in the mid-ninth century BC as a tribal people in eastern and southern Syria, and the north of the Arabian peninsula (Myers 2010, p. 18). It must be noted that existing explanations of the term "Arab" in Semitic languages—including those in which Arab is referred to "west," "sunset," "desert," "nomadic," and "merchant"—may not be culturally convincing. The ancients living in the harsh environment usually related themselves to some divine sources. In fact, several different ethnonyms that are found in Assyrian texts are roughly transliterated as "Arab": Arabi, Arubu, Aribi, Urbi, and so on. As a result, I believe that the word "Arab" is likely derived from Abu—a Sumerian god of plants and vegetation that was originally read "Wabu" by the ancient Mesopotamians.

Over the course of the past thousands of years, and thanks to humans' continuing efforts on the invention of new syllables and new vocabularies, the frequency of the syllable "wa" in human languages has been declining over time. For example, in the "Declaration of Independence" of the United States of America, which was drafted in AD 1776, only 0.75% of the English words include the syllable "wa." However, in the "Hymn to the Nile," written in the Egyptian hieroglyphs in the New Kingdom (c. 1550–1069 BC), about 1.11% of the words include the syllable "wa," and that, in "The Epic of Gilgamesh"—an epic poem written in the Sumerian cuneiform in about 2600 BC and compiled in a dialect of Akkadian sometime between 1300 and 1000 BC that is often regarded as the oldest written story on earth, the frequency of the words including the syllable "wa" is as high as 1.75%.[16] Obviously, the older the written document, the higher is the frequency of the syllable "wa" in it.

To be certain, at the earliest stage when humans were evolving bipedalism, they were still not able to speak "ma" and "ba" ("pa"); however, like many other similar animals, they could scream with the sound "wa." Consequently, the following inferences seem to be reasonable:

(i) If the pronunciation of a term (or any part thereof) is (or is similar to) [wā] in a language at a specific time, then it is also [wā] in that language before that time, though it is not necessarily so thereafter; and

(ii) If the pronunciations of a term (or any part thereof) are both [wā] and other, more twisted syllables in a given family of languages, the term should have been pronounced [wā]—not any other, more twisted syllables—in the proto-language of all these languages.

---

[16]Calculated by author based on the English translations of "The Epic of Gilgamesh" (available at http://www.ancienttexts.org/library/mesopotamian/gilgamesh/) and of the "Hymn to the Nile" (available at http://www.reshafim.org.il/ad/egypt/texts/hymn_to_the_nile.htm)—all accessed 2017-04-24. The figures for the "Epic of Gilgamesh" and the "Hymn to the Nile" can be underestimated since the syllable 'wa' may have mutated when the original texts were translated into English.

To be even more certain, "wa" first appeared in the ancestral languages of all humans, and its variants include, inter alia, "va," "wo," "vo," and "we." Other, more twisted syllables and words did not come into being until later stages when cultures became more complicated. For example, the ancient Egyptians originally knew Thebes (an ancient Egyptian city located east of the Nile about 800 km south of the Mediterranean) as Waset, Wo'sen or Wase. With its ruins lying within the modern Egyptian city of Luxor, Thebes (Waset) was the main city of the fourth Upper Egyptian nome (Sceptre nome) and was the capital of Egypt during the Middle Kingdom (c. 2055—1640 BC) and much of the New Kingdom (c. 1550–1069 BC). Waset began to be known as Niwt-'Imn ("city of Amun") from the end of the New Kingdom (Huddlestun 2003) and as other, more twisted names (such as Thebes and Luxor) later on.

In short, the word "wa" has the meanings of, for example, "house," "land," "homeland," and "motherland," and its extended meanings include physical and moral protections. In addition, "wa" has also frequently served as the key syllable for the vocabularies in almost all human languages, especially in indigenous languages. Tens of thousands of years ago, humans' language perhaps was not different from those of other primates (such as gorillas and chimpanzees). Only after their cultures grew larger and became more complicated, did humans from different parts of the world begin to find it necessary to diversify their common, wa-based ancestral language (see Fig. 3.1).

3.3 Religion Is Created by and for the Weak

Religion is a major determinant of humans' societal attitudes and behaviors. According to the Oxford Advanced Learner's Dictionary, "religion" is defined as "belief in the existence of a supernatural ruling power, the creator and controller of the universe, who has given to man a spiritual nature which continues to exist after the death of the body" (OALD 1974, p. 712). The development of religion has taken different forms in different cultures. Some religions place an emphasis on belief, while others emphasize practice. In many places, religion has been associated with public institutions such as education, hospitals, the family, government, and political hierarchies.

It is quite reasonable to believe that civilizations were quite an unintentional invention of human beings. More precisely, they were the by-products of human beings' struggles for their survival. To be certain, had human beings been strong enough as compared with their enemies, they would not have invented any advanced tools and weapons for their own; had they run as fast as they expect, they would not have invented any fast-running vehicles, neither would they have invented airplanes so that now they can fly as high as birds do. However, over the course of the past tens of thousands of years, our distant ancestors' steady efforts have unintentionally created various advanced civilizations, all being—believe it or not—the by-product of their passive struggles.

Fig. 3.1 Civilizations came from Wa: Linguistic evidence *Notes* (1) "Hua" means "China or Chinese nation." (2) "Shiva" (or Siva or Siwa), one of the principal deities of Hinduism, is believed to have derived from the Harappan civilization. (3) "Pharaoh" is the title of the ancient Egyptian kings. (4) "Ur" and "Uruk"—two of the earliest Sumerian city-states—mean the places of earth-goddess and sky-god, respectively. (5) "Wak'a" means "god of protection" or "sacred object or place" in Quechua (or Kichwa)—an indigenous language in Andean South America. (6) "Waka'" means "place of gods" in Nahuatl (or Nawatl)—a Mayan language in Mesoamerica. *Source* Author

It seems apparent that one thing religion or belief helps us do is to deal with problems of human life that are significant, persistent, and intolerable. One important way in which religious beliefs accomplish this is by providing "a set of ideas about how and why the world is put together that allows people to accommodate anxieties and deal with misfortune" (Monoghan and Peter 2000, p. 124). Thus, it is reasonable to assume that all existing religions were created for those who believed that they had been far weak in the world they lived. On the other hand, most of existing religions have been created, either individually or collectively, by those who faced various difficulties or thought to have been weak themselves.

Confucianism combines a political theory and a theory of human nature. The theory starts with a doctrine of political authority. The legitimate ruler derives authority from heaven's command or the mandate of heaven (tianming). The ruler bears responsibility for the well-being of the people and therefore for peace and order in the empire. Confucian philosophy presupposes that humans are essentially social animals whose mode of social interaction is shaped by li (convention or ritual), which establishes value distinctions and prescribes activities in response to those distinctions. Education in the li, or social rituals, is based on the natural behavioral propensity to imitate models. Ideally, the ruler should himself be such a model and should appoint only those who are models of de (virtue) to positions of prominence. People are naturally inclined to emulate virtuous models; hence, a hierarchy of merit results in widespread natural moral education. Lunyu, commonly known in English by the title of "Analects of Confucius," became the basis of the Chinese social lifestyle and the fundamental religious and philosophical point of view of most traditionalist Chinese intellectuals throughout history since the Han dynasty. It is one of the most influential texts in East Asian intellectual history.

Confucius (or Kongzi as called in Chinese pinyin form) was born in 551 BC in the state of Lu (now in the southern area of Shandong province), which was in troubled times during the Spring and Autumn Period (770–476 BC). According to the Records of the Grand Historian, written by Sima Qian, the marriage between his father and mother was an illicit union (i.e., his father was a very old man and his mother was only in her late teens when they got married).[17] At the tender age of three, Confucius lost his father and was brought up, in poverty, by his mother. During his early 20 s, Confucius worked in various government jobs, including those as a bookkeeper and a caretaker of sheep and horses. At the age of 30, when his official career floundered, he decided to recommend himself as political advisers to state rulers. However, his career was not successful. He could not carry out his political ideal in his own state (Lu) and had to leave for other states, in the hope that he would be heard, his politics be practiced and his ideal be actualized somewhere else.

For 13 years, Confucius and his disciples traveled from one state to another. In the end when he realized that there was no hope as such, he decided to devote the rest of his life to teaching disciples and editing ancient classics, through which he expected that the disciples would carry on his will and bring his teachings to later generations. In 483 BC, Confucius returned to his native land of Lu and stayed there for his last years till 479 BC. In fact, Confucius's hard life and moral achievements are well summarized by the well-known saying of Mencius (372–289 BC):

> Thus, when Heaven is about to confer a great office on any man, it first exercises his mind with suffering, and his sinews and bones with toil. It exposes his body to hunger, and subjects him to extreme poverty. It confounds his undertakings. By all these methods it stimulates his mind, hardens his nature, and supplies his incompetencies.[18]

Founded in Palestine by the followers of Jesus Christ in the first century, Christianity is now the most influential religion in the Western society. It is generally agreed that Jesus was born around the beginning of the first century. The designation for the first century, or Anno Domini (AD), meaning "in the year of the lord," is in reference to the birth of Jesus, despite modern consensus that he was born before this time. Even though there has not been any detailed (and convincing, sometimes) description about Jesus Christ's family and his early life, it is generally believed that

---

[17]See Sima (91 BC, vol. 47, No. 17).

[18]Cited from Mencius (c. 300 BC, Book VI, Chap. XV).

Jesus was not born in a wealthy family and that he had but a depressed childhood of his own. For example, when Mary (Jesus's mother) was due to give birth, she and Joseph (Jesus's father) traveled from Nazareth to Joseph's ancestral home in Bethlehem to register their marriage in the census ordered by Caesar Augustus. "While there Mary was giving birth to Jesus, and as they found no room in the inn, she placed the newborn in a manger" (Luke 2: 6–7). In addition, as described in the New Testament:

> Jesus came into conflict with his neighbors and family… Because people were saying that Jesus was crazy, Jesus' mother and brothers came to get him… But Jesus responded that his followers were his true family.[19]

While scholars dispute some Bible stories (particularly the Creation and even some of the Gospels), there is no doubt that the Bible does contain at least some historic truth about Jesus. All his hard experiences impelled Jesus to conduct teachings, preaching, and religious activity. In addition, recent archeological work does indicate that Capernaum, a city important in Jesus's ministry, was poor and small, without even a forum or an agora. This archaeological discovery resonates well with the scholarly view that Jesus advocated reciprocal sharing among the destitute in that area of Galilee.[20]

In 1054, Christianity was split into two churches: Roman Catholicism and Orthodox (or Eastern Orthodox, mainly adopted in Russia and Central Europe). Since the sixteenth century, as a result of the Protestant Reformation, often referred to simply as the Reformation, there has been a further division of Western Christianity. The schism was initiated by Martin Luther (AD 1483–1546) and other early Protestant Reformers. Luther, born in Thuringia (Saxony) in what is now the country of Germany, is widely acknowledged to have started the Reformation with his 1517 work entitled "The Ninety-Five Theses." Luther began by criticizing the selling of indulgences, insisting that the Pope had no authority over purgatory and that the Catholic doctrine of the merits of the saints had no foundation in the Gospel. The attacks widened to cover many of the doctrines and devotional Catholic practices.

The Protestant Reformation was initiated within Germany, and other reform impulses arose independently of Luther. The largest groupings were the Lutherans and Calvinists, or Reformed. Lutheran churches were founded mostly in Germany, the Baltics, and Scandinavia. This was largely because people living in these regions, compared with those who were living in the core Roman Catholic area, had been largely ignored or marginalized in political, economic, and cultural affairs. For example, Poggio Bracciolini (AD 1380–1459), an Italian scholar who had served as Apostolicus Secretarius (papal secretary), had complained the backwardness of Germany in 1416. This has been described by Stephen Greenblatt:

> At the bathhouse in Baden [in Germany], Poggio was amazed by what he saw: "Old women as well as younger ones," he wrote to a friend [Niccolò de' Niccoli (1364 – 1437) – an Italian Renaissance humanist] in Florence, "going naked into the water before the eyes of

---

[19] See Mark (3: 21, 31–32, and 34–35).
[20] See, for example, Gowler (2007, p. 102) and Charlesworth (2006, ed., p. 127).

men and displaying their private parts and their buttocks to the onlookers." There was a sort of lattice between the men's and women's baths, but the separation was minimal: there were, he observed, "many low windows, through which the bathers can drink together and talk and see both ways and touch each other as is their usual custom." Poggio refused to enter the baths himself, not, he insisted, from any undue modesty but because "it seemed to me ridiculous that a man from Italy, ignorant of their language, should sit in the water with a lot of women, completely speechless."[21]

However, backwardness and inferiority could also serve as incentives for cultural change and advancement. In his famous essay "The Protestant Ethic and the Sprit of Capitalism," Max Weber argued that the profit-maximizing behavior, which is so characteristic of the bourgeoisie, could be explained under fully developed capitalist conditions by its sheer necessity to survive in the face of competition. It was the product of an autonomous impulse to accumulate far beyond the needs of personal consumption, an impulse which was historically unique. Weber traced its source to the "worldly asceticism" of reformed Christianity, with its twin imperatives to methodical work as the chief duty of life and to the limited enjoyment of its product. The unintended consequence of this ethic, which was enforced by the social and psychological pressures on the believer to prove (but not earn) his salvation, was the accumulation of capital for investment. The larger participation of Protestants (compared with that of Catholics) in modern business life was also more striking, as Weber observed:

> Among journeymen, for example, the Catholics show a stronger propensity to remain in their crafts, that is they more often become master of craftsmen, whereas the Protestants are attracted to a larger extent into the factories in order to fill the upper ranks of skilled labor and administrative positions.[22]

Founded by Muhammad (also spelled Muhammed or Mohammed, AD 570–632), Islam dates back to around AD 610. Although belonging to the Banu Hashim clan, one of Mecca's prominent families, Muhammad had a difficult early lifetime. His father, Abdullah, died almost six months before Muhammad was born. According to Islamic tradition, soon after his birth, Muhammad was sent to live with a Bedouin family in the desert, as desert life was considered healthier for infants. At the age of six, Muhammad's biological mother, Amina, died and he became orphaned. For the next two years, he was under the guardianship of his paternal grandfather Abd al-Muttalib. When Muhammad was eight, his grandfather also died. He then came under the care of his uncle Abu Talib, the new leader of Banu Hashim. According to Islamic historian William Montgomery Watt, there was a general disregard by guardians in taking care of weaker members of the tribes in Mecca during the sixth century, "Muhammad's guardians saw that he did not starve to death, but it was hard for them to do more for him, especially as the fortunes of the clan of Hashim seem to have been declining at that time."[23]

---

[21] Cited from Greenblatt (2011, p. 174). The quotes are from a letter of Poggio to Niccoli, May 18, 1416. It is worth noting that Niccoli's and Poggio's cursive scripts have developed into Italic and Roman types, respectively.

[22] Cited from Weber (1904, p. 7).

[23] Cited from Watt (1974, p. 8).

With its followers of about one-fifth of the global population, Islam is the largest religion by number of adherents and the fastest-growing major religion in the world. Islamic adherents can be found from the Atlantic across the northern half of Africa and the Middle East to most part of Asia. "Islam" is the infinitive of the Arabic verb "to submit," Muslim is the present participle of the same verb; thus, a Muslim is one submitting to the will of Allah—the only God of the universe—of which Mohammed is the Prophet. Muslim theology, Tawhid, defines the Islamic creed, whereas the law, Shariah, touches on virtually every aspect of life and society, providing guidance on multifarious topics from banking and welfare, to family life and the environment. The Koran (Qur'an) is accepted as the ultimate guide and anything not mentioned in the Koran is quite likely to be rejected. The Five Pillars of Islam, or the duties of a Muslim, are:

(i) the recital of the creed
(ii) prayer
(iii) fasting
(iv) almsgiving and
(v) the pilgrimage.

The most important prayers are the obligatory prayers who perform five times a day at definite hours. During the month of Ramadan in the midsummer in the lunar year, Muslims are required to fast from sunrise to sunset with no food, no drink, and no smoking. The fast is meant to develop both self-control and sympathy for the poor. By almsgiving, the Muslim shares with the poor. The pilgrimage to Mecca is a well-known aspect of Islam.

Sunni, whose name comes from the word "Sunnah" (referring to the exemplary behavior of the Islamic prophet Muhammad), is the largest denomination of Islam. The differences between Sunni and Shia Muslims arose from a disagreement over the choice of Muhammad's successor and subsequently acquired broader political significance, as well as theological and juridical dimensions. According to Sunni tradition, Muhammad did not clearly designate a successor and the Muslim community acted according to his sunnah in electing his father-in-law Abu Bakr (AD 573–634) as the first caliph. This contrasts with Shi'a view, which holds that Muhammad intended his son-in-law and cousin Ali ibn Abi Talib (AD 556–661) to succeed him. Political tensions between Sunnis and Shias continued with varying intensity throughout Islamic history, and they have been exacerbated in recent times by ethnic conflicts.

At present, Sunni Muslims constituted the majority of the world's Muslim population. Shia Islam is the second-largest branch of Islam. In addition, the Ibadi movement, also called Ibadism or Ibāḍiyya, is a school of Islam dominant in Oman and a few of other Muslim communities in the Middle East and Africa.

Founded in ancient India by Siddhartha Gautama, Buddhism is one of the most influential religions in Asia. Different from Confucius, Jesus Christ, and Muhammad, who are the founders of Confucianism, Christianity, and Islam, respectively, and each of whom had a poor family or an early difficult life, Siddhartha was born in a wealthy family. Reliable factual data on the life of Siddhartha Gautama are very scarce. Historians estimate that Siddhartha was born in Lumbini (in present-day Nepal) and lived from around 563 BC to around 485 BC. Siddhartha grew up as a son of a royal family, confined within his palace, leading a life of luxury enjoyed by the very wealthy and privileged. This lifestyle made him more and more delicate and sensitive. The following is a recollection of his youth:

> I was delicate, most delicate, supremely delicate. Lotus pools were made for me at my father's house solely for my use; in one blue lotuses flowered, in another white, and in another red. I used no sandal wood that was not from Benares. My turban, tunic, lower garments and cloak were all of Benares cloth. A white sunshade was held over me day and night so that I would not be troubled by cold or heat, dust or grit or dew. Yet even while I possessed such fortune and luxury, I thought, "When an unthinking, ordinary person who is himself subject to aging, sickness, and death, who is not beyond aging, sickness, and death, sees another who is old, sick or dead, he is shocked, disturbed, and disgusted, forgetting his own condition. I too am subject to aging, sickness, and death, not beyond aging, sickness, and death, and that I should see another who is old, sick or dead and be shocked, disturbed, and disgusted – this is not fitting." As I reflected thus, the conceit of youth, health, and life entirely left me.[24]

At the time when Siddhartha Gautama lived, northern India was composed of numerous independent states competing for resources. This was a time when the traditional religious order in India was being challenged by a number of new philosophical and religious schools that were not in line with the orthodox Indian religious views. The Vedic philosophy, theology, and metaphysics, along with the growing complexity of rituals and sacrificial fees, were also questioned. Materialistic schools were running wild in India, undermining the reputation and authority of the priestly class, leading to a temporary religious anarchy which contributed to the development of new religions. By the time Siddhartha was born, the intellectual decay of the old Brahmanic orthodoxy had begotten a strong skepticism and moral vacuum which was filled by new religious and philosophical views. At the heart of Buddhism, there are the Four Noble Truths:

(1) existence is suffering
(2) suffering has a cause, namely craving and attachment
(3) there is a cessation of suffering, which is Nirvana and
(4) there is a path to the cessation of suffering, which includes the Noble Eightfold Path—that is, right view, right intention, right speech, right action, right livelihood, right effort, right mindfulness, and right concentration.

Nirvana is the ultimate goal of the Buddhism. It represents the extinction of all cravings and the final release from suffering. To the extent that such ideal reflects the thinking of the mass of people, the society's values would be considered antithetical to such goals as acquisitions, achievement, or affluence.

Two major extant branches of Buddhism are generally recognized: namely Theravada (meaning "school of elder monks") and Mahayana Buddhism. The oldest surviving Buddhist school, Theravada, also called the Hinayana (lesser vehicle), is relatively conservative, and generally closest to early Buddhism. Mahayana (greater

---

[24]Cited from Gethin (1998, pp. 20–21).

vehicle) flourished in India from the fifth century onward. Even though both Theravada and Mahayana traditions accept the Buddha (Siddhartha Gautama) as the founder, Theravada considers him unique, but Mahayana considers him one of many Buddhas. Though a branch of Mahayana, Tibetan Buddhism not only accepts all the basic concepts of Mahayana, but it also includes a vast array of spiritual and physical techniques designed to enhance Buddhist practice. At present, these three different traditions of Buddhism can be found in the following geographical or cultural areas:

- Theravada Buddhism: Sri Lanka, Myanmar, Laos, Thailand, Cambodia as well as small portions of China, Vietnam, Malaysia, and Bangladesh
- Mahayana Buddhism: China (mainly in the Han-dominated areas), Korea, Japan, most of Vietnam, and Singapore
- Tibetan Buddhism: Tibet, Bhutan, Nepal, the Himalayan region of India, Kalmykia, and Mongolia and its surrounding areas.

3.4 Lucretius, Poggio, and Sima Qian[25]

More than 600 years ago, in the winter of 1417, a young man in his late thirties, after a long trip from Italy, plucked a very old manuscript off a dusty shelf in a remote monastery in Germany. That was the last surviving manuscript (De Rerum Natura), translated into English as "On the Nature of Things" (Lucretius 2001). The book is a beautiful poem but one that had the most dangerous ideas: that the universe functions without the aid of gods, and that matter is made up of very tiny material particles that are in eternal motion, randomly colliding and swerving in new directions. This ancient book had been almost entirely lost to history for more than a thousand years.

However, in his book *The Swerve: How the World Became Modern* (winner of the 2011 National Book Award and the 2012 Pulitzer Prize), Stephen Greenblatt, Cogan University Professor of the Humanities at Harvard University, states:

> The return [of Lucretius' book] to circulation has not been merely a major source of inspiration for a wide range of modern philosophers, including Gassendi, Bergson, Spencer, Whitehead, and Teilhard de Chardin. In fact, it also fueled the Renaissance – a riveting tale of the great cultural swerve in the Western World, inspiring artists such as Sandro Botticelli and Leonardo da Vinci and thinkers such as Giordano Bruno; shaped the thought of Galileo and Freud, Darwin and Einstein; and had a revolutionary influence on writers such as Montaigne and Shakespeare and – in the hands of Thomas Jefferson who would have become the third President of the United States from 1801 to 1809 - left its trace on the Declaration of Independence in 1776.[26]

The book hunter was Poggio Bracciolini (AD 1380–1459)—an Italian humanist and calligrapher. Poggio had served as Apostolicus Secretarius (papal secretary) in Rome. After July 1415, Antipope John XXIII had been deposed by the Council

---

[25]This section draws heavily on my book "An Economic Inquiry into the Nonlinear Behaviors of Nations" (Guo 2017, pp. 32–35).

[26]Cited from Greenblatt (2011, pp. 8f, 183, and 262f).

of Constance and the Roman Pope Gregory XII had abdicated—the papal office remained vacant for two years. To be masterless in the early fifteenth century was for most men an unenviable, even dangerous state (Greenblatt 2011, p. 20). This was indeed a difficult period for Poggio—he did not quickly find a new position for himself. However, had not been for that difficult period, Poggio would not have had any opportunity for his pursuit of book hunting in 1416 and 1417; neither would he have been willing to help in the copying and circulation of the book—one that had one of the most dangerous ideas at the time but the one that changed the course of history.

The author of "On the Nature of Things" is Titus Lucretius Carus (c. 99–c. 55 BC). Of Lucretius's life remarkably little is known: only that he was an accomplished poet; and that he was devoted to the teachings of Epicurus. Almost everything else we know about him is a matter of conjecture, rumor, legend, or gossip. The Lucretii were an old, Roman aristocratic clan. However, since slaves, when freed, often took the name of the family that had owned them, it is also possible that the author was a former slave and freedman of that same noble family (Greenblatt 2011, p. 53). According to the Internet Encyclopedia of Philosophy (IEP)—a peer-reviewed academic resource, some scholars have imagined that this lack of information is the result of a sinister plot—a conspiracy of silence supposedly conducted by pious Roman and early Christian writers bent on suppressing the poet's antireligious sentiments and materialist blasphemies (IEP 2015). Yet perhaps more vexing for our understanding of Lucretius than any conspiracy of silence has been the single lurid item about his death that appears in a fourth-century chronicle history by the great Church Father St. Jerome (c. AD 340–420):

> 94 [sic] BC... The poet Titus Lucretius is born. He was later driven mad by a love philter and, having composed between bouts of insanity several books (which Cicero afterwards corrected), committed suicide at the age of 44.[27]

Many, if not all well-known book authors had unlucky or even miserable experiences. In China, the best-known historical book is Shiji (Records of the Grand Historian), the first general history written in Chinese in the form of a series of biographies. Written by Sima Qian (c. 145–86 BC), it covers all the developments in the fields of politics, economy and culture from the legendary Huangdi (Yellow Emperor) down to Emperor Wu (156–87 BC) of the Western Han dynasty.

Sima Qian created five forms of historical writings, including emperors' biographies (basic annals), memorials to the emperors (tables), treatises, hereditary houses of nobles and princes, and biographies of historical figures. Among these five forms, the emperors' biographies, hereditary houses of the nobles and princes, and the biographies of historical figures have had an extraordinarily far-reaching influence upon Chinese literature of later ages.

However, Sima Qian's finalization of this great book had only been promoted by a fatal disaster of his own. For example, Sima Qian wrote the following in the Epilogue to his book Shiji:

---

[27] Cited from http://www.iep.utm.edu/lucretiu/. Accessed 2015-12-3.

Next, let me tell you why I devoted myself to this book. Affected by the Li Ling incident [of 99 BC], I received a castration [a serious punishment in ancient China] from the court. Oh, that was even worse than killing me – I had become useless! Then I asked myself: Might most of the poem and book authors be those who had serious hurts? King Wen of the Zhou, when serving as the earl of the West, was in captivity; but he elaborated the Book of Changes; Confucius was in a desperate situation and wrote The Spring and Autumn Annals; Qu Yuan was banished, and only then he composed the Li Sao; Zuoqiu Ming lost his sight, and he wrote The National Languages; Sun Bin had his knees amputated, and then The [Sun Bin] Art of War was drawn up; Lv Buwei was exiled to Sichuan, but he complied Lv's Spring and Autumn; Han Fei was thrown into prison in the state of Qin, and he wrote To Admonish and The Indignation; and the 300 articles included in The Book of Songs were all written as the emotional outlets for the pent-up feelings of the sages.[28]

Alas, without the classical literature mentioned by Sima Qian, it is unbelievable what the Chinese culture would have looked like! To develop his ideas further, Sima Qian continued to write:

All of these men had something eating away at their hearts; they could not carry through their ideas of the Way, so they gave an account of what had happened before while thinking of those to come. Why didn't I use my time to write something? As a result, I decided to write the Historical Records from the era of Emperor Huang until the beginning of Emperor Wu.[29]

Indeed, all these well-known works were authored by those who felt highly depressed. As a matter of fact, all the sages (Confucius, Siddhartha Gautama, Jesus Christ, and Muhammad) as we mentioned earlier, as well as Titus Lucretius Carus, Poggio Bracciolini, and Sima Qian, were either mistreated or unlucky or had a difficult life themselves. However, they have all contributed to the world civilizations—in fact, they have all become the important components of the world civilizations. Is there any civilization, nation or individual who has achieved a great success without having any costs or sacrifices at the earlier stage?

3.5 Case Study: The Cherokee and Vai Writing Systems

Cherokee is an Iroquoian language spoken by the Cherokee people in the USA. The Iroquoian languages are a Native American language family in North America. Known for their general lack of labial consonants, the Iroquoian languages are polysynthetic and head-marking (Lounsbury 1978, pp. 334–43). Today, almost all surviving Iroquoian languages are severely endangered. However, the Cherokee language is an exception. A Southern Iroquoian language, Cherokee is a polysynthetic language and uses a unique syllabary writing system (Montgomery-Anderson 2008). After the Cherokee syllabary, which includes 85 characters instead of 26 letters of English, was completed by Sequoyah (c. 1770–1843) in the early 1820s, it achieved

---

[28] Translated by author based on Sima (91 BC, vol. 130, No. 70). Words within square brackets are added by author.
[29] Ibid.

almost instantaneous popularity and spread rapidly throughout the Cherokee society; and, by 1825, the majority of Cherokees could read and write in their newly developed orthography (McLaughlin 1986, p. 353; Walker and Sarbaugh 1993, pp. 70–2).

In West Africa, Vai, alternately called Vy or Gallinas, is a Mande language, spoken by the Vai people, roughly with a population of 104,000 in Liberia and of some 15,500 in Sierra Leone.[30] Vai means water in Vai; and similar words in other languages include, but not limited to, wai (in Proto-Nuclear Polynesian), wair (in Proto-Oceanic, Proto-Eastern Malayo-Polynesian, and Proto-Central-Eastern Malayo-Polynesian), and wahir (in Proto-Malayo-Polynesian), all of which are derived from the common ancestral word "wa." Vai is noteworthy for being one of the few African languages to have a writing system that is not based on the Latin or Arabic script. The Vai syllabic writing system is devised for the Vai language by Momolu Duwalu Bukele in what is now Grand Cape Mount county, Liberia (Coulmas 1996, pp. 537–9). Vai is one of the two most successful indigenous scripts in West Africa in terms of both the number of current users and the availability of literature written in the script (Unseth 2011, pp. 23–32).

It is interesting to note that the Cherokee syllabary of North America provided a model for the design of the Vai syllabary. The Vai syllabary emerged about AD 1832 or 1833. The link appears to have been related to a Cherokee who emigrated to Liberia after the invention of the Cherokee syllabary (which in its early years spread rapidly among the Cherokee) but before the invention of the Vai syllabary. One such man, Cherokee Austin Curtis, married into a prominent Vai family and became an important Vai chief himself. It is notable that the romantic "inscription on a house" that first drew the world's attention to the existence of the Vai script was in fact on the home of Curtis, a Cherokee.[31] Then, why is the Vai writing system, which is used by the Vai speakers in West Africa, structurally influenced by the Cherokee script in the United States?

Given its geographical proximity to many Eurasian civilizations, West Africa should have more opportunities to develop a writing system that is based on the Latin or Greek letters. Then, why was the Vai writing system borrowed from the Cherokee script but not from the Latin or Greek letters? Of course, the Cherokee-Vai marriage (as mentioned above) was the key factor. But the answer is still not satisfactory. Other factors might also matter. In particular, there must have been more cultural similarities between the Vai- and Cherokee-speaking communities than between the Vai- and Latin-/Greek-speaking communities. Think that the Vai-European marriage could have happened in the early 1820s or 1830s? Even though there is no record about this kind of marriage, it is unlikely that it could have happened. However, the Vai–Cherokee marriage did happen successfully at that time.

Even worthier of noting is the life of Sequoyah—the inventor of the Cherokee syllabary. There were very few primary documents describing Sequoyah's life. Some anecdotes were passed down orally, but these often conflict or are vague. According

---

[30]Data source: http://www.ethnologue.com/show_language.asp?code=vai (accessed 2016-11-18).

[31]See Tuchscherer and Hair (2002) for more details.

to Davis (1930), Sequoyah was born in the Cherokee town of Tuskegee in about AD 1770. His mother, known to be Cherokee, had a name Wut-teh or Wurte—both of which can be roughly treated as the variants of wadi. The exact place and date of Sequoyah's birth are unknown, although it is believed that he spent his early years with his mother in the village of Tuskegee, Tennessee. Sequoyah was not an uncommon name among the Cherokees and is fairly common in Oklahoma at the present time.

Like those of many common English names, the original meaning of Sequoyah or Sequoia has been lost and its derivation is rarely considered. The names Sequoyah and Sequoia are both spellings given by missionaries, and probably come from the Cherokee name sikwa, a hog or originally an opossum. This is either a reference to a childhood deformity or a later injury that left him disabled.[32] It is interesting to note that the suffix of -wa (or -va or -wai, depending which tribes the speakers come from) is a locative ending meaning a place or an enclosure. This is very similar to those of many other indigenous languages in Andean South America and in the Old World as well. Sequoyah, regardless of his physical disadvantage, must have inherited the wadi gene from his mother and, above all, he must have worked very hard.

Since humans' migration out of Africa, various complicated cultures and civilizations have made humans behave, over time, more and more different from their earlier generations. Since the development of any culture or civilization consists of inventing new things, humans, given their brain capacities each are held fixed, must forget or disregard some, if not all, old tings. As a result, over the course of the past thousands of years, the human features of these civilizations have born significant changes. However, there are still two exceptions: northern America and southwestern Africa had been almost isolated from each other and from the Eurasian civilizations during most of the pre-Columbian era. Nevertheless, the Vai and Cherokee peoples, though each belonging to a different race, should have been more culturally similar to each other than to those elsewhere. This may explain why the two peoples living far away from each other are still able to use similar writing systems. Both Vai and Cherokee are closer to the common ancestral language of humans than are the Indo-European languages.

References

Anderson S (2012) Languages: a very short introduction. Oxford University Press, Oxford
Bancel PJ, de l'Etang AM (2008) The age of mama and papa. In: Bengtson JD (eds) In Hot Pursuit of Language in Prehistory: Essays in the four fields of anthropology. John Benjamins Publishing, Amsterdam, pp 417–38
Bonner P (1982) Kings, commoners and concessionaires. Cambridge University Press, Cambridge

---

[32] Sources: http://thewildwest.org/nativeamericans/native-american-faces/92-sequoyah (accessed 2016-11-18) and Davis (1930).

Bower B Jesus and archaeol (January 27, 2011) Hints of earlier human exit from Africa: Stone tools suggest a surprisingly ancient move eastward. Science News. https://www.sciencenews. org/article/hints-earlier-human-exit-africa. Accessed Nov 11 2014

Bowler JM, Johnston H, Olley JM, Prescott JR, Roberts RG, Shawcross W, Spooner NA (2003) New ages for human occupation and climatic change at Lake Mungo, Australia. Nature 421:837–840

Charlesworth JH (2006, ed.) Jesus and archaeology. Wm. B. Eerdmans Publishing, Cambridge

Chomsky N (2000) The architecture of language. Oxford University Press, Oxford

Coulmas F (1996) The blackwell encyclopedia of writing systems. Wiley-Blackwell, Oxford

Croft W (2012) Verbs: aspect and causal structure (Oxford Linguistics). Oxford University Press, Oxford

Dalley S (2000) Myths from Mesopotamia (Revised edn). Oxford University Press, Oxford

Davis JB (1930) The life and work of Sequoyah. Chronicles of Oklahoma. 8(2):149–80. http:// digital.library.okstate.edu/chronicles/v008/v008p149.html. Accessed 16 Nov 2016

Eagly AH, Wood W (1999) The origins of sex differences in human behavior: evolved dispositions versus social roles. Am Psychol 54(6):408–423

Fitch W Tecumseh (2010) The evolution of language. Cambridge University Press, Cambridge

Gamkrelidze TV, Ivanov VV (1995) Indo-European and the indo-europeans: a reconstruction and historical analysis of a proto-language and a proto-culture (Trends in Linguistics: Studies and Monographs vol. 80), 2nd Ed. De Gruyter Mouton, Boston, MA

Gethin R (1998) The foundations of buddhism. Oxford University Press, Oxford

Gowler DB (2007) What are they saying about the historical jesus?. Paulist Press, New York

Gračanin A, Bylsma LM, Vingerhoets Ad JJM (2018) Why only humans shed emotional tears: evolutionary and cultural perspectives. Human Nature 29(2), https://doi.org/10.1007/s12110-018-9312-8

Greenblatt S (2011) The swerve: how the world became modern. W.W. Norton and Company, New York

Guo R (2017) An economic inquiry into the nonlinear behaviors of nations: dynamic developments and the origins of civilizations. Palgrave Macmillan, New York

Guo R (2018). The civilizations revisited: the historians may be wrong, really. Draft

Hatley R (1984) Mapping cultural regions of Java. In: Hatley R, Schiller J, Lucas A, Martin-Schiller B (eds) Other Javas away from the kraton. Monash University Press, Clayton, VIC, pp 1–32

Huddlestun JR (2003) Nahum, Nineveh, and the Nile: the description of Thebes in Nahum 3:8–9. J Near East Stud 62(2):97–98

Hughes SS, Hughes B (2001) Women in ancient civilizations. In: Michael A (ed) Agricultural and pastoral societies in ancient and classical history. Temple University Press, Philadelphia, PA, pp 116–50

Jakobson R (1962) Why 'mama' and 'papa'? In: Jakobson R (ed) Selected writings, Vol. I: phonological studies. Mouton & Co., Hague, pp 538–45

Kimutai S, Gichoya D, Milgo E (2013). Isolated swahili words recognition using Sphinx4. International Journal of Emerging Science and Engineering 2(2): 51–57

Kraemer S (1991). The origins of fatherhood: an ancient family process. Family Process 30(4): 377–392.

Kuper H (1997) The swazi: a south african kingdom, 2nd edn. Harcourt School Publishers, San Diego, CA

Lounsbury FG (1978) Iroquoian languages. In: Bruce GT (ed) handbook of north American Indians, Vol 15: Northeast. Smithsonian Institution, Washington, DC

Lucretius (2001). De Rerum Natura (on the nature of things) (trans: Smith MF). Hackett Publishing Company, Inc., Indianapolis

Mayr E (1982) The growth of biological thought: diversity, evolution, and inheritance. Belknap Press of Harvard University Press, Cambridge, MA

McLaughlin WG (1986) Cherokee renascence in the new republic. Princeton University Press, Princeton, NJ

Mencius (c. 300 BC) (1999) Analects of mencius (English-Chinese Edition). Foreign Languages Press, Beijing

Monaghan J, Just P (2000) Social and cultural anthropology. Oxford University Press, New York

Montgomery-Anderson B (2008). Citing verbs in Polysynthetic languages: the case of the Cherokee-English dictionary. Southwest Journal of Linguistics, 27: 53–76

Myers EA. (2010). The ituraeans and the Roman Near East: reassessing the sources. Cambridge University Press, Cambridge

OALD (1974) Oxford advanced learner's dictionary, 3rd edn. Oxford University Press, Oxford

O'Brien SJ, Wildt MBD. (1986). The cheetah in genetic peril. Scientific American 254: 68–76.

Sapir E (1985) Selected writings in language, culture and personality (Editor: D.G. Mandelbaum). University of California Press, Berkeley, CA

Sima Q (91 BC) (1997) Shiji (Records of the Grand Historian) (in Chinese). Taihai Press, Beijing

Smith BL, Brown BL, Strong WJ, Rencher AC (1975) Effects of speech rate on personality perception. Lang Speech 18(2):145–152

Sunquist F, Sunquist M (2002). Wild cats of the world. The University of Chicago Press, Chicago, IL

Tomasello M (2008) Origin of human communication. The MIT Press, Cambridge, MA

Trimble M (2012) Why humans like to cry: tragedy, evolution, and the brain. Oxford University Press, Oxford

Tuchscherer K, Hair PEH (2002) Cherokee and West Africa: examining the origins of the Vai script. History in Africa 29:427–486

Unseth P (2011) Invention of scripts in West Africa for ethnic revitalization. In: Fishman JA, García O (Eds) Handbook of language and ethnic identity: the success-failure continuum in language and ethnic identity efforts. Oxford University Press, New York

Walker W, Sarbaugh J (1993) The early history of the Cherokee syllabary. Ethnohistory 40(1):70–94

Watt WM (1974) Muhammad: prophet and statesman. Oxford University Press, Oxford

Weber M (1904; 1930) The protestant ethic and the spirit of capitalism. Allen & Unwin, London

Wells S, Read M (2002) The journey of man—a genetic odyssey. Random House, New York

Williams CE, Stevens KN (1972) Emotions and speech: some acoustical correlates. J Acoust Soc Am 52(4):1238–1250

Woods C (2005) On the Euphrates. Zeitschrift für Assyriologie 95:7–45

Zhao M, Kong QP, Wang HW, Peng MS, Xie XD, Wang WZ, Jiayang Duan JG, Cai MC, Zhao SN, Cidanpingcuo Tu YQ, Wu SF, Yao YG, Bandelt HJ, Zhang YP (2009) Mitochondrial genome evidence reveals successful Late Paleolithic settlement on the Tibetan Plateau. PNAS 106(50):21230–21235

Chapter 4
Environment Matters, But Not the Way You Think (I)

Abstract In this chapter, we will compare three areas of distinct geographies and climates: (i) equatorial and tropical, (ii) dry or desert in the Northern Hemisphere, and (iii) semiarid or temperate in the Southern Hemisphere. Our empirical findings show that, while different environments could result in different cultures and civilizations, it is the unfriendly environment—as long as it could sustain humans—that created the first and the most powerful civilizations. Cultures and civilizations could only be created by those who were environmentally threatened and hence struggled to seek protections for their own. Not all cultures or civilizations could become powerful civilizations; some might fail eventually. Catastrophic events and natural disasters could destroy civilizations; so did friendly and comfortable environment.

Keywords Civilization · Environmental threat · Global history · River valley Writing system

4.1 "That's What I'm Doing Right Now!"

Would you like a grand new Lamborghini, a seashore villa or a luxury ocean journey? Would you like more free time, more sleeping time and, at the same time, more money to spend? Who wouldn't? The problem is simply that the resources available to satisfy these wants, or desires, are virtually limited. They are scarce. Hard choices arise from scarcity. If it were not scarcity, we would never bother to change our previous habits, making choices in between, constructing economic structures and market mechanisms to produce and distribute; and trying to maintain them work smoothly and efficiently.

While most resources and goods are scarce, some are not—for example, the air that we breathe. A resource or good that is not scarce, even when its price is zero, is called a free resource or good. Human beings, however, are mainly concerned with scarce resources and goods. It is the presence of scarcity that motivates not only the productivity of human capital but also the study of how society allocates

© Springer Nature Singapore Pte Ltd. 2019
R. Guo, *Human-Earth System Dynamics*,
https://doi.org/10.1007/978-981-13-0547-4_4

resources and goods. Below is a story of this kind, which has been frequently told as the "Mexican Fisherman" joke[1]:

One day, an investment banker from New York City was spending his vacation at the pier of a small coastal Mexican village when a small boat with just one fisherman docked. Inside the small boat were several yellowfin tuna. The American asked how long it took him to catch them.

"Only a little while," the Mexican replied.

"Then, why didn't you stay out longer and catch more and larger fish?" asked the American.

The Mexican replied that the amount of the fish was enough to support his family's needs.

"But what do you do with the rest of your time?" The American then asked.

The Mexican fisherman said, "I sleep late, fish a little, play with my children, have an afternoon's rest under a coconut tree. In the evenings, I go into the community hall to see my friends, have a few beers, play the drums, and sing a few songs…"

The American scoffed, "You should spend more time fishing and with the proceeds, buy a bigger boat with the proceeds from the bigger boat you could buy several boats, eventually you would have a fleet of fishing boats. Instead of selling your catch to a middleman you would sell directly to the processor, eventually opening your own cannery. You would control the product, processing and distribution. You would need to leave this small coastal fishing village and move to Mexico City, then Los Angles and eventually New York City where you will run your expanding enterprise."

The Mexican fisherman asked, "But, how long will this all take?"

The American replied, "10, maybe 20 years."

"But what then?"

The American laughed and said: "When the time is right you would sell your company stock to the public and become very rich, you would make millions."

"Millions? Then after that?"

The American said, "Then you would retire. Move to a small coastal fishing village where you would sleep late, fish a little, play with your kids…"

"That is what I'm doing right now," said the fisherman and went his way.

More than 150 years ago, Henry Thomas Buckle (1821–1862)—an English historian—resolved to direct all his reading and to devote all his energies to the preparation of some great historical work. At first, Buckle planned a history of the Middle Ages, but later he had decided in favor of a history of civilization. It is a gigantic unfinished work, of which the plan was, as the first part, to state the general principles of the author's method and the general laws that govern the course of human progress; and, as the second part, to exemplify these principles and laws through the histories of certain nations of prominent and peculiar features (such as Spain and Scotland, the USA, and Germany). Buckle's fame rests mainly on his History of Civilization in England. The completed work was to have extended to 14 volumes, with the following chief ideas (Buckle 1913)[2]:

- That, while the theological dogma of predestination is a barren hypothesis beyond the province of knowledge, and the metaphysical dogma of free will rests on an erroneous belief in the infallibility of consciousness, it is proved by science, and especially by statistics, that human actions are governed by laws as fixed and regular as those that rule in the physical world;

- That climate, soil, food, and the aspects of nature are the primary causes of intellectual progress—the first three indirectly, through determining the accumulation and distribution of wealth, and the last by directly influencing the accumulation and distribution of thought, the imagination being stimulated and the understanding subdued when the phenomena of the external world are sublime and terrible, the understanding being emboldened and the imagination curbed when they are small and feeble;
- That the great division between European and non-European civilizations turns on the fact that in Europe man is stronger than nature, and that elsewhere nature is stronger than man, the consequence of which is that in Europe alone has man subdued nature to his service;
- That the advance of European civilization is characterized by a continually diminishing influence of physical laws, and a continually increasing influence of mental laws; and
- That the mental laws that regulate the progress of society cannot be discovered by the metaphysical method, that is, by the introspective study of the individual mind, but only by such a comprehensive survey of facts as enabling us to eliminate disturbances, that is, by the method of averages.

Buckle is remembered for treating history as an exact science. Many of his ideas have passed into the common literary stock, and have been more precisely elaborated by later writers on sociology and history because of his careful scientific analyses. However, his ideas about the division between European and non-European civilizations and about the primary causes of intellectual progress seem to be incorrect. In fact, as just mentioned in the above fisherman story, it is the abundance of fisheries that eventually induced the fisherman not to have, for better and worse in the long run, changed his old, simple cultural tradition to a new, more complicated one. Before delving into my argument that the environment does not decide or influence existing cultures and civilizations in the way that Buckle and many other historians have thought, let us first have a brief analysis of how the environment has played a role in the evolution of human civilizations.

As a matter of fact, some scholars, among them Ester Boserup (1910–1999), have believed that food surplus was not the incentive for the eventual creation of more complex civilizations. Boserup's work challenges the assumption dating back to Malthus's time (and still held in many quarters) that agricultural methods determine population (via food supply). By way of contrast, Boserup argued that it is population that determines agricultural methods. The major point of her book "The Conditions of Agricultural Growth: The Economics of Agrarian Change under Population Pressure" is that "necessity is the mother of invention."[3]

---

[3]See Boserup (1965, p. 13). Later, she developed this idea further (Boserup 1976, 1985, pp. 185–210).

Following Boserup's "demand determines supply" theory, others have argued that agricultural systems, such as those in early Mesopotamia or along the banks of the Nile River (where annual floods inundated the fields), tended to be more intensive and to exploit the environment in a more ordered and systematic way. All these created conditions in which more settlements could exist on foods whose annual yields were at least roughly predictable. The more specialized ecosystem created by these efforts supported more concentrated, rapidly growing populations, and thus civilization.[4] Unfortunately, the above theory—partly due to its incomplete narrative when it is used to describe the real story of cultural formation—has not received much attention from historians. As a result, mainstream historians, when identifying the key factors contributing to the birth of ancient civilizations, have still applied their "supply determines demand" theory.[5]

Three is a so-called equatorial paradox in the explanation of contemporary development pattern of the world. For example, after controlling such variables as labor, machinery, soil treatment, and irrigation, Gallup et al. (1999) find that agriculture in the tropics secures a 30–50 % decrease in productivity relative to temperate-zone agriculture production. Indeed, the real world has a special scenario at present: places in higher latitudes, especially in the Northern Hemisphere, experience higher standards of living, and reap climatic advantages and better opportunities to input resources. As latitude increases north or south from the equator, levels of real GDP per capita increase (Easterly and Levine 2003). In addition, Parker (2000, pp. 3-6) finds that a country's latitude explains up to 70 percent of cross-country variances in per capita income.

One popular theory to explain this "equatorial paradox" is that development is less necessary in the tropics, as opposed to the need to invent agriculture and economy in order to prosper and survive. These environments "were seen as producing less civilized, more degenerate peoples, in need of salvation by western colonial powers" (Gilmartin 2009, p. 117). Another explanation for this fact is that humans originated as tropical mammals, so those located in cold climates feel under pressure to restore their physiological homeostasis by, for example, agriculture and wealth-creation to produce more food, better housing, heating, warm clothes, etc. (Parker 2000, p. 122). Conversely, those in warmer climates are more physiologically comfortable simply due to temperature, and so have less incentive to work to increase their comfort levels.

Then, what roles have the natural and environmental factors played in the whole evolution and development process of humankind?

---

[4]See, for example, Scarre and Fagan (2016, p. 29).

[5]See Sect. 5.1 in Chap. 5 for a detailed description of existing theories on civilizations.

4.2 Good Environment, Bad Environment

For a long history of their existence throughout the world, human beings had lived as hunter-gatherers in small, dispersed places or villages which were, as far as we can tell, completely autonomous. A hunter-gatherer or forager society is one in which most or all food is obtained from wild plants and animals. Not until perhaps 5000 BC (or even earlier) did villages begin to aggregate at various river valleys. But, once this aggregation process began, it continued at a progressively faster pace, which led, around 4000 BC, to the formation of the first agricultural society in history. In contrast to hunter-gatherers, agriculturists have relied mainly on domesticated species. Then what have driven human beings as hunter-gatherers to become agriculturists? Or, to put it in another way, why did human beings decide to create civilizations throughout the world thousands of years ago?

Indeed, many human and cultural issues, especially those relating to the process of the rise and fall of cultures and civilizations, have still remained unexplained. For example, given that humans' migrations out of the African continent have followed the "Win-Stay Lose-Shift" law (as discussed in Chap. 1), why had the African natives—the first and the largest winner of intra-human competitions—not been able to advance their civilizations as powerful as those created elsewhere? Why have the Caucasoid and the Mongoloid in Eurasia—both physically weaker than the Negroid in southern Africa—had their civilizations much earlier and stronger than the latter? Last but not least, why did Andean South America—which has much worse natural and environmental conditions than those of the Amazonia and most, if not all places in North America—give birth to the earliest civilization in the Americas?

A hydraulic or riverine culture (also known civilization) is a social or government structure which maintains power and control through exclusive control over access to water. Hydraulic culture arises through the need for flood control and irrigation, which requires central coordination and a specialized bureaucracy (Wittfogel 1957, p. 67). Often associated with these terms and concepts is the notion of a water dynasty. This body is a political structure which is commonly characterized by a system of hierarchy and control often based around class or caste. Power, both over resources (food, water, energy) and a means of enforcement such as the military are vital for the maintenance of control. The government of a typical hydraulic empire, according to Wittfogel's hypothesis, is usually a centralized one, with no trace of an independent aristocracy.

Though tribal societies had structures that were usually personal in nature and exercised by a patriarch over a tribal group related by various degrees of kinship, hydraulic hierarchies gave rise to the established permanent institution of impersonal government. In the fifteenth century, for example, the Ajuran Empire was the only hydraulic empire in Africa. As a water dynasty, the Ajuran state monopolized the water resources of the Jubba and Shebelle rivers. Through hydraulic engineering, it also constructed many of the limestone wells and cisterns of the state that are still operative and in use today. The rulers developed new systems for agriculture and taxation, which continued to be used in parts of the Horn of Africa as late as the

Fig. 4.1 Bali's rice terrace: Life is easy with the Subak irrigation system

nineteenth century (Njoku 2013, p. 26). However, it must be noted that Wittfogel's hypothesis cannot be sufficiently supported by the evidence elsewhere—including that in the Orient on which Wittfogel's research was focused.

Subak, the name of water management (irrigation) system for paddy fields on Bali Island, Indonesia, was first developed in the ninth century (see Fig. 4.1). Along the rivers in Bali, various small groups of farmers meet regularly in water temples to manage their irrigation systems. This has been a tradition for more than a thousand years. In total Bali has about 1,200 water collectives, in each of which between 50 and 400 farmers manage the water supply from one source of water. For the Balinese, irrigation is not simply providing water for the plant's roots, but water is used to construct a complex, pulsed artificial ecosystem, which consists of five terraced rice fields and water temples covering nearly 20,000 ha (Lansing 1987). The five sites, which were enlisted as a UNESCO world heritage site in June 2012, exemplify the interconnected natural, religious, and cultural components of the traditional subak system, where the subak system is still fully functioning, where farmers still grow traditional Balinese rice without the aid of fertilizers or pesticides, and where the landscapes overall are seen to have sacred connotations.[6]

The overall subak system exemplifies the philosophical principle called "Tri Hita Karana"—a traditional philosophy that draws together the realms of the spirit, the

---

[6]See http://whc.unesco.org/en/list/1194/ (accessed 2015-11-5).

human world and nature for life on the island of Bali.[7] Did someone have to design Bali's water temple networks, or could they have emerged from a self-organizing process? In order to find an answer to most of this question, Stephen Lansing, a professor of anthropology at the University of Arizona, developed a computer model. At the beginning of each year the artificial subaks in the model are given a schedule of crops to plant for the next twelve months, which defines their irrigation needs. Then, based on historic rainfall data, Professor Lansing and his colleague simulated rainfall, river flow, crop growth, and pest damage. They tested the model by simulating conditions for two cropping seasons, and compared its predictions with real data on harvest yields for about half the subaks. The model did surprisingly well, and the result it produced is barely visible from within the horizons of Western social theory:

> We created the simplest rule we could think of to allow the subaks to learn from experience. At the end of a year of planting and harvesting, each artificial subak compares its aggregate harvests with those of its four closest neighbors. If any of them did better, copy their behavior. Otherwise, make no changes. After every subak has made its decision, simulate another year and compare the next round of harvests. The first time we ran the program with this simple learning algorithm, we expected chaos. It seemed likely that the subaks would keep flipping back and forth, copying first one neighbor and then another as local conditions changed. But instead, within a decade the subaks organized themselves into cooperative networks that closely resembled the real ones.[8]

In contrast to Bali, China has a quite different scenario. The Loess Plateau, also known as "Huangtu Gaoyuan" in Chinese, is a plateau that covers a large area of land in the upper and middle reaches of the Yellow River (Huanghe). Loess is the name for the silty sediment that has been deposited on the plateau over the ages. It is a highly erosion-prone soil susceptible to the forces of wind and water. In fact, the soil of this region has been called the "most highly erodible soil on earth," The Loess Plateau and its dusty soil cover almost all of Shanxi and Shaanxi provinces, as well as parts of Gansu Province, the Ningxia Hui autonomous region, and the Inner Mongolia autonomous region in China. The plateau generally has an arid or semiarid climate, with extensive monsoonal influence. Winters are cold and dry, while summers are very warm and in many places hot. Rainfall tends to be mainly concentrated in summer; in the remaining seasons (spring in particular), water is extremely of shortage.

In the Bali Island, the Subak irrigation system, once constructed, does not need any extra energy or labor input to keep it working. However, people living in the Loess Plateau have not been so lucky. Since cultivable land is usually much higher than the banks of the Yellow River (see Fig. 4.2), the Loess Plateauers have to input more energies so as to make a harvest that could sustain their life. In summer, water

---

[7]The literal translation of the "Tri Hita Karana" philosophy is roughly the "three causes of well-being" or "three reasons for prosperity" (i.e., harmony among people; harmony with nature or environment; and harmony with God).

[8]Cited from Lansing (2006, p. 14). (Italic is added by author.) Note that the simulation model was constructed on the basis of the data on all 172 subaks lying between the Oos and Petanu rivers in central Bali, including rainfall, river flows, irrigation schedules, water uptake by crops such as rice and vegetables, and the population dynamics of the major rice pests.

Fig. 4.2 Loess Plateau: Life is never easy along the Yellow River

is seldom needed in the Plateau; however, since there usually are more rainfalls than needed in summer, people living there have to make collective management of their land in order to prevent the latter from being destroyed by floods. Alas, life has never been an easy thing there! However, throughout their histories, it seems that the Loess Plateauers have done a better job than the Subakers. At ancient times, the Loess Plateau had contributed to the early Chinese civilization, of which the Dadiwan culture (c. 7800—c. 4800 BC) was located in today's Gansu Province.

Till now, after briefly comparing the Subak irrigation system in the Bali Island and the agricultural activity along the Yellow River, we can reach a consensus: water control or irrigation (management) system and other water- or river-related activity do not always lead to advanced (or powerful) cultures or civilizations. Moreover, even if rulers of the early dynasties or kingdoms were cruel and ferocious, there are still conditions under which farmers could choose either subordination to the rulers or simply migrating out of the rulers' territory for a better life. Given that early agricultural communities had no armies or strict border control measures, why had most, if not all lower-ranking farmers still been willing to be subordinated to their rulers? The most likely fact is that they were facing other environmental risks or threats (or even death) that could be overcome only through a certain-sized, and somewhat centralized, cooperative organization. If it is this case, without civilization, ancient humans would have faced other, more serious situations.

Fig. 4.3 Sacred Valley: Life falls short of the best, but still better than the worst *Note* Agricultural terraces near the town of Písac, Sacred Valley, Peru. *Source* Benutzer Torox, 2001 (Wikimedia Commons)

In his travel memoir *The Malay Archipelago* (1869), Alfred Russel Wallace—a British naturalist, explorer, geographer, anthropologist and biologist and co-author of some of Charles Darwin's writings—wrote of his experience in Bali, as the following:

> I was both astonished and delighted; for as my visit to Java was some years later, I had never beheld so beautiful and well-cultivated a district out of Europe. A slightly undulating plain extends from the seacoast about ten or twelve miles inland, where it is bounded by a fine range of wooded and cultivated hills. Houses and villages, marked out by dense clumps of coconut palms, tamarind and other fruit trees, are dotted about in every direction; while between them extend luxurious rice-grounds, watered by an elaborate system of irrigation that would be the pride of the best cultivated parts of Europe.[9]

The term "elaborate system of irrigation" used by Wallace is now called "Subak"—the name of water management (irrigation) system that was just mentioned earlier. With so many natural and geographical advantages, why has Bali, like many other fertile regions in both the Old and the New worlds, not given birth to an advanced (powerful) indigenous civilization that can be seen in many other, environmentally circumscribed places in the rest of the world? Bali was inhabited around 2000 BC by Austronesian people who migrated originally from Southeast Asia and Oceania through Maritime Southeast Asia.[10] However, for a long period of time, the Balinese

---

[9]Cited from Wallace (1869 (2011), p. 116).

[10]See Taylor (2003, pp. 5 and 7).

culture, like those of the rest of Indonesia, was strongly influenced by the Hindu and Chinese cultures, but not vice versa. From the sixteenth century till World War II (1939–1945), the Indonesian archipelago (including Bali) had been ruled by the Dutch government. Then, why did Bali not give birth to an indigenous culture or civilization that was as powerful or influential as those in Eurasia?

From east to west, the Bali Island is approximately 153 km wide and spans, from north to south, approximately 112 km, with a total area of 5,780 sq. km. Bali's central mountains include several peaks over 3,000 m in elevation. The highest mountain, Agung, which is also known as the "mother mountain," is an active volcano (in 1963, an eruption killed 2,000 people). The Ayung River (with the same name as and, of course, originating from Mt. Ayung) is the longest river on the island of Bali. It runs about 75 km from the northern mountain range and discharges into the Badung Strait at Sanur near Denpasar—the provincial capital and the largest city of Bali near the southern coast. Bali's volcanic nature has contributed to its exceptional fertility and its tall mountain range provides the high rainfall that supports the highly productive agriculture sector.

Located just 8° south of the equator, Bali has a fairly even climate year round. Daytime temperatures at low elevations vary between 20°C and 33°C. The west monsoon is in place from approximately October to April, bringing significant rainfalls. The natural and environmental conditions in Bali have influenced the every sphere of the Balinese people, including the cultural formation. For example, unlike most of other peoples who use lunisolar calendars (including the Gregorian calendar which is the de facto international standard), the Balinese apply a 210-day Pawukon calendar that has its origins in the Hindu religion. Since the Bali Island is located around the equator, a calendar with dates that may distinguish seasonable changes is not required in the Balinese society. In other words, there were no serious climate changes or that those changes did not seriously affect Bali's social and economic activities.

I am not to say that the Balinese 210-day calendar is backward as compared with the Gregorian calendar. But it is the latter as well as many others used in the Eurasian civilizations that can better predict the seasonable changes within a year. The ancient Balinese had no crying need of the Gregorian calendar since there were no drastic seasonable changes in the Bali Island. However, it is humans' consistent efforts toward the creation of a more accurate calendar that have eventually promoted the advancement of various technologies, sciences and, to a broader extent, civilizations.[11] In Bali, there have been almost no cyclical, river-related floods or disasters, a must-occur event found in almost all of the earliest cultures or civilizations of the world—both the Old and the New. Throughout its history, Bali has had a few of earthquakes.[12] However, this does not provide any incentives for cultural evolution and development.

---

[11] See Sect. 7.3 Chap. 7 for a more detailed analysis.

[12] For example, the earthquakes in 1917 and 1976 killed 1,500 and 573 people, respectively. Source: https://mceer.buffalo.edu/infoservice/reference_services/indonesian_earthquake.asp (accessed 2016-10-20).

The earliest effort for me to analyze the environmental influences on civilizations started, rather accidentally, in the summer of 2009. To be more precise, it stemmed from my comments on Professor Eric R. Force's (2008) paper published in Geoarchaeology (John Wiley and Sons) as well as his reply to my comments.[13] The article was selected by the Science magazine as one of "The Top 10 ScienceNOWs of 2008," According to this article, earthquake-prone areas along the edges of tectonic plates were, at least in Asia and Europe, far more likely to give birth to the great ancient civilizations than the less dynamic landscapes (Force 2008). The findings immediately received attention from many prestigious magazines and world-class news agencies, with a striking title "Creative Destruction,"[14] However, Force's theory has left the birth of some major ancient civilizations, including those in Egypt and China—two of the world's greatest ancient civilizations—unexplained. Neither did he analyze the Western Hemisphere.

If earthquakes occur more frequently in a place than they do elsewhere, the place may be defined as the one that has been more cyclically threatened by natural disasters (earthquakes). Does this matter to the differing behaviors of civilizations and nations? A comparison of Chile and China still has broader implications.

Chile is one of the world's most earthquake-prone countries because just off the coast, the Nazca tectonic plate plunges beneath the South American plate, pushing the towering Andes cordillera to ever higher altitudes. Since earthquakes have huge ramifications, both political and practical, they have prompted the Andean nation to improve its alert systems for both quakes and tsunamis. For the Chileans, the key to surviving high magnitude quakes is to live and work in seismically safe buildings, while being aware of how frequent nature around them can also change. Chile has been decimated by earthquakes before. Since Chile has seen its fair share of earthquakes it has worked hard to prepare and protect against others. Since the 1960s, Chile's seismic codes have been enforced for all new construction based on what they call the "strong columns weak beam" system. The country's building codes are now recognized as some of the best in the world. From 2010 to 2015, as many as ten earthquakes, measured at 7.0 Richter magnitude scale (or RMS) or greater, were recorded in Chile. The average death toll resulting from each of these quakes, however, was only about 54.[15]

On the other hand, China is a country that only occasionally sees deadly earthquakes in its seismic areas. As a result, China, not like many other earthquake-prone countries in the rest of the world, has not invented or applied the quake-resistant building techniques, especially in its economically underdeveloped provinces, to stem future disasters. And this looks to be quite rational—economically and technologically. Who are willing to waste a large amount of financial and human resources for a geological event that will not happen within a period of decades or even longer? Consequently, whenever an infrequent earthquake occurred in China, China usually

---

[13] See Guo (2009) and Force (2009) for these two short papers.

[14] See, for example Britannica Online Encyclopedia (2009), Reebs (2008), ScienceNOW Staff (24 December 2008), and Malakoff (22 August 2008).

[15] Source: Author based on miscellaneous news clippings.

suffered much heavier quake-related casualties. For example, in 2008 an earthquake in Wenchuan County, Sichuan Province, measured at 7.9-8.0 RMS, has killed over 80,000 people. Prior to that, in 1976 a deadliest earthquake (measured at 7.8 RMS) hit Tangshan city, near Beijing, killing a population of 1/4 million or so.

Indeed, the more frequent occurrence of earthquakes and of other disasters can provide more incentives for people to protect themselves. While all disasters are harmful, disasters that occur cyclically or regularly still induce humans to enhance their "response-to-challenge" capabilities more significantly than they otherwise do. More specifically, if humans have grasped some knowledge about the cyclicity of disasters or have known that some disasters are bond to have come within a certain (or short) period of time, then they are already prepared to minimize, if not to get rid of, the casualties and property losses that may result from these disasters. All these cyclical natural phenomena or disasters have promoted the advancement of civilizations in the past thousands of years; and they will do so in the future.

However, earthquakes are not periodic or regularly repeating events; in other words, earthquakes are not a natural phenomenon that has clocklike behaviors like the rising and setting of the Sun. In Mesopotamia, Egypt, and China, earthquakes and other seismic disasters are not regularly occurring events, neither can they be predictable. Therefore, it is unlikely that they would influence humans' decisions on long-term capacity-building and other socioeconomic activities.

As a matter of fact, river flood is usually different from earthquake in that the former is cyclic or annual, while the latter is of irregularity and thus can have positive influences on the capacity-building of humans and other socioeconomic activities.

4.3 Old World, New World

In the Old World, after biological factors are held fixed, geographical and environmental factors are the most important dummies to explain the differences between the various cultures concerned. In China, the changes of the Yellow River's course have been spectacular, and the river mouth has sometimes changed catastrophically by hundreds of kilometers. It has had dozens of major and numerous minor changes in the course of the past thousands of years, each leading to great amount of not only human casualties but also property losses (Guo 2018, Chap. 5). All of these features have influenced the lifestyles of the Chinese people, especially of those with close proximity to the Yellow River. For example, after a comparison of the traditional architectures between the provinces of Henan, Shandong, and Fujian, we can find that the houses at the Yellow River Valley, especially at the lower reaches of the river, are much simpler and, of course, include fewer valuable materials. Since the majority of the Han populations living in Southeast China descend from those who immigrated from the valley of the Yellow River, only geographical features can explain that difference. People living along the Yellow River must have frequently abandoned their homes in order to escape from the unruly, disastrous floodwaters.

The difficulties in securing sufficient food within the Valley of the Yellow River have built the economical foundations for the Chinese cuisine. In contrast to the Westerners, the Chinese have a much smaller percentage of fat and meat as the main ingredient in their daily diet. This instantly reminds me of the hypothesis that it is the shortage of food in quantity and category that drove the Chinese to develop many cooking methods (including braising, boiling, braising with soy sauce, roasting, baking, grilling, scalding, deep-frying, steaming, drying, and salt-preserving) in order to make their food more delicious. In addition, the scarcity of food has resulted in a distinctive eating habit (i.e., dishes are placed in the center of a table so that everybody can share the meal) in ancient China. More often than not, all of the above conditions have also contributed to the development of a collectivist-style culture in China.

Resource scarcity and environmental hardship have also shaped other cultures as well. In the Mongol Plateau, winters are bitter cold, with strong, cold winds blowing into the region from north and west. As a result, the ancient Mongols living there must have had an intergenerational dream of possessing warm and safe shelters or yurts of their own. This can be witnessed by the fact that, in Mongolian, Urga (or Waga in proto-form), the old name of today's Ulaanbaatar, represents "palace" and that, in the Mongolian dialect, Ordos or Urdus (in proto-form: Wadus) is referred to "palaces." Now, Ordos (plural of Ordo or Wadu in proto-form) represents both a Mongol subgroup and a city in Inner Mongolia of China. The Mongol Plateau is a desert and steppe region, most of whose soil is a mixture of clay and sand and, as a result, is poorly suited for agriculture. Consequently, it is natural to understand that many key terms relating to the Mongol culture are derived from "wa"—the first common ancestral word that is believed to have the meanings crucial to the daily life of ancient humans. This can also be witnessed by the fact that Arvaikheer (likely derived from Awa Kheer), now a city in central Mongolia, has the meaning of "barley steppe" and that the Uurga (in proto-form: Waga, meaning "lasso") is a traditional Mongolian event celebrating nomads' horsemanship skills shown by catching horses.

It is worth recalling that that due to the fact that ancient humans had only been able to pronounce far small number of syllables than we are now, the syllables "ga" and "ka" were similar to each other in both pronunciations and meanings at ancient times, which are even so in some modern languages including Japanese. As a result, the term "Waga" mentioned above may be derived from or even has the same meanings of the common ancestral word "Waka" and its various variants—terms that were adopted to denote, among others, "city-state," "god of protection" or "sacred object or place" in the ancient Mesopotamian, Mesoamerican and Andean South American cultures (Guo 2018). In addition, the Proto-Mongolian words "Wadu" and "Awa" as mentioned earlier are also the common ancestral words that were widely used in ancient Mesopotamia.

Historic times are marked apart from prehistoric times when records of the past begin to be kept for the benefit of future generations (Carr 1961, p. 108)—that is, with the development of writing. Writing can naturalize a hegemonic discourse. Instead of simply expressing power, writing is a complex system of communication involving writers, massagers, media, and readers (Houston 2004). Thus, writing has been one of the major inventions for civilizations. However, humans' diverse writing systems were decisively influenced by both the scarcity of natural resources and the uniqueness the environment that were available to them. Let us have a brief comparison of the three oldest writing systems of the world—the Sumerian cuneiforms, the Egyptian hieroglyphs and the Chinese characters.

The Sumerian cuneiform and Egyptian hieroglyphic scripts each consists of a combination of logo-phonetic, consonantal alphabetic and syllabic signs. At its early stage, their writing systems were basically logographic in nature, and a sign represented a content word (such as a thing or an action). This nature looks like that of other early writing systems (such as that of Chinese characters). Since the ancient Sumerians wrote on clay tablets that were quite abundant in Mesopotamia, the Sumerian cuneiforms, each of which usually includes two or more independent signs, had been loosely written in space (see Fig. 4.4)[16] For example, the cuneiform script for Ur—name of the ancient Sumerian city-state—is loosely written as independent signs (□□□). As a result, the Sumerian cuneiform, unlike the Chinese writing system to be discussed later, had had an opportunity to gradually develop into a combined system where a set of signs could be used to represent logograms and phonograms or syllabograms. In the cuneiform texts of the Ur period (i.e., the late third and early second millennium), logograms were used to write content words and the base (root) of a word, while phonograms were used to write bound morphemes and loan words.

By way of contrast, the ancient Chinese first wrote on oracle bones—turtle shells, ox scapulae, or other bones that were scarce for agriculturists (if not for hunter-gatherers). As a result, they had to write more efficiently in order to save writing space (see Fig. 4.4). As for the Chinese character "guo" (in traditional form: 國) for "state" or "country," it is written as a large square (□ denoting "a land with walled boundaries") inside which there is another Chinese character "或" that is composed of the characters "ge" (戈, denoting a weapon used in ancient China) and "kou" (口, denoting a human mouth or population).[17] So much information is included in a single square! In most circumstances, it cannot be accomplished by either the Sumerian cuneiform script or the Egyptian hieroglyphs. Here, the scarcity of material for writing in ancient China did induce the ancient Chinese to use 國 (instead of □戈口) for "state" or "country." However, this spatially optimized writing system might have also been responsible for the Chinese writing system not to gradually evolve into an alphabetic one. The drawback of a purely logographic writing system is of course that the number of signs needed to represent all the words of a language will run into the thousands.

Like Ur, which was an ancient Sumerian city-state and initially pronounced "wa" (see Fig. 3.1 in Chap. 3), the Chinese character for state or country (now read as "guo" in Mandarin Chinese, "ge" in Hakka, "kue" in Wu, and "gwo" in Cantonese) was likely pronounced "wa" (or any variant of it) in Proto-Chinese. In addition, like many other indigenous languages in the Old World, Han-Chinese, especially some

---

[16]This is also similar to that of the Egyptian hieroglyphic script whose writing surface was made of the pith of papyrus plant and was quite abundant across the Nile delta in ancient Egypt.

[17]Note that the earliest forms of the Chinese character 國 also include, among others, 或 and 馘 (in which 王 denotes 'king'), each of which is also composed of the components (口 and 戈).

Fig. 4.4 The Sumerian cuneiforms, Egyptian hieroglyphs and Chinese characters *Notes* (1) The Sumerian cuneiforms (c. 26th century BC) are shown in the down left side; the Egyptian hieroglyphs from the tomb of Seti I (reign c. 1294-1279 BC) are shown in the upper left side; and the oracle bone script (c. 13th century BC) is shown in the right side. (2) There are 48 Sumerian cuneiforms and more than 100 Chinese characters. *Sources* Wikimedia Commons (under the Creative Commons Attribution-Share Alike 3.0 Unported license)

of its dialects (such as Wu, Hakka, and Cantonese, which are also the early versions of or even the proto-languages of Han-Chinese), frequently uses the syllable "wa."

Even though the creation of a language has been driven by the crying demand of humans who were physically weak (see Sect. 3.1 in Chap. 3), the specific linguistic system of any ethnic group may also be significantly influenced by the environment in which that ethnic group lives or lived. For example, Han-Chinese language—one that has been used by the ethnic majority in China—is usually referred to as a monosyllabic language. To understand the differences between the Han language and many of those of the Indo-European phylum, we need to investigate the initial conditions under which all these languages were born. Different from Mesopotamia and the Nile Valley—two areas from which the Western civilizations and languages originate, the Yellow River Valley was a much more difficult place for people to live there.

Table 4.1 Chinese dialect differences in Beijing, Shandong, Shanghai and Henan

Speaker	English	Beijing dialect	Shandong dialect	Shanghai dialect	Henan dialect
A	Who is it?	zhe shi shui ya?	jie si shei?	sa nin?	sei?
B	It's me.	shi wo nin na.	jie si wo.	wu a.	wo.
A	What are you doing?	ni gan ma qu?	shang na qu?	sa qi?	zhua?
B	I'm going to use the toilet.	wo sha pao niao.	shang bian suo.	sha si.	niao!

While it is difficult to explain how China's monosyllabic and Europe's multisyllabic languages have been determined, the environment must have been one of the most important factors influencing the past language evolutions. To provide more consistent evidence, let us control for other variables (including race or ethnic variation) and look at how China's oral languages reflect environmental differences among the following areas:

- Beijing area: Surrounded by the Yanshan Mountains on the north and northeast and by the Taihang Mountains on the west, it has almost no flood-related disasters.
- Shandong area: Surrounded by seas on three sides, it has no unruly rivers, especially in the Shandong peninsula.
- Shanghai area: Located in the delta area of the Yangtze River, it was more seriously hit by river floods than Shandong.
- Henan area: Located the lower reaches of the Yellow River, it has suffered China's most deadly flooding in history.

Here, the Beijing area, especially the northern part of Beijing, is defined as a place free of natural disasters, which is followed by Shandong and Shanghai, with Henan having historically suffered the most serious natural disasters (mainly river floods). The most intriguing fact is that, when a given expression (say, "Who is it?") is spoken, different dialects were created in these four areas. For example, local Beijingers usually speak four characters "zhe shi shui ya?" while the Henanese often say "sei?" (see Table 4.1). All this reflects the basic idea that people living in difficult and sometimes dangerous areas had to learn how to save time in communicating with each other.

The above logic may also be applied to the analysis of cultural and language evolutions in Japan and Korea. The idea that Japanese and Korean belong to a putative Altaic language family has been generally discredited; and, as a result, historical linguists have generally classified them each as a language isolate.[18] However, one thing is almost certain that Japanese and Korean are more similar to Altaic and/or Turko-Mongolic rather than to Chinese languages. During the past thousands of years, and compared with the Han-Chinese (especially those living in the Yellow River Valley),

---

[18] See, for example, Song (2005, p. 15) and Campbell and Mixco (2007, pp. 7 and 90–91).

the Japanese and, to a lesser extent, the Koreans, have not been seriously affected by the frequent occurrence of natural and environmental disasters. A hypothesis is as follows: since the Japanese and the Koreans did not encounter some, if not all of the difficulties and dangers with which the Han-Chinese were faced, their languages are not as efficient as the Chinese language; or, more precisely, Japanese and the Korean do not include more shorten sentences than Chinese does. (Of course, Chinese language also differs from region to region, all conforming to the law that tightened geographical and environmental influences usually result in shorten dialects). For example, when speaking "Who is it?" in their own languages, the Japanese say "do chi ra sa ma de su ka?" (or "a na ta wa da re?" in a shorter version) and the Koreans use "nu gu sei yao?" Obviously, they each use more syllables than the Chinese usually do (shown in Table 4.1).

Without doubt, people living in the environmentally unfriendly areas of the Old World have developed complicated cultural traditions much earlier than those living elsewhere. Of course, large-scale irrigation, where it occurred, did contribute significantly to increasing the power and scope of the civilization. However, the point at issue is not how a hydraulic empire increased its power but how it arose in environmentally challengeable places (see Fig. 4.2). And to this issue existing theories (including Wittfogel's hydraulic hypothesis, which will be discussed in Sect. 5.1 in Chap. 5) does not appear to hold the key. Remember that hydraulically related activity has not only led to despotism, as insisted by Wittfogel, but it has also invented various forms of "democratic" governance (such as the cooperative water networks in Bali, Indonesia). Of course, all these institutional inventions—either despotic, cooperative, or democratic—can be defined as "cultural complexity" and thus are pertinent to the core elements of various human civilizations.

Why did influential civilizations usually arise in the environmentally challengeable—though not the abominable—places? History did not leave much detail about the rise and fall of the Norte Chico civilization in Andean South America, except that the archaeological finds suggest that it has Multipotamian characteristics. We may also learn something about a late-coming, and also the wadi-based, civilization that has natural and geographic conditions similar to those of the Norte Chico.

Located in the Andean region of present-day Peru, the Sacred Valley is 20 km from north of Cusco—the capital of the Inca Empire from AD 1438 to 1533. The valley was formed by the Urubamba River, also known as Willkanuta River (in Aymara, "house of sun") or Willkamayu (in Quechua). The Sacred Valley of the Incas is called Willka Qhichwa in Kichwa (or Quechua in Spanish)[19]—the still spoken lingua franca of the Inca Empire. It is fed by numerous rivers tributaries descending through adjoining valleys and gorges. The valley was appreciated by the Incas due to its special geographical and climatic qualities. It was one of the empire's main points for the extraction of natural wealth, and one of the most important areas for maize production in Peru northwards from Pisac. The Incas built extensive agricultural

---

[19]Note that all the terms of Qhichwa, Kichwa and Quechua means "temperate valley" in Kichwa (or Quechua in Spanish), which is similar to the term 'wadi' in the Old World (Guo 2018, Chap. 7).

cultivation and irrigation systems that still work today on the sides of mountains and hills (see Fig. 4.3).

On the vast majority of these agricultural terraces, the Incas planted potatoes, crops and other plants. Reasons for creating stepped agricultural "fields" are various. If you notice on the map, the Sacred Valley region is surrounded by very high mountains. There is little space in the valley, so the usage of steps actually increases the area available for agriculture. Another reason is the fact that they could better control the amount of water used for the irrigation of the plants. Benefits include defense against possible landslides and floods. In this way, the water does not accumulate and run down on the towns below. The rocks used for creating the steps strengthen the sides of the mountains, thus protecting what is in the valleys from possible mudslides during heavy rainfall (Covey 2003). Nevertheless, the stepped agriculture is complex, requires hard work for creation, but, whenever completed, ensures food over a long period of time. Remarkably, the Sacred Valley is Peru's productive agricultural region today. Local people use the old terraces to produce their food, just like their ancestors did many hundreds of years ago.

During the golden age of the Inca Empire, the Sacred Valley must have been much more agriculturally productive than the Loess Plateau (see Fig. 4.2) in the Yellow River Valley that is the cradle of one of the greatest civilizations in the Old World. Like the Chinese living near the Yellow River, the Incas had had to cope with floods that could have destroyed their agricultural fields and homes in the valleys. Higher ground protects the plantations from flood-related disasters. Sometimes, the Urubamba River, though far less unruly than the Yellow River, can be terrifying when its affluent and intense rain increase its volume.[20] However, the agricultural terraces in the Sacred Valley are still not as productive as Bali's Subak irrigation system (see Fig. 4.1). In addition, the Bali Island in Indonesia is almost free from any serious river-related floods or disasters.

When the Chinese were anxiously waiting for the rain to come to their dry land in the Loess Plateau, the Incas were—leisurely and freely—controlling the irrigation of their terraces by diverting small quantities of water from mountain rivers. In this way, the threat of drought was significantly reduced, if not eliminated, in the Sacred Valley. Among all the three peoples—the Balinese, the Chinese, and the Andean Natives—the Balinese once had the simplest life, without any sorrow and anxiety. However, a brief comparison of the Chinese, the Incas, and the Balinese civilizations simply reveals that the strength of a civilization is negatively determined by the friendliness of the natural and geographical environments therein. More specifically, over the courses of their respect histories, the Chinese, though having lived a miserable life, still possessed a more powerful civilization than the Incas did; while the Incas, though having less productive terraces and more terrifying flooding experiences than those of the Balinese, still advanced their civilization better than the latter did.

---

[20]For example, in early 2010 the Urubamba River has shown its force once again, twisting railway lines, demolishing buildings.

Hundreds of thousands of years ago, when one or more groups of humans left the African continent, those who remained in southern Africa might have the first laugh. Yes, nature selected the latter as they were more suited to the environment of the African continent. However, after generations of struggles against the nature and between themselves, the successors of those who were not selected by nature and had to migrate out of Africa have been living quite well in the rest of the world—at least not worse than their counterparts, or the successors of the earlier winners, in Africa. However, after taking into account the Paleo-Indian migration from Eurasia to the Americas that occurred tens of thousands of years ago, we can only but have a different scenario: For a long period of time prior to the European colonization from the sixteenth century onwards, the Americas as a whole had lagged far behind Eurasia—technologically, economically, and culturally. If all the humans living in the African, Eurasian and American continents have the same ancestor and are still not different from each other in gene, then why have there been so technological, economical, and cultural differences throughout the world?

Historically, in most places of the world, natural resources were not abundant enough for human beings to sustain their daily lives. Without good reason, the transformation from the nomadic life to an agricultural society was first accomplished by those who had not been able to obtain enough food provided by nature. This, as a result, provides incentives for human beings to invent agriculture and other more complicated (or "advanced" as we now usually say) cultures. Compared with hunter-gatherers, agriculturalists could, through learning and inventing, more freely decide the varieties of their food supplies. Even if nature could provide abundant foods (including wild fruits and animals), humans might sometimes still find it necessary to create an agricultural society for their own. This was decided by many other factors including, for example, the one that humans could get rid of the competition with their natural enemies; or the one that humans could decide where, when and how to produce what they wanted.

4.4 New World, Old Issues

A glance at Fig. 4.5 simply shows that the Native Americans usually have a lower average height than the other peoples (including Whites-Europeans) living in the New World. If physical weakness was an advantage for cultural advancement, then, why had there been no powerful civilization in the New World during the pre-Columbian era? In other words, why had the Native Americans not been able to advance their indigenous cultures as powerful as the Eurasian civilizations? These are very serious questions. If the reasons have nothing to do with the differences of anthropological factors (according to our theoretical and empirical analyses stated in Chaps. 2 and 3, physically weaker humans should have been more prepared to advance their cultures or civilizations), then the reasons must have been the intercontinental differences.

Thus, the following is almost certain that it is the environment—not human factors—in the New World that did not make the cultures and civilizations therein as

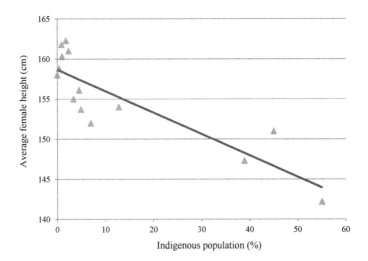

Fig. 4.5 Average female height and indigenous populations, the Americas *Source* Drawn by author based on Table 4.2

powerful (advanced) as those in the Far East and in the Old World. Again, as stated elsewhere in this book, it is the good environments—not the bad environments—that were responsible for the abortion or failure of some early indigenous cultures or civilizations.[21] Examples in this regard include the Subak irrigation system of the Bali Island, Indonesia, as already described in Sect. 4.2. Even though it is difficult to precisely define what a good or bad environment is, Americas' crops (such as maize in Mesoamerica and potato in the Andes, to name but two) are generally known to have agricultural advantages over the Old World during the pre-Columbian era. Throughout history, and thanks to these easy-to-plant and large-in-output crops, there has been a far lower frequency of large-scale famines in the New World than in the Old World.[22]

Genetic studies suggest that the first inhabitants of the Americas shared a single ancestral population, one that developed in isolation, conjectured to be Beringia (Wells and Read 2002, pp. 138–140). The long-lasting isolation of these peoples in Beringia must imply that all these indigenous peoples as well as their descents who are now living throughout the Americas have been genetically homogeneous (at least as compared with those living in Eurasia). On the other hand, the environments have varied from place to place in the Americas, so do the indigenous cultures there. We may thus believe that, like in the Old World, all the indigenous cultures and civilizations in the Americas have been the result of the bad (vis-à-vis good)—though

---

[21]This does not say that some sudden and catastrophic disasters would not destroy cultures and civilizations.

[22]The only pre-Columbian food shortages or famines that have been recorded for Mesoamerica include the persistent drought (c. AD 850) in the Maya society and the famine (AD 1454) in Mexico (Benedict 2000, p. 123).

still not the worst—environments there. We may further conclude that the main, if not the only reason why the indigenous cultures and civilizations in the Americas have not been as strong as those in the Old World is that the environments are still not worse than those in the Old World.

There have been as many as over one million different societies throughout human history, of which only about two hundred or so societies survive (Elwell 2013, p. 103). Early cultural (or sociocultural) evolution theories claimed that societies started out in a primitive state and gradually became more civilized over time. In the nineteenth century, there were attempts to explain how culture developed in its evolutionary process. However, it is the neo-evolutionary thinkers who brought back evolutionary thought and developed it to be acceptable to contemporary anthropology. Neo-evolutionism is a social theory that tries to explain the evolution of societies by drawing on Charles Darwin's theory of evolution and discarding some dogmas of the previous social evolutionism. It is concerned with long-term, directional, evolutionary social change and with the regular patterns of development that may be seen in unrelated, widely separated cultures.

Table 4.2 provides estimates for some human and cultural features of the major countries in the Americas. Here, my definition of indigenous peoples does not include those with partial indigenous ancestry. Obviously, except Greenland—an Arctic country within the Kingdom of Denmark, most of the other countries that have the largest indigenous peoples (as a percentage of the overall population) are located either in Mesoamerica or in the central and north Andes (including Bolivia, Colombia, Ecuador, Peru, and Venezuela) that surround or are in close proximity to Andean Peru—cradle of the Native American cultures. It is noteworthy that all of these countries (again, Greenland is excluded) are either the successors of two indigenous American civilizations (i.e., the Olmec in Mesoamerica and the Norte Chico in Andean South America) or those with close proximity to them. Is it not quite queer? But it is still not the queerest.

The World Health Organization (WHO) defines that a country is overweight if its body mass index (BMI)—an indicator that is defined as a person's weight in kilograms divided by the square of his height in meters—is greater than or equal to 25. According to this definition, all the American countries shown in Table 4.2 are now overweight. While what the BMI really implies still remains a subject of argument, an overly high value of BMI is by no means good for human health and cultural development. If we look at the Americas' BMI values with respect to the proportions of indigenous populations, then a negative correlation can be found (see Fig. 4.6). In other words, it suggests a positive correlation between the BMI and the proportion of non-Hispanic White populations. Of course, many other factors are also responsible for the overweight problem in the Americas and elsewhere. However, as will be seen later, after income level's influences on the BMI are fixed (since countries with higher income levels usually have greater BMI figures than those with lower income levels), the overweight problem is more serious in the Americas.

According to the statistically estimated results shown in Sect. 5.2 in Chap. 5, the BMI of peoples living in the Americas, Oceania, and other islands that had been isolated from the Eurasian civilizations during the pre-Columbian era tends to increase

Table 4.2 The human and cultural features of selected American countries

Country	Pre-Colombian culture(s)	Indigenous population (%)	Average female height (cm)	BMI (kg/m^2)
North America				
Canada	HG/SFS	1.80	162.30	27.00
USA	HG/SFS	0.90	161.80	28.50
Mesoamerica				
Belize	SFS/CFS	16.70	NA	28.45
Costa Rica	SFS	2.40	NA	26.55
El Salvador	SFS/CFS	1.00	160.30	27.00
Guatemala	SFS/CFS	38.90	147.30	26.15
Honduras	SFS/CFS	7.00	152.00	26.05
Mexico	HG/SFS/CFS	12.80	154.00	27.75
Nicaragua	SFS	5.00	153.70	26.55
Panama	SFS	6.00	NA	26.60
South America				
Argentina	HG/SFS	2.38	161.01	27.25
Bolivia	HG/SFS/CFS	55.00	142.20	25.50
Brazil	HG/SFS	0.40	158.80	25.60
Chile	HG/CFS	4.60	156.10	27.45
Colombia	HG/SFS	3.40	155.00	25.60
Ecuador	SFS/CFS	25.00	NA	26.65
Guyana	HG/SFS	9.10	NA	25.85
Paraguay	HG/SFS	1.70	NA	25.45
Peru	CFS	45.00	151.00	25.90
Suriname	HG/SFS	2.00	NA	26.85
Uruguay	HG/SFS	0.00	158.00	26.45
Venezuela	HG/SFS	2.70	NA	27.00

Notes (1) BMI=body mass index, HG=hunter-gatherers, SFS=simple farming societies, and CFS=complex farming societies (tribal chiefdoms or civilizations). (2) All data on the indigenous and mixed populations are as of 2010-15; some figures are based on the results of population-wide genetic surveys while others are based on self-identification or observational estimation. (3) The data on the BMI are as of 2010. The BMI is defined as a person's weight in kilograms divided by the square of his height in meters (kg/m^2). The WHO definition is that a BMI greater than or equal to 25 is overweight

Source Guo (2017, p. 51)

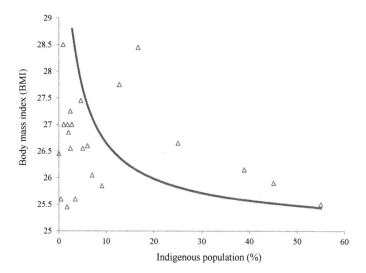

Fig. 4.6 Body mass index (BMI) and indigenous populations, the Americas *Source* Drawn by author based on Table 4.2

by about 0.460 kg/m ^{2} in 1980 and by about 1.022 kg/m ^{2} in 2010 as compared with that of peoples living in the rest of the world. Since the coefficient has more than doubled from 1980 to 2010, we may conclude that from 1980 to 2010 the geographical influences on overweight and obesity have sharply increased in countries of the Americas, Oceania, or any islands that had been isolated from the Eurasian civilizations during the pre-Columbian era. Since other explanatory variables such as economic and racial variables are also included in the regressions, the above figures are purely generated by the environment alone. If overweight or obesity is the factor that has negative influences on cultural advancement, then we may conclude that the environment does not encourage cultures to advance in the Americas, Oceania, and other islands that had been isolated from the Eurasian civilizations.

It should be noted that the estimated results have different implications at different circumstances. Specifically, if the BMI is lower than or near to the level of underweight or malnourishment, then there would be good news for the Americas (especially in 1980) that the White population has advantages in health improvement (represented by the BMI) over both the Yellow and the Black populations; and that living in the New World is a much easier thing than that in the Old World. More specifically, these findings are approved by the following evidence: that the minor and statistically insignificant coefficient on the dummy "White" (i.e., 0.065, which is statistically insignificant) in 1980, implies that the Americas, especially when compared with the countries dominated by the racial groups of "Yellow" (with a coefficient of −1.830, which is statistically significant at greater than the 1% confidence level), was experiencing a faster human development than Asia.

However, as for the year 2010, in which the Americas had already one of the largest shares of overweight and obese populations in the world and that overweight and obese issues were already a problem in many, if not all Eurasian countries, the findings are bad news for the Americas but good news for Asia. Haven't these changing features of the environment and human beings also been forming part of the nonlinear or cyclical civilizations of today?

The environments in the Americas have almost not changed during the past thousands of years. Then, can they explain why North America never gave birth to an indigenous civilization?[23] Maybe it is a mere coincidence; maybe not. However, one thing is certain that these continents, though quite far away and different from each other, tend to increase the average BMI of the populations living there. This might be good news in the 1980 s during which the BMI was still not very high. However, since more and more people living there have become overweight or obese, this is no longer good news. Then, why the Whites-dominated countries have more serious overweigh problems than other peoples in the Americas (also in Oceania and any islands that had been isolated from the Eurasian civilizations during the pre-Columbian era) than elsewhere?

The Americas have been deeply affected by the European expansions. Spain first conquered most of the Caribbean islands and overran the two great New World empires: the Aztec Empire (in today's Mexico) and the Inca Empire (in today's Peru). From there, Spain conquered about half of South America and part of North America. Portugal also expanded in the Americas, conquering half of South America and calling their colony Brazil. Other powers to arrive in the Americas were the Swedes, Dutch, English, and French. In the Americas, it seems that only the most remote peoples managed to stave off complete assimilation by Western and Western-fashioned governments. These include some of the northern peoples (i.e., Inuit), some peoples in the Yucatán, Amazonian forest dwellers, and various Andean groups. Nevertheless, contacts between the Old and New worlds promoted the transfer of goods unique to one hemisphere to another.

More than 500 years have passed since Christopher Columbus found the New World. During the post-Columbian era, the White population has successfully colonized the Americas as a whole. What is more, the Europeanization has effectively reduced, if not annihilated, the American Indians in many American countries, especially in Uruguay, Brazil, and the USA (see Table 4.2). In Amazonia, for example, even though hundreds of native languages are still spoken, most of these languages are each spoken by only a handful of indigenous people, and thus are critically endangered. Why have the indigenous peoples survived more easily within or near their traditional cultural centers than elsewhere? This is a big question and it seems that it has never received a convincing answer. Nevertheless, if our previous analysis of the natural and environmental influences on cultural evolution and development is correct, then the following facts and inferences seem to be rational:

---

[23] There existed several indigenous civilizations in Mesoamerica and Andean South America. But these civilizations were much less powerful than those in the Old World.

- Columbus and his followers always chose the most fertile and environmentally friendly places to settle in (fact).
- There are more natural and environmental challenges in the centers of the indigenous American civilizations than elsewhere (fact).
- Populations responsible for or influenced by more advanced civilizations or cultural traditions are less likely to be conquered or assimilated (inference).
- Indigenous Americans can be more easily found in Mesoamerica and the central and north Andes than elsewhere (inference).

Over the course of the past thousands of years, the criteria humans have used to define the terms "fertile and environmentally friendly place" and "natural and environmental challenge" may have slightly changed. However, it seems that the fundamental criterion has never changed. Unlike their Native American counterparts who (as losers) have to reside in the regions with various (naturally and environmentally) disadvantageous places, the White Europeans (as winners) are now occupying most, if not all of the environmentally friendly places of the Americas. However, it should be noted that it is the relatively infertile places that had helped the Native American Indians to create various indigenous cultures or civilizations, though the latter being still not as powerful as those in the Old World.

The White Europeans have already achieved various economic and cultural miracles in the New World. Can they sustain these miracles in the long run? It is a hard question. However, most of the Whites-dominated areas in the Americas had never given birth to an indigenous civilization during the pre-Columbian era. I do not intend to say that the White Europeans and other newcomers from the Old World cannot sustain their current, comfortable lifestyle of their own in the future. However, as having stated in this chapter and will be proved in the following chapter, favorable environmental and external factors usually become disincentives (whereas unfavorable environmental and external factors may become incentives) for humans to advance economic and cultural developments.

Think that the natural and environmental conditions that did not lead to the birth of indigenous civilizations in North America have changed during the past thousands of years? Think again!

References

Benedict RG (2000) The great maya droughts: water, life, and death. University of New Mexico Press, Albuquerque, NM

Boserup E (1965) The conditions of agricultural growth: the economics of agrarian change under population pressure. Allen & Unwin, London

Boserup E (1976) Environment, population, and technology in primitive societies. Popul Dev Rev 2(1):21–36

Boserup E (1985) The impact of scarcity and plenty on development. In: Rotberg RI, Rabb TK (eds) Hunger and history: the impact of changing food production and consumption patterns on society. Cambridge University Press, Cambridge and New York, pp 185–210

Britannica Online Encyclopedia (2009) Creative destruction. Britannica Online Encyclopedia. http:/
    /www.britannica.com/bps/additionalcontent/18/35247242/Creative-Destruction. Accessed 8 Oct
    2016
Buckle HT (1913) History of civilization in England, 2nd edn. Hearst's International Library Co.,
    London
Campbell L, Mixco MJ (2007) A glossary of historical linguistics. University of Utah Press, Salt
    Lake City, UT
Carr EH (1961) What is history?. Random House Inc., New York
Covey AR (2003) A processual study of Inka state formation. J Anthropol Archaeol 22(4):333–357
Easterly W, Levine R (2003) Tropics, germs, and crops: How endowments influence economic
    development. J Monet Econ 50:3–39
Elwell FL (2013) Sociocultural systems: principles of structure and change. University of Wash-
    ington Press, Seattle
Force ER (2008) Tectonic environments of ancient civilizations in the eastern Hemisphere. Geoar-
    chaeol An Int J 23(5):644–653
Force ER (2009) Birth of ancient civilizations: Reply to comments of Rongxing Guo. Geoarchae-
    ology: An. Int J 24(6):849–850
Gallup JL, Sachs JD, Mellinger AD (1999) Geography and economic development. Int Reg Sci
    22:179–224
Gilmartin M (2009) Colonialism/imperialism. In: Gilmartin M, Mountz A, Shirlow P (eds) Carolyn
    Gallaher, Carl T Dahlman. Sage Publications Ltd, Key Concepts in Political Geography. London
    and New York, pp 115–123
Guo R (2009) On the birth of ancient civilizations—Comments on a paper by Eric R force. Geoar-
    chaeology Int J 24(6):846–848
Guo R (2017) An Economic Inquiry into the Nonlinear Behaviors of Nations: Dynamic Develop-
    ments and the Origins of Civilizations. Palgrave Macmillan, New York
Guo R (2018) Civilizations revisited: the historians may be wrong, really. University Press, Hong
    Kong
Houston SD (2004) The archaeology of communication technologies. Annu Rev Anthropol
    33:223–250
Lansing J Stephen (1987) Balinese "water temples" and the management of irrigation. Am Anthropol
    89(2):326–341
Lansing J Stephen (2006) Perfect order: recognizing complexity in Bali. Princeton University Press,
    Princeton, NJ
Malakoff D (22 August 2008) Did rumbling give rise to Rome? ScienceNOW Daily News. Available
    at: http://sciencenow.sciencemag.org/cgi/content/full/2008/822/3. Accessed 6 Oct 2016
Njoku RC (2013) The history of Somalia. Greenwood Histories of the Modern Nations. Greenwood,
    Santa Barbara, CA
Parker PM (2000) Physioeconomics: the basis for long-run economic growth. The MIT Press,
    Cambridge, MA
Reebs S (2008) Creative destruction—Ancient civilizations rose near tectonic boundaries.
    Natural History Magazine. www.naturalhistorymag.com/samplings/11343/creative-destruction.
    Accessed 8 Oct 2016
ScienceNOW Staff (24 December 2008) The top 10 ScienceNOWs of 2008. ScienceNOW Daily
    News
Scarre C, Brian MF (2016). Ancient Civilizations (4th Edition). Routledge, London
Song JJ (2005) The Korean language: structure, use and context. Routledge, London
Taylor JG (2003) Indonesia: peoples and histories. Yale University Press, New Haven and London
Wallace AR (1869; 2011) The malay archipelago: the land of the orang-utan and the bird of paradise
    (2nd edition). John Beaufoy Publishing, Hong Kong
Wells S, Read M (2002) The journey of man—a genetic odyssey. Random House, New York
Wittfogel K (1957) Oriental Despotism: A Comparative Study of Total Power. Yale University
    Press, New Heaven, MA

Chapter 5
Environment Matters, But Not the Way You Think (II)

Abstract Although civilization has been the most far-reaching achievement in human history, the origin of civilization is still imperfectly understood. It seems that existing theories have not given a satisfactory answer to the question how various environmental (geographic) factors matter. Now, the question is that, if it is the fertility of the crescent-shaped region that gave birth to the earliest human civilization, then why many other fertile areas, including those of southern Africa (also the place with by far the longest history of human occupation), North America, and Oceania, have never given birth to a powerful indigenous civilization? Over the course of human history, the environment has mattered to human and cultural behaviors, but not in the way historians have suggested. And, under certain conditions, some unfavorable boundary and external factors can incentivize civilizations and nations to develop and advance in the long run, if not in the short run.

Keywords Human evolution · Civilization · Environment · External threat
Long-run growth

5.1 A Review of the Theories of Civilization

Being part of a group offered physical protection that the solitary hunters did not have given the hunters concerned confidence in their ability to predict the outcome of their expeditions. Without such confidence, the members of the first organizations might well have starved. People joined organizations to make their lives more secured, and those organizations depended on other organizations to perform certain activities in a predictable manner (Stevenson and Moldoveanu 1995). As people turned from hunting to farming, then to more complicated (or advanced) civilization, the link between organizations and the need for predictability became more complex.

An important evolutionary theorist of the late nineteenth century, the Russian geographer Peter Kropotkin, in his book *Mutual Aid: A Factor of Evolution* (1902), advocated a conception of Darwinism. He used biological and sociological arguments in an attempt to show that the main factor in facilitating evolution is cooperation

© Springer Nature Singapore Pte Ltd. 2019
R. Guo, *Human-Earth System Dynamics*,
https://doi.org/10.1007/978-981-13-0547-4_5

between individuals in free-associated societies and groups. This was in order to counteract the conception of fierce competition as the core of evolution. Kropotkin summed up Darwinism as the following:

> The animal species, in which individual struggle has been reduced to its narrowest limits, and the practice of mutual aid has attained the greatest development, are invariably the most numerous, the most prosperous, and the most open to further progress. The mutual protection which is obtained in this case, the possibility of attaining old age and of accumulating experience, the higher intellectual development, and the further growth of sociable habits, secure the maintenance of the species, its extension, and its further progressive evolution. The unsociable species, on the contrary, are doomed to decay.[1]

The first relatively sophisticated theories about the origins of civilization were formulated by the Australian archaeologist and philologist Vere Gordon Childe (1892–1957). Childe claimed that a "Neolithic Revolution," which witnessed the beginning of farming, was followed by an "Urban Revolution." He then theorized that this second revolution saw the development of metallurgy and the appearance of a new social class of full-time artisans and specialists who lived in much larger settlements, that is, cities. In addition, Childe proposed ten traits that were present in the oldest cities:

- There were larger than earlier settlements;
- They contained full-time craft specialists;
- The surplus was collected together to a god or king;
- They witnessed monumental architecture;
- There was an unequal distribution of social surplus;
- Writing was invented;
- The sciences developed,
- Naturalistic art developed;
- Trade with foreign areas increased; and
- The state organization was based on residence rather than kinship.[2]

In the 1960s, many Mesopotamian archaeologists argued that the term "Urban Revolution" puts undue emphasis on the city at the expense of social change, that is, the development of social classes and political institutions. Robert McCormick Adams, for example, pointed out that both early Mesopotamian and American civilizations followed a basically similar course of development in which kin groups, who controlled land communally, were replaced by the growth of private estates owned by noble families.[3]

Another modern theory is what Robert L. Carneiro called the "automatic" theory in his 1970 paper published in the Science magazine. According to this theory, the invention of agriculture automatically brought into a surplus of food, enabling some individuals to divorce themselves from food production and to become potters, weavers, smiths, masons, and so on, thus creating an extensive division of labor

---

[1]Cited from Kropotkin (1902, p. 293).

[2]Cited from McNairn (1980, pp. 98–102).

[3]Cited from Scarre and Fagan (2016, p. 29).

(Carneiro 1970). Out of this occupational specialization, there developed a political integration which united a number of previously independent—usually adjacent in geography—communities into a state.

A close examination of history indicates that a coercive theory can account for the rise of the civilization. Force, and not enlightened self-interest, is the mechanism by which to promote, step by step, cultural evolution from autonomous villages to the state. Napoleon Alphonseau Chagnon has advanced the argument that the violence in Yąnomamö (also spelled Yanomami or Yanomama)—a group of approximately 35,000 indigenous people who live in some 200–250 villages on the border between Venezuela and Brazil in the Amazon rainforest—has fueled an evolutionary process in which successful warriors have more offspring. For example, in his (1968) book *Yanomamö: The Fierce People*, Chagnon wrote:

> Most wars are merely a prolongation of earlier hostilities, simulated by revenge motives. The first causes of hostilities are usually sorcery, murders, or club fights over women in which someone is badly injured or killed. Occasionally, food theft involving related villages also precipitates raiding. This was the causes of the first raids between Kaobawa's [a headman] group and the Patanowa-teri [village]; they split from each other after a series of club fights over women. Each group made a new garden and returned periodically to the old one to collect peach-palm fruit, a crop that continues to produce after the garden itself has gone to weeds. Someone stole the peach-palm fruit belonging to a man in the other group, resulting in another food theft for revenge, a club fight, and then raiding...[4]

There is little question that, in one way or another, war has played a decisive role in the rise and fall of cultures or civilizations. In fact, the view that war lies at the root of the state is by no means new. 2,500 years ago, Heraclitus, a pre-Socratic Greek philosopher, wrote that "war is common to all and strife is justice, and that all things come into being through strife necessarily."[5] Historical or archaeological evidence of war is found in the early stages of state formation throughout the world. However, although warfare was surely a key mover in the origin of civilizations, it was the only factor, neither was it the prime factor. Like in much of the animals' world, wars have been found in many parts of the human world where advanced civilizations never emerged. After all, they have not always ended with the victories of ethically just or culturally advanced belligerents. Thus, while warfare may be a necessary condition for the rise and fall of the civilizations, it is not a sufficient one. While we can identify war as an instrument for cultural evolutions, we also need to specify the initial conditions under which humans gave rise to the civilizations.

In his 1957 work *Oriental Despotism*, Karl August Wittfogel emphasized the role of irrigation work, the bureaucratic structures needed to maintain them and the impact that these had on society, coining the term "hydraulic empire" to describe the system. In his view, many societies, mainly in Asia, relied heavily on the building of large-scale irrigation work. To do this, the state had to organize forced labor from the population at large. As only a centralized administration could organize the building and maintenance of large-scale systems of irrigation, the need for such

---

[4]Cited from Chagnon (1972, p. 123).
[5]Cited from http://www.iep.utm.edu/heraclit/, accessed 2016-9-1.

systems made bureaucratic despotism inevitable in Oriental lands. This structure was uniquely placed to also crush civil society and any other force capable of mobilizing against the state. Such a state would inevitably be despotic, powerful, stable, and wealthy. Wittfogel states:

> The patterns [of organization and social control] come into being when an experimenting community of farmers or protofarmers finds large sources of moisture in a dry but potentially fertile area... [A] number of farmers eager to conquer arid lowlands and plains are forced to invoke the organizational devices which—on the basis of premachine technology—offer the one chance of success: they must work in cooperation with their fellows and subordinate themselves to a directing authority.[6]

Wittfogel's theory, when applied to China, has been criticized by scholars such as Joseph Needham who argued essentially that Wittfogel was operating from ignorance of basic Chinese history (Needham 1959). As a matter of fact, the hydraulic despotism has only been the by-product of a riverine civilization. Even though it has existed in the history of human civilization, using the modern terms of despotism and democracy may not be appropriate when the origin of ancient civilizations is analyzed. More often than not, creating a culture or civilization might have been initial goal of the most, if not all people concerned.

Civilization might not have satisfied everyone; instead, it simply was an automatic, collective reaction or response to either the challenges from their common threats or other, natural or environmental disasters. Without a civilization, everyone concerned would have died.

5.2 Why North America Had No Civilization?[7]

Thanks to a long, peaceful development, the average human body mass or weight has increased throughout the world. Body mass index (BMI) is defined as a person's weight in kilograms divided by the square of his height in meters (kg/m^2). The World Health Organization (WHO) definition is that a BMI under 18.5 is considered underweight and possibly malnourished, a BMI greater than or equal to 25 is overweight, and a BMI greater than or equal to 30 is obesity. The WHO provides the age-standardized mean BMI data of over 200 countries in 1980 and 2010. The data show that

- Pacific island nations have the highest average BMI value in the world,
- Among high-income countries, the USA has the single highest BMI value (over 28 kg/m^2), and
- Among high-income countries, between 1980 and 2010, the BMI value rises most in the USA (by more than 1 kg/m^2 per decade).

---

[6]Cited from Wittfogel (1957, p. 18).
[7]This section heavily draws on Guo (2017, pp. 268-74.).

Even though the underweight or malnourished people can be found throughout the world, especially in poor and underdeveloped areas, there is not any country whose average figure of the BMI is less than 18.5. As a result, unless stated otherwise, in what follows in this appendix, the BMI is simply used as a positive indicator of overweight or obesity. According to a recent study by the WHO, more than 1.6 billion people in the world are either overweight or obese. According to the data released by the WHO, as of 2010, countries with the highest rates of overweight or obese populations at ages 15 or older are estimated as the following (note: all figures are in percent, by male and female, respectively):

1. Nauru: 96.9/93.0
2. Cook Islands: 93.4/90.3
3. Micronesia: 93.1/91.1
4. Tonga: 91.4/92.1
5. Samoa: 81.1/84.1
6. Niue: 80.9/86.7
7. USA: 80.5/76.7
8. Argentina: 77.7/71.2
9. Palau: 77.1/84.5
10. Kiribati: 76.1/77.1
11. Australia: 75.7/66.5
12. Venezuela: 74.4/67.3
13. New Zealand: 73.9/74.2
14. Mexico: 73.6/73.0
15. Malta: 73.3/67.6
16. Dominica: 70.8/80.8
17. Kuwait: 69.5/80.4
18. Uruguay: 69.3/64.4
19. Chile: 68.4/73.3.[8]

Note that, except Kuwait, which is located in the area influenced by the ancient Mesopotamian civilization, none of the other countries is the one or involved in any larger region that gave birth to a great indigenous civilization in history. Of course, Kuwait should be excluded from our analysis since the country has been heavily dependent on petroleum exports. Then, can we conclude that Micronesia, Tonga, the USA, Samoa, Australia, and Malta were good at raising fat people? Of course, it is meaningless to compare countries with different economic conditions.

The USA, even though not listed at the top of the world's richest countries, has the highest average body mass among all the countries with similar levels of per capita GDP. If excluding Qatar, United Arab Emirates, Kuwait, Bahrain, and Oman, whose incomes have mainly come from petroleum exports, we may find that the average body mass in the USA largely exceeds those in Singapore and Brunei—two Asian countries—by 23.0 kg and 20.9 kg, respectively, and those in the Netherlands and

---

[8]Source: https://apps.who.int/infobase/Comparisons.aspx (accessed 2016-6-18).

Norway—two European countries—by 13.2 kg and 13.2 kg, respectively.[9] Obviously, these differences of population fatness are not due to economic factors (e.g., Singapore and Brunei have the higher levels of per capita GDP than the USA). Neither are they explained by anthropological or racial factors (e.g., the ethnic majorities of the Netherlands, Norway, and the USA all belong to the same subset of the Caucasoids).

What have caused some countries to have high rates of overweight or obese populations? It seems that there are multiple factors associated with overweight and obesity. Genetically, the environment and human behavior play important roles in the development of obesity. Excess energy intake and the decreasing energy expenditure are vital components in this growing epidemic. Physical inactivity is also an important factor related to obesity. Two proxy measures for this factor are car ownership and amount of television viewing. Other important factors include the availability of food and the access to facilities for physical activity and exercise. However, some of these factors must be simplified in international analyses.

In this research, the prevalence of overweight or obesity, represented by the body mass index (BMI), is determined by a set of factors—economic, geographic, and cultural. In order to yield statistically consistent results, we need to quantify all the factors concerned. Specifically, the explanatory variables are defined as the following:

(i) GNIPC denotes per capita gross national income, which is measured by the World Bank Atlas method in current US dollars and by the purchasing power parity (PPP) rates for the years 1980 and 2010, respectively.

(ii) "White," "Yellow," and "Black" are three dummies, denoting that if a country is dominated by Caucasoid (White), Mongoloid (Yellow), or Negroid (Black), it has a value "1"; otherwise, it has a value "0." It should be noted that aboriginals in the countries which had been isolated from the Eurasian civilizations during the pre-Columbian era are defined as a different group from the White, Yellow, and Black groups.

(iii) SSA is a dummy, denoting that if a country is in sub-Saharan Africa (if yes, it has a value "1"; otherwise, it has a value "0"). The reason why countries in North Africa and Egypt are differently treated from those in sub-Saharan Africa is that they have long had such diverse connections with the Mediterranean and Southwest Asian world (Connah and Hobbs 2001, p. 16).

(iv) AOI is also a dummy, denoting that if a country is in the Americas, Oceania, or any islands that had been isolated from the Eurasian civilizations during the pre-Columbian era (if yes, it has a value "1"; otherwise, it has a value "0").

Restricted by data availability, we choose two years 1980 and 2010, in the quantitative analyses. Using the Ordinary Least Square (OLS), we obtain the following results [10]:

---

[9]Cited from Guo (2017, p. 219–20).

[10]Data source: Annexes A.2 and A.3.

1980 : BMI $= 16.877 + 0.862ln$GNIPC $+ 0.065$White $- 1.830$Yellow $+ 0.057$Black $- 1.088$SSA $+ 0.460$AOI

$\quad\quad\quad$ (0.752) (0.089^a)$\quad\quad\quad$(0.341)$\quad\quad$(0.535^a)$\quad\quad$(0.373)$\quad\quad\quad$(0.417^a)$\quad$(0.292^c)

$\quad\quad$ (N = 118, R-squared = 0.724, F = 48.480, SE = 1.026)$\hfill$(5.1)

2010 : BMI $= 17.899 + 0.898ln$GNIPC $- 0.692$White $- 2.687$Yellow $- 0.403$Black $- 1.258$SSA $+ 1.022$AOI

$\quad\quad\quad$ (1.259) (0.132^a)$\quad\quad\quad$(0.491)$\quad\quad$(0.664^a)$\quad\quad$(0.485)$\quad\quad\quad$(0.611^b)$\quad$(0.415^a)

$\quad\quad$ (N = 178, R-squared = 0.552, F = 35.305, SE = 1.543)$\hfill$(5.2)

In Eqs. (5.1) and (5.2), lnGNIPC denotes the natural log of GNIPC (per capita gross national income); and N, F, SE, and R-squared represent number of observations, F-statistic, standard error of regression, and the squared coefficient of correlation, respectively. The figure within each pair of parentheses represents the standard error of the estimated coefficient concerned; and superscripts "a", "b," and "c" denote that estimates are statistically significant at greater than the 1%, 5%, and 10% confidence levels, respectively.

The estimated coefficients on GNIPC, shown in Eqs. (5.1) and (5.2), indicate that the body mass index (BMI) is positively related to per capita GNI (GNIPC) in both 1980 and 2010. The estimated coefficients on the three racial groups ("White," "Yellow," and "Black") are quite complicated. Specifically, in both 1980 and 2010 the BMI becomes lower in countries that are dominated by "Yellow" populations than in those that are dominated by other racial groups or aboriginals. To be more precise, the BMI in countries dominated by the "Yellow" population, as compared with countries dominated by any other racial groups or aboriginals, tends to be reduced by about 1.830 kg/m ^{2} in 1980 and by about 2.687 kg/m ^{2} in 2010. However, the estimated coefficients on "White" and "Black" are statistically insignificant in both 1980 and 2010, indicating that the "White" and "Black" populations have a much smaller, if any, contribution to the changes of the BMI than the "Yellow" population. It still needs more careful explanations for why there have been so many differences between the "Yellow" and other racial groups. However, the difficulties in securing sufficient food within the valley of the Yellow River—probably the result of frequent natural disasters—laid the economical foundations for Chinese cuisine. For example, unlike the Whites and many other aboriginals, the Chinese have a much smaller percentage of fat and meat as the main ingredient in their daily diet.

For the years 1980 and 2010, the BMI is lower in countries when SSA $= 1$ (i.e., for countries of sub-Saharan Africa) and is higher in countries when AOI $= 1$ (i.e., for countries of the Americas, Oceania, or any islands that had been isolated from the Eurasian civilizations during the pre-Columbian era). Specifically, according to the estimated coefficients on SSA (i.e., -1.088 in 1980 and -1.258 in 2010), the BMI in sub-Saharan Africa tends to reduce by about 1.088 kg/m^2 in 1980 and by about 1.258 kg/m^2 in 2010 as compared with that in the rest of the world. By contrast, according to the estimated coefficients on AOI (i.e., 0.460 in 1980 and 1.022 in 2010), the BMI in the Americas, Oceania, and other islands that had been isolated from the Eurasian civilizations during the pre-Columbian era tends to increase by about 0.460 kg/m^2 in 1980 and by about 1.022 kg/m^2 in 2010 as compared with that in areas that have been included in the rest of the world. Since the estimated coefficient on AOI has more than doubled from 1980 to 2010, we may conclude that from 1980 to 2010 the geographical influences on the body mass index have sharply increased in countries of the Americas, Oceania, or any islands that had been isolated from the Eurasian civilizations during the pre-Columbian era.

There are some geographic and environmental explanations for the above finding. For example, in North America Native Americans, including American Indians and Alaska Natives, survived largely on meat, fish, plants, berries, and nuts. According to a special survey of American Indians performed as part of the 1987 National Medical Expenditure Survey, on average, more than 30% of all adult Native Americans are overweight or obese, with both males and females being consistently more overweight and obese than the total US population (Broussard et al. 1991). Of course, Native American diets and food practices have possibly changed more than any other ethnic group in the USA. And, as judged by Dr. Boyd Eaton and Professor Loren Cordain, experts in the so-called Paleolithic diet, the hunter-gatherers had the health benefits of a diet rich in protein and high in fiber from a variety of plant foods (Eaton et al. 1989; and Cordain and Eaton 1997). However, the territories of the Native Americans, which are marked by specific natural boundaries, such as huge mountains and vast oceans, must suggest that living there can be safer and less repressed than that in the rest of the world (especially in the Eurasian continent). In certain conditions, the lack of external threats also means that the lack of incentives for people living there to advance their cultural complexity.[11]

Frankly speaking, the above estimated coefficients have different implications at different circumstances. For example, if all the countries concerned have the BMI lower than or near to the level of underweight or malnourishment, the negative coefficient on the dummy of "Yellow" (i.e., -1.830) in Eq. (5.1) indicates that in 1980 the "Yellow" population were in a disadvantageous position as compared with "White" and "Black" populations and aboriginals. By way of contrast, in 2010 when more and more counties have become overweight or obese, the negative coefficient on the dummy of "Yellow" (i.e., -2.687) in Eq. (5.2) indicates that in 2010 the Yellow population tends to be less overweight and obese than the "White" and "Black" populations and aboriginals. In the meantime, the negative coefficients on the dummies SSA in both 1980 and 2010 suggest that living in southern Africa has been much more difficult than that in the rest of the world. If this result can be used to represent the early conditions of southern Africa, then it would be easy to understand why humans (i.e., Homo sapiens) originated in southern Africa had more competiveness than those living in other continents. However, we still need more evidence to explain why it is the Africa-originated Homo sapiens who eventually dominated the world.

The most intriguing finding here is that the estimated coefficients on the dummy AOI are positive in both 1980 and 2010, suggesting that living in the Americas, Oceania, and other islands that had been isolated from the Eurasian civilizations during the pre-Columbian era is much easier than that in the rest of the world. This must have been good news before the 1980s, especially for those countries whose

---

[11]In my other research, the in-depth cases studies of the relations between external threats and national development are discussed (Guo, 2017, pp. 71–105).

BMI figures were lower than or near to the underweight or malnourishment level. However, since more and more countries concerned have the BMI figures that are of overweight or obesity at present, it is not good news for the New World as a whole. I have analyzed this topic in more details in another book (Guo 2017, pp. 207–76).

Then, why is it North America, Oceania and, to a less extent, Latin America and the Caribbean—not the other continents of the world—that have had worsening population fatness problems? Is this a mere coincidence? If not, have they been characterized by any common or similar environmental factors? Remember that all the three continents have not given birth to any indigenous civilizations that were as powerful as those created in Eurasia and northern Africa. Why do I mention this? Maybe North America and Oceania have similar natural and geographic environments that did not help to invent an agricultural society or to advance cultural complexity? Think that why peoples living in Micronesia, Tonga, the USA, and Samoa—regardless of their great economic divergences—are much fatter than those in the rest of the world? Have the natural and geographic environments of these continents tended to make peoples living there fatter?

In short, if the natural and environmental conditions have not changed throughout the world during the past thousands of years, then, compared with the Old World, the Americas, Oceania, and any other islands that had been isolated from the Eurasian civilizations during the pre-Columbian era should have been the ideal places for humans to make their lives. At the same time, however, they did provide disincentives for indigenous peoples to make any more complicated cultural traditions and civilizations there.

Indeed, had the opportunity cost of living in a society in which most or all food is obtained by foraging (collecting wild plants and pursuing wild animals) still been much lower than that of cultivating plants and breeding animals for food, nobody would have been willing to learn hard to live in an advanced life.

5.3 External Threats as (Dis)incentives

[I]f abroad there are no hostile states or other external calamities, his kingdom will generally come to ruin. From these things we see how life springs from sorrow and calamity, and death from ease and pleasure.

— Mencius (372—289 BC)

At the beginning of mankind, life was uncertain, brutish, and short. Was the creature behind the bush of the hunter's lunch, or was it looking for lunch? A moment's hesitation and the hunter went hungry or satisfied another hunter's appetite. Over time, the hunter was able to predict, just by watching the creature's shadow, whether it was suitable prey. Groups of hunters put their individual experiences to collective use: If some people flushed and chased prey, and then others ambushed, the probability that everyone would eat increased.

Compared with human evolution that has lasted for millions of years, civilization has only had a history of thousands of years. Indeed, many phenomena relating to civilizations have still not been quite clear. For example, of the earliest indigenous civilizations throughout the world, each civilization has different characteristics (in terms of language, writing, and religion, among others) from the others. Furthermore, humans' evolution and development during the civilizational era have followed a much more complicated mechanism than they did in remote antiquity. What were the key factors or mechanisms that led to the diverse developments of these civilizations?

The creation of civilization was not a unique event but a recurring phenomenon—otherwise, it would be hard to understand why civilizations arose independently in different places and at different times. Where the appropriate conditions existed, the civilization emerged. Without good reason, climate and agriculture work hand in hand with the output of production. Only when ideal weather conditions become available, can agriculture produce the surplus supply needed to maintain humans' daily lives. On the other hand, even though the specific environments or conditions under which the ancient civilizations were born are necessary, their influences on cultures and civilizations are too complicated to be illustrated in a single way. And our analysis in Chap. 4 shows that many comfortable places and environmentally friendly places have never given birth to an indigenous civilization.

And, many external threats still have exerted positive influences on the long-run socioeconomic performances of the some, if not all nations of today. To delve into them in details, let us conduct an international comparison. Since existing countries are diversified in terms of both domestic instability (DI) and external threats (ET), we may first compare four groups of nations after they are classified by low (L) and high (H) scores of DI and ET: LDILET, LDIHET, HDILET, and HDIHET. In each group, selected countries are shown as the following[12]:

- LDILET countries: Sweden, Switzerland, Luxembourg, New Zealand, Hong Kong, Sao Tome and Principe, Poland, Tunisia, Malta, and Trinidad and Tobago;
- LDIHET countries: Vietnam, Denmark, India, Canada, Mauritius, Japan, Oman, The Netherlands, Cyprus, the United Arab Emirates, and Libya;
- HDILET countries: India, Ethiopia, France, Brazil, Israel, Benin, Tanzania, Uzbekistan, Colombia, Kyrgyz Republic, and Chad; and
- HDIHET countries: the Russian Federation, China, Kazakhstan, Vietnam, Iran, Malaysia, Tajikistan, Denmark, the UK, Turkmenistan, and The Philippines.

The economic situations of the above countries are compared in Table 5.1, showing that nations with low DI scores have higher GDP per capita than nations with high DI scores; and that nations with high ET scores have higher GDP per capita than nations with low ET scores. Does this mean that domestic instability always retards while external threats always encourage long-run economic growth? Since many other factors also play important roles in the determinants of macroeconomic performance, without a comprehensive, econometric analysis, this question cannot be easily answered.

What would have happened in Japan if the latter has not allied with the USA in the postwar period? Would it have grown as fast as it did? Michael Beckley and his

---

[12]Data source: Annex A.4.

Table 5.1 Average per capita GDPs (in PPP $) by different types of nations, 2010

	Low ET nations	High ET nations
Low DI nations	34.563	34.904
	(23.282)	(17.108)
High DI nations	9.775	16.934
	(12.005)	(12.753)

Notes (1) Figures within parentheses are standard errors. (2) PPP = purchasing power parity; DI = domestic instability; and ET = external threats
Source Calculated by author based on the World Bank Database and Annex A.4 at the end of this book

colleagues asked this intriguing counterfactual question. Constructing a "synthetic" Japan drawing on data from other postwar countries, they show statistically that Japan would have grown much more slowly than it did. They complement this new technique with a consideration of some of the key US interventions including not only the provision of financial support, the tolerance for moderate defense spending, and the US openness to Japanese exports but even interference in Japanese politics to keep the Socialists from gaining office (Beckley et al. 2018). This analytical result may be correct for a short-term scenario. In the long-run economic analysis, it may not be so.

Many phenomena with regard to the social and economic development of the contemporary world cannot be explained by traditional economic theories. For example, external threats, which can be represented by various threats of attacks or sanctions that are exerted from external sources, are generally considered to be harmful for the improvement of domestic investment environment, which in turn discourage cross-border trade and the inflows of foreign capital, among others. However, a time series comparison of South Korea and Taiwan reveals that external threats have almost served as a positive factor contributing to their respective GDP growth rates for most, if not all years from 1960 to 2015. In addition, it is a puzzle that the unified Germany as a whole has won fewer Olympic medals than either East or West Germany did during the 1977–1988 Games (Guo 2017, pp. 71–106). In order to have a better explanation of a country's dynamic pattern of social and economic development, one must pay attention to the country's boundary and external conditions (especially those that may result in psychological reactions or pressures on human and cultural behaviors).

In next section, we will conduct a quantitative analysis of the determinants of long-run economic growth. Indeed, threats posed by immediate neighbors may provide a chance for governments that have suppressed economic and technological progress to correct their policy mistakes or to be outcompeted relatively quickly. Specifically, as shown in Eq. (5.3) in next section, the threshold of domestic instability (DI*) increases with respect to experts of goods and services as percent of GDP (i.e., EXPORT). In other words, the threshold is larger in nations with large EXPORT values than in those with small EXPORT values.

Usually, smaller nations have greater—while larger nations have smaller—degrees of economic dependence on the outside world. In the meantime, since a country's economic dependence on the outside world can be approximately expressed by its export (or import), we may conclude that smaller nations have greater—while larger nations have smaller—values of DI*. This can be theoretically and empirically explained as the following. First, geographically large nations usually are risk-bearing economies. The underlying factor is that large nations frequently engage in a range of diverse activities, so that a fall in the return from any one unit of economy does not induce policymakers to either care about it or take measures to restore it. Secondly, the hinterland of a larger nation usually has a longer distance from the border and thus is less significantly affected by any external threats than that of a smaller nation does.

To summarize up, our estimated results show that some countries have domestic instability (DI) scores that are smaller than, and others have domestic instability (DI) scores that are larger than, their respective thresholds of DI (i.e., DI*). As a result, external threats may have different (positive and negative) effects on the long-run growth performance of different countries. If these results are correct, then the positive effects of external threats or the scenario that Mencius predicted at the beginning of this section, which had been the scenario of China's Warring States period (475–221 BC) can still be witnessed by some (and usually geographically small and/or politically stable) nations of the contemporary world. However, it does not exist in the other (and usually geographically large and/or politically instable) nations. More specifically, we find that:

I. Hong Kong, Singapore, Luxembourg, Ireland, Seychelles, Malta, Equatorial Guinea, the United Arab Emirates, Belgium, the Netherlands, Malaysia, Republic of Congo, Vietnam, Hungary, Switzerland, Czech Republic, Slovak Republic, Slovenia, Turkmenistan, Libya, Qatar, Denmark, Bahrain, Estonia, Oman, Kuwait, Norway, Mauritius, Swaziland, Austria, and so on would most benefit from any external threats;

II. Afghanistan, Nepal, Eritrea, Central African Republic, Timor-Leste, Pakistan, Burundi, Haiti, Bangladesh, Sudan, Tajikistan, Sierra Leone, Colombia, Guinea-Bissau, Kenya, Sri Lanka, Cameroon, Dominican Republic, Niger, Burkina Faso, Uganda, Brazil, Mali, Senegal, Turkey, the USA, and so on would suffer most seriously from any external threats; and

III. Macedonia, Liberia, Croatia, Portugal, Morocco, Algeria, and so on would neither benefit nor suffer from any external threats.

In short, even though external threats are helpful in some circumstances, they may be harmful elsewhere, especially in countries whose external threats are extremely unbearable or in which external threats and domestic risks or challenges exist concurrently. To be sure, not all external threats and psychological pressures are helpful—to serve as incentives for domestic development, they must have some easy-to-be-predictable or -manageable components.

5.4 A Model of Long-Run Growth[13]

Traditional growth theories and models have usually focused on a nation's short-run development, represented by annual economic growth rates. Consequently, they paid little attention to factors that could have long-run, nonlinear influences. As a matter of fact, many environmental and external factors that have been absent from traditional growth theories and models could also exert influences on macroeconomic performances. However, the mechanism of long-run national growth is usually different from, if not more complicated than, that of short-run national growth. Sometimes, the factors on which long-run national growth depends interact with each other.

Assume that the dependent variable is lnGDPPC—i.e., the natural log of 2010's per capita gross domestic product (GDP) in purchasing power parity (PPP). Regarding the explanatory variables, let us first look at the following[14]:

- LATITUDE = North/South latitude of a country, represented by the degrees from Earth's equatorial plane (data are collected by author);
- NRR = total natural resources rents as a percentage of GDP (%);
- GER = gross enrolment ratio, primary, both sexes (%) (if data are not available in some countries, those from the years near 2010 are adopted);
- FDI = net inflows of foreign direct investment as a percentage of GDP (%);
- EXPORT = experts of goods and services as a percentage of GDP (%); and
- WAR = a dummy variable, which has a value of "1" if a war or an armed conflict occurred in a country from 2005 to 2010 or of "0" otherwise (data are collected by author).

The inclusion of the LATITUDE variable in the long-run economic growth is justified in Easterly and Levine (2003), Gallup et al. (1999) and Parker (2000, pp. 3–6). NRR is the sum of oil rents, natural gas rents, coal rents (hard and soft), mineral rents, and forest rents, which are estimated based on sources and methods described in World Bank (2011).

The estimated results involving all the above explanatory variables are reported as Regression (1) in Table 5.2. The statistically significantly estimated coefficients do suggest that a country's economic prosperity is positively related to its distance from Earth's equatorial plane (represented by LATITUDE) and its external economic openness (represented by EXPORT); and that wars or armed conflicts (represented by WAR) have always retarded economic progress. While the positive effect of EXPORT and the negative effect of WAR on economic performance are quite understandable, the positive effect of LATITUDE is not. Since the estimated coefficient on LATITUDE is 0.035 and that the dependent variable is the natural logarithm of per capita GDP, we may easily calculate that for countries on both the Northern and the Southern Hemispheres, an increase of each degree of latitude from Earth's equatorial plane would tend to raise the per capita GDP by 1.04 (i.e., $\exp(0.035) \approx 1.04$)

---

[13]This section heavily draws on Guo (2017, pp. 122–9).

[14]Except those that are stated otherwise, the data on the following variables are as of 2010 and from the World Bank Database (available at http://data.worldbank.org/).

Table 5.2 Determinants of long-run economic performance: Estimated results

Explanatory variable	Regression (1)	Regression (2)	Regression (3)	Regression (4)
Constant	7.007^a (0.466)	10.023^a (0.601)	7.259^a (0.436)	7.540^a (0.473)
LATITUDE	0.035^a (0.004)	0.023^a (0.004)	0.029^a (0.004)	0.035^a (0.005)
NRR	0.005 (0.005)	0.005 (0.004)	0.004 (0.005)	0.004 (0.005)
GER	0.005 (0.004)	−0.002 (0.004)	0.002 (0.004)	0.005 (0.004)
FDI	−0.011 (0.007)	−0.010^c (0.006)	−0.007 (0.006)	−0.004 (0.006)
EXPORT	0.017^a (0.003)	0.014^a (0.002)	0.016^a (0.003)	–
WAR	−0.624^a (0.214)	−0.417^b (0.187)	−0.473^b (0.198)	−0.574^a (0.221)
DI	–	−0.361^a (0.051)	–	–
ET	–	0.127^b (0.051)	0.797$^{a;d}$ (0.144)	–
DI·ET	–	–	−0.118$^{a;d}$ (0.023)	−0.042^a (0.011)
ET·EXPORT	–	–	–	0.007^a (0.001)
N	151	151	151	151
F	27.041	33.983	28.001	21.920
SE	0.892	0.770	0.818	0.906
R-squared	0.518	0.646	0.601	0.506

Notes (1) The Ordinary Least Square (OLS) method is applied to all the regressions. (2) The dependent variable is the natural log of per capita GDP (lnGDPPC). (3) Superscripts "a," "b," and "c" denote statistically significant at greater than the 1%, 5%, and 10% confidence levels, respectively. Superscript "d" denotes that multicollinearity problems may exist. (4) N, F, SE, and R-squared represent number of observations, F-statistic, standard error, and the squared coefficient of correlation, respectively

PPP dollar. How has cold climate helped countries advance their long-run economic performances? It seems that traditional growth theories do not have an answer to it. But the findings here do support the hypothesis that unfavorable environmental factors may become incentives (whereas favorable environmental factors may become disincentives) for humans and nations to advance economic and cultural developments.

In Regression (1), the estimated coefficients on the three other variables (NRR, GER, and FDI) are statistically insignificant, showing that natural resources, early-stage human capital, and the inflow of foreign capital have no significant influences on the current status of economic prosperity. Obviously, our findings are quite different from many existing empirical studies in which short-run economic growth rates (rather than long-run economic growth or prosperity as in ours) were selected as dependent variables.[15] For example, the estimated coefficient on FDI (net inflows of foreign direct investment as a percentage of GDP)—a factor that has usually been treated by economists to contribute to short-run economic growth—is found to be negative and statistically insignificant.

There are many differences between the determinants of short- and long-run economic growth (Putterman and Weil 2010). In addition, some shortcomings do exist in Regression (1). For example, is not quite convincing that the estimated coefficient on the variable GER is statistically insignificant. One explanation may be that, thanks to the world-wide efforts during the past decades, the gross enrolment ratios (primary, both sexes) have been converged in both developed and developing nations in 2010. Other educational variables (say, years of schooling and government expenditure on education) may be adopted to explain macroeconomic performance. Unfortunately, the data on these variables are not available for many of the countries in the World Bank Database.

Throughout history, physical terrain, political fiat, and conquest have divided the world. The result is over 200 independent states and dependencies, areas of special sovereignty, and other miscellaneous entities that have either friendly or antagonistic relations with each other. Broadly, political risk or threat refers to the complications resulting from what are commonly referred to as political decisions—or any political change that alters the expected outcome and value of a given action by changing the probability of achieving objectives. The level of political risk or threat in a given country does not necessarily correspond to the degree of political freedom in that country. In his Nobel Prize address in December 1993, Robert Fogel conjectured that a link may exist between long-run economic growth and fundamental principles in physiology:

> Recent findings in the biomedical area call attention to what may be called the thermodynamic and physiological factors in economic growth. Although largely neglected by theorists of both the 'old' and the 'new' growth economics, these factors can easily be incorporated into standard models.[16]

In order to compile the different degrees of external threats, we seek to identify and quantify the political and military factors and traits that are causally associated with, or that can predict, international tensions. For ease of simplification, we use two indicators to equally measure the index of external threats: (1) the number of cases of boundary and territorial disputes and (ii) military expenditure as a percentage of

---

[15] Selected literature relating to theoretical and empirical analyses of the determinants of short-run economic growth would include Barro (1991, 1997, 2003), Moral-Benito (2007), and Ciccone and Jarociński (2010).

[16] Cited from Fogel (1994, p. 385).

GDP.[17] Specifically, if a country has no boundary or territorial disputes with the rest of the world, then its score of external threats is "0"; and since Russia has the largest number of boundary and territorial disputes, its score of external threats is "5." Similarly, we define the country with the lowest military expenditure as a percentage of GDP to have a score of "0" and the one with the highest military expenditure as percentage of GDP to have a score of "5." The overall index is defined as a scale of from 0 (no external threats) to 10 (highest degree of external threats).

Social and political unrest or upheaval can be defined as those events or developments that pose a serious extra-parliamentary or extra-institutional threat to governments or the existing political order. Research has shown that macro-level indicators can be quantified and modeled like other types of risk. For example, the Economist Intelligence Unit (EIU) produces a political risk index which incorporates two categories of sub-risk into a calculation of political stability (EIU 2009). There are 15 indicators in all—12 for the underlying vulnerability (inequality, state history, corruption, ethnic fragmentation, trust in institutions, status of minorities, history of political instability, proclivity to labor unrest, level of social provision, a country's neighborhood, regime type, and regime type and factionalism) and three for the economic distress index (growth in incomes, unemployment, and level of income per head). The overall index on a scale of 0 (no vulnerability) to 10 (highest vulnerability) has two component indexes—an index of underlying vulnerability and an economic distress index. The overall index is a simple average of the two component indexes. The index of political instability, which shows the level of threats posed to governments by social protest, is derived by combining measures of economic distress and underlying vulnerability to unrest. The index covers the period 2009/10.[18]

Indeed, threats posed by immediate neighbors may provide a chance for governments that have suppressed economic and technological progress to correct their policy mistakes or to be outcompeted relatively quickly. After including the domestic instability (DI) and external threats (ET) variables, the data on which are available in Annex A.4, we now obtain Regression (2) (shown in Table 5.2) in which DI has a negative effect (statistically significant at the 1% confidence level) and ET has a positive effect (statistically significant at the 5% confidence level) on economic prosperity.

It must be noted that the view that external threats are helpful cannot be approved in all circumstances. Sometimes, external threats may be harmful, especially in countries whose external threats are extremely unbearable or in which external threats and domestic risks or challenges exist concurrently. Bearing in mind that ET may have nonlinear influences on economic performances, we include an interactive term (DI·ET) and the estimated results are shown in Regression (3) in Table 5.2. However, the values of Variance Inflation Factor (VIF) are as large as 7.8 for the variables of ET and DI·ET, implying that multicollinearity may exist in the regression and that the

---

[17]The data on the number of cases of boundary and territorial disputes and on military expenditure as a percentage of GDP are from Guo (2007) and the World Bank Database (available at http://data.worldbank.org/), respectively.

[18]See Annex A.4 for the data on political instability scores of a total of 165 countries.

estimated coefficients may not be statistically reliable. For example, even though the estimated coefficients on ET are statistically significant at the 5% and 1% confidence levels in Regressions (2) and (3), respectively, their values are unusually different from each other—i.e., 0.127 in Regression (2) and 0.797 in Regression (3).

In order to overcome the above-mentioned multicollinearity problem, we use another interactive term (ET·EXPORT) to replace the variable of ET and obtain Regression (4). Now, in addition to the fact that the estimated coefficients on the variables of DI·ET and ET·EXPORT are statistically significant at greater than the 1% confidence level, the VIF values of the all the explanatory variables are now smaller than 2, suggesting that there is no multicollinearity problem in the regression.[19] After letting the partial differential of the dependent variable with respective to ET be zero in Regression (4), we obtain a threshold for domestic instability (DI*):

$$DI^* = 0.007/0.042 EXPORT = 0.167\,EXPORT \tag{5.3}$$

Obviously, the threshold (DI*), which is not held fixed value in Eq. (5.3), suggests that

(i) If a country's value of DI is less than 0.156EXPORT, then the marginal effect on ET (i.e., $-0.042DI + 0.007EXPORT$) in Regression (4) is greater than 0, suggesting that external threats always have a positive effect on economic prosperity; and

(ii) If a country's value of DI is larger than 0.156EXPORT, then the marginal effect on ET (i.e., $-0.042DI + 0.007EXPORT$) in Regression (4) is less than 0, suggesting that external threats always have a negative effect on economic prosperity.

In all circumstances, a country's long-run economic performance is always jointly determined by its domestic and external factors. And the gap between each country's DI and its threshold (DI*) can help us clarify how existing countries can benefit (if DI < DI*) or suffer (if DI > DI*) from any external threats. After calculating each country's marginal effect on external threats (ET), which is represented by $-0.042DI + 0.007EXPORT$) in Regression (4) in Table 5.2, we observe:

I. Hong Kong, Singapore, Luxembourg, Ireland, Seychelles, Malta, Equatorial Guinea, the United Arab Emirates, Belgium, the Netherlands, Malaysia, Republic of Congo, Vietnam, Hungary, Switzerland, Czech Republic, Slovak Republic, Slovenia, Turkmenistan, Libya, Qatar, Denmark, Bahrain, Estonia, Oman, Kuwait, Norway, Mauritius, Swaziland, Austria, and so on would most benefit from any external threats;

II. Afghanistan, Nepal, Eritrea, Central African Republic, Timor-Leste, Pakistan, Burundi, Haiti, Bangladesh, Sudan, Tajikistan, Sierra Leone, Colombia, Guinea-Bissau, Kenya, Sri Lanka, Cameroon, Dominican Republic, Niger, Burkina Faso, Uganda, Brazil, Mali, Senegal, Turkey, the USA, and so on would suffer most seriously from any external threats; and

III. Macedonia, Liberia, Croatia, Portugal, Morocco, Algeria, and so on would hardly benefit (or suffer) from any external threats.

---

[19]Due to space limitations, we have not reported the results of the VIF test here.

All the nations included in each of the above three groups are listed according to the decreasing order of the absolute values of marginal effects on external threats.

References

Barro RJ (1991) Economic growth in a cross section of countries. Quart J Econ 106:407–444
Barro RJ (1997) Determinants of economic growth: a cross-country empirical study. MIT Press, Cambridge, MA
Barro RJ (2003) Determinants of economic growth: A cross-country empirical study. Am J Agr Econ 85(450):1087–1088
Beckley M, Horiuchi Y, Miller J (2018) America's role in the making of Japan's economic miracle. J East Asian Stud 18(1):1–21. https://doi.org/10.1017/jea.2017.24
Broussard BA, Johnson A, Himes JH, Story M, Fichtner R, Hauck F, Bachman-Carter K, Hayes J, Frohlich K, Gray N (1991) Prevalence of obesity in American indians and alaska natives. Am J Clin Nutr 53(6)(S):1535–1542
Chagnon, NA (1968[1972]). Yanomamo: the fierce people. Second Edition. Holt, Rinehart and Winston, New York
Ciccone A, Jarociński M (2010) Determinants of economic growth: Will data tell? Am Econ J Macroecon 2(4):222–246
Connah G, Hobbs D (2001) African civilizations: an archaeological perspective, 2nd edn. Cambridge University Press, Cambridge
Cordain L, Eaton B (1997) Evolutionary aspects of diet: Old genes, new fuels. Nutritional changes since agriculture. World Rev Nutr Diet 81:26–37
Easterly W, Levine R (2003) Tropics, germs, and crops: How endowments influence economic development. Journal of Monetary Economics 50:3–39
Eaton S Boyd, Shostak M, Konner M (1989) The paleolithic prescription: a program of diet & exercise and a design for living. Harpercollins, New York
EIU (2009) Political instability index: Vulnerability to social and political unrest. Economist Intelligence Unit (EIU), London, UK. March 19. http://viewswire.eiu.com/index.asp?layout=VWArticleVW3&article_id=874361472. Accessed 30 Dec 2015
Fogel R (1994) Economic growth, population theory, and physiology: The bearing of long-term processes on the making of economic policy. Am Econ Rev 84(3):369–395
Gallup JL, Sachs JD, Mellinger AD (1999) Geography and economic development. Int Reg Sci 22:179–224
Guo R (2017) An economic inquiry into the nonlinear behaviors of nations: dynamic developments and the origins of civilizations. Palgrave Macmillan, New York
Kropotkin P (1902) Mutual aid: a factor of evolution. McClure Phillips & Co, New York
McNairn B (1980) The method and theory of V. Edinburgh University Press, Gordon Childe. Edinburgh
Moral-Benito E (2007) Determinants of economic growth: A Bayesian panel data approach. Rev Econ Stat 94:566–579
Needham J (1959) Book review: oriental despotism: a comparative study of total power (by K.A. Witttogel). Sci Soc 23:58–65
Parker PM (2000) Physioeconomics: the basis for long-run economic growth. The MIT Press, Cambridge, MA
Putterman L, Weil DN (2010) Post-1500 population flows and the long-run determinants of economic growth and inequality. Quart J Econ 125(4):1627–1682
Scarre C, Fagan BM (2016) Ancient Civilizations, 4th edn. Routledge, London and New York
Stevenson HH, Moldoveanu MC (1995) The power of predictability. Harvard Business Review, July–August Issue. https://hbr.org/1995/07/the-power-of-predictability. Accessed 20 Nov 2016

Wittfogel K (1957) Oriental despotism: a comparative study of total power. Yale University Press, New Heaven, MA

World Bank (2011) The changing wealth of nations: Measuring sustainable development in the new millennium. The World Bank, Washington DC

Chapter 6
Civilization as Responses to Cyclical Challenges

Abstract Why were indigenous civilizations usually associated with arid river valleys instead of other geographical features? Over the course of the past thousands of years, various natural disasters and threats have made humans—either individually or collectively—institutionally and intellectually more powerful than otherwise circumstances. However, most of these natural disasters and threats, as long as they occur randomly or irregularly, would not induce humans to advance their cultures and civilizations. In short, it is the cyclical disasters and threats (especially annual or seasonable river floods)—not other irregular disasters and threats—that have enabled humans to create brilliant civilizations of today. In addition, Mesopotamia (or Multipotamia)—land through which two (or more) independent rivers run—are also found to have served as hedging mechanisms for civilizations to grow and advance.

Keywords Civilization · River flood · Natural disaster · Cyclical challenge Multipotamia

6.1 What Do the Myths Say?

Since their migration out of Africa, Homo sapiens had appeared and populated Eurasia, Australia, and the Americas. After that, except for some simple agricultural techniques and other cultural traditions invented by humans in different parts of the world, not much had happened for tens of thousands of years. Then, civilizations began to appear in Mesopotamia by about 3500 BC, India and Pakistan by about 3300 BC, Egypt by about 3100 BC, coastal Peru by about 2500 BC, China by about 2000 BC, and Mesoamerica by about 1500 BC.

Why did human civilizations emerge almost simultaneously throughout the world? There have been various myths. Some myths emerged in historical times, and these can be dated, but many are prehistoric.[1]

---

[1]By "prehistory," it means the knowledge of the past in an area where either no written records exist or the writing of a culture is not understood.

© Springer Nature Singapore Pte Ltd. 2019
R. Guo, *Human-Earth System Dynamics*,
https://doi.org/10.1007/978-981-13-0547-4_6

The prehistoric myths were passed down from one generation to the next by word of mouth in the age before writing was first introduced. Of all the myths, none has generated more interests and stimulated more research than the story of the Great Flood. The flood myths or deluge myths are, taken collectively, stories surviving from prehistory, of a Great Flood which has generally been taken as mythical. Flood stories are common across a wide range of cultures, extending back into prehistory. In Africa, many African cultures or peoples have an oral tradition of a flood myth, which include Pygmy, Kikuyu, Yoruba, Mandingo (in Ivory Coast), Bakongo (in western Congo), Cameroon, Kwaya (in Lake Victoria), Mbuti, and Mandin peoples. For example, the Maasai flood myth is stated as follows:

> Once upon a time the rivers began to flood. Then god told two people to get into a ship. He told them to take lots of seed and to take lots of animals. The water of the flood eventually covered the mountains. Finally the flood stopped. Then one of the men, wanting to know if the water had dried up, let a dove loose. The dove returned. Later he let a hawk loose, which did not return. Then the men left the boat and took the animals and the seeds with them.[2]

The Genesis flood narrative indicates that God intended to return the Earth to its pre-creation state of watery chaos by flooding the Earth because of humanity's misdeeds and then remake it using the microcosm of Noah's ark. Thus, the flood was no ordinary overflow but a reversal of creation (Bandstra 2009, p. 61). The narrative discusses the evil of mankind that moved God to destroy the world by the way of the flood, the preparation of the ark for certain animals, Noah, and his family, and God's guarantee (the Noahic Covenant) for the continued existence of life under the promise that he would never send another flood (Cotter 2003, pp. 49–50). The Genesis flood narrative makes up chapters 6–9 in the Book of Genesis, in the Bible. Below is a short excerpt:

> In the six hundredth year of Noah's life, in the second month, on the seventeenth day of the month, on the same day all the fountains of the great deep burst open, and the floodgates of the sky were opened. And the rain fell upon the land for forty days and forty nights. On the very same day Noah and Shem and Ham and Japheth, the sons of Noah, and Noah's wife and the three wives of his sons with them, entered the ark, they and every beast after its kind, and all the cattle after their kind, and every creeping thing that creeps on the land after its kind, and every bird after its kind, all sorts of birds. So they went into the ark to Noah, by twos of all flesh in which was the breath of life. And those that entered, male and female of all flesh, entered as God had commanded him; and the Lord closed it behind Him. (Genesis 7:11–16)

Furthermore, in the New International Version of the Holy Bible, the flood is described in further details, as the following:

> For forty days the flood kept coming on the earth, and as the waters increased they lifted the ark high above the earth. The waters rose and increased greatly on the earth, and the ark floated on the surface of the water. They rose greatly on the earth, and all the high mountains under the entire heavens were covered. The waters rose and covered the mountains to a depth of more than fifteen cubits... Every living thing on the face of the earth was wiped out; people and animals and the creatures that move along the ground and the birds were wiped from the earth. Only Noah was left, and those with him in the ark. (Genesis 7: 17–20; 23)

---

[2]Cited form Lynch and Roberts (2010, p. 45).

The Genesis flood narrative is considered to be derived, at least partially, from the Mesopotamian versions. This is predominantly because biblical mythology that is found in Judaism, Christianity, Islam, and Mandeanism shares overlapping consistency with far older written Mesopotamian stories of the Great Flood, and that some of the early Hebrews are believed to have lived in Mesopotamia during the Babylonian captivity.[3] In the Sumerian King List, the flood motif is used to divide Sumerian history into pre-flood and post-flood periods. The pre-flood kings had enormous life spans, whereas post-flood life spans were much reduced. The Sumerian flood myth found in the Deluge tablet was the epic of Ziusudra, who heard the Divine Counsel to destroy humanity, in which he constructed a vessel that delivered him from great waters.[4] Further discoveries produced several versions of the Mesopotamian flood myth, with the account closest to that in the Book of Genesis found in a 700 BC Babylonian copy of the Epic of Gilgamesh. In this work, the hero, Gilgamesh (the fifth king of Uruk, an ancient city of Sumer, whose supposed historical reign is believed to lie within the period from 2700 to 2500 BC), meets the immortal man Utnapishtim, and the latter describes how the god Ea instructed him to build a huge vessel in anticipation of a deity-created flood that would destroy the world (Speiser 1969, pp. 72–98). For example, Tablet XI, in the Epic, says:

Six days and seven nights
came the wind and flood, the storm flattening the land.

…

It is Ea who knows every machination!'
La spoke to Valiant Enlil [the wind god], saying:
'It is yours, O Valiant One, who is the Sage of the Gods.
How, how could you bring about a Flood without consideration
Charge the violation to the violator,
charge the offense to the offender,
but be compassionate lest (mankind) be cut off,
be patient lest they be killed.
Instead of your bringing on the Flood,
would that a lion had appeared to diminish the people!
Instead of your bringing on the Flood,
would that a wolf had appeared to diminish the people!
Instead of your bringing on the Flood,
would that famine had occurred to slay the land!
Instead of your bringing on the Flood,
would that (Pestilent) Erra [the plague god] had appeared to ravage the land![5]

---

[3] See, for example, Roux (2001, pp. 21–22), Fant and Reddish (2008, pp. 21ff) and Cohn (1999, p. 5).

[4] See Bandstra (2009, pp. 61 and 62). In the Atrahasis version, the flood is a river flood (Lambert and Millard 1970).

[5] Source: http://www.ancienttexts.org/library/mesopotamian/gilgamesh/tab11.htm (accessed 2018-03-18). The words within square brackets are inserted by the author.

The history of China as a continuously recorded literary tradition begins with the ancient documents transmitted to posterity through the Shiji (Records of the Grand Historian) of Sima Qian, which begin with the reign of Huangdi (the Yellow Emperor)—a legendary hero in China's prehistoric era. According to the Shiji, the fourth successor of the Yellow Emperor was Yao. Beginning with the reign of Emperor Yao, additional literary sources become available, including the Book of Documents (collected and edited by Confucius), describing the events of Yao's reign.[6] The Great Flood of China (also known as the Gun-Yu myth) was a major flood event that continued for at least two generations, which resulted in great population displacements among other disasters, such as storms and famine. According to mythological and historical sources, the flood was dated to the late period of the third millennium BC, during the reign of Yao. Treated either historically or mythologically, the story of the Great Flood and the heroic attempts of the various human characters to control it and to abate the disaster is a narrative fundamental to Chinese culture. Among other things, the Great Floods of China are the key to understanding the history of the founding of China's first dynasties in history. For example, the following story was told by Mencius (372–289 BC):

> In the time of Emperor Yao [about the 22nd century BC], the waters, flowing out of their channels, inundated the Central Kingdom. Big snakes and dragons occupied it, and the people had no place in which they could settle themselves. In the low grounds they made nests for themselves on the trees or raised platforms, and in the high grounds they made caves. It is said in the Book of History, 'The waters in their wild course warned me.' Those 'waters in their wild course' were the waters of the great inundation. Emperor Shun dispatched Yu the Great to reduce the waters to order. Yu dug open their obstructed channels and conducted them to the sea. He drove away the snakes and dragons [italic added by author] and forced them into the grassy marshes. On this, the waters pursued their course through the country, even the waters of the Jiang [Yangtze], the Huai, the He [Yellow river] and the Han, and the dangers and obstructions which they had occasioned were removed. The birds and beasts which had injured the people also disappeared, and after this men found the plains available for them.[7]

A brief glance at the world history simply reveals that civilizations tended to grow up in river valleys for a number of reasons. The most obvious is access to a usually reliable source of water for agriculture and human needs. Plentiful water, and the enrichment of the soil due to annual flooding, made it possible to grow excess crops beyond what was needed to sustain an agricultural village. This allowed for some members of the community to engage in non-agricultural activities such as construction of buildings and cities (the root of the word "civilization"), metalworking, trade, and social organization. Additional advantages of locating near a river included easy transportation by water as well as good hunting and fishing.

It has been generally recognized that all of the world's independent, indigenous civilizations arose in or near river valleys, viz. Mesopotamia (i.e., the Tigris–Euphrates river valleys), the Nile Valley, the Indus–Ghaggar-Hakra river valleys, and the Yellow River Valley. Earlier agricultural societies (5,000 to 6,000 years ago) were

---

[6]Cited from Wu (1982, p. 65).

[7]Cited from Mencius (c. 300 BC, Teng Wen Gong II).

largely subsistence cultures. The riverine civilizations had enough food to provide for most, if not all classes of people other than just farmers. These societies all used agricultural surpluses to establish civilizations with cities and trade and to create greater sophistication in the arts, sciences, government, and even a leisure class. Cities enabled societies much more sophisticated than primitive agriculture allowed. The first beginnings of a higher level urban–rural society began in Mesopotamia about 4000 BC. Other civilizations appeared shortly thereafter.

Existing archaeological and palaeoenvironmental evidence has proved that the development of complex societies in the Middle Holocene (c. 5000 BC—3000 BC) was largely the consequence of the responses of the precursor societies to deteriorating environmental conditions. This deterioration was associated principally with the orbitally driven weakening and southward retreat of the northern hemisphere monsoon belt. For example, in all the regions examined by Professor Nick Brooks of the University of East Anglia in Norwich, UK, the emergence of complex societies coincided with or followed a period of increased aridity:

> A general trend toward desiccation after about 8 kyr BP [8,000 years before present] was punctuated by shorter (decadal to centennial scale) episodes of increased aridity. While desiccation trajectories were mediated by local and regional factors and feedback processes such as the collapse of vegetation systems, there appear to have been episodes of accelerated aridification that were coherent throughout the monsoon belt. One such event occurred around 6 kyr BP, and may have been associated with cooling in the North Atlantic. Enhanced regional aridity following this event coincided with sociocultural change, particularly in the Eastern Sahara, Egypt and Mesopotamia. Regional data suggest another episode of accelerated change at the end of the sixth millennium BP, when discontinuities are apparent in archaeological records from across the Afro-Asiatic desert belt, and abrupt environmental changes are suggested by records from northern Africa, Western Asia, China and northern South America.[8]

Transient environmental shocks appear to have resulted in a variety of outcomes depending on the nature of the societies on which they impact. However, the relationship between the environment and sociocultural change is not straightforward, usually with a given environmental phenomenon having a single type of societal outcome. For example, it has been argued that the development of agriculture, which formed the basis for the increases in social complexity in the Middle Holocene, was associated with a succession of responses to both climatic amelioration and deterioration (Hole 1991).

Exploration of the world has produced increasing evidence that terrible floods occurred throughout the world, with several high mountains demonstrating geological scoring and drift materials demonstrating that they had been covered by rapid floodwaters (Bros 2005, pp. 44–45). While scholars have offered possible explanations for the origins of the flood myth, the general mythological exaggeration and implausibility of the story are widely recognized by relevant academic fields. The acknowledgment of this follows closely the development of understanding of the natural history and especially of the geology and paleontology of the planet. A dramatic rise in sea level since the end of the last glacial episode is shown in

---

[8]Cited from Brooks (2006).

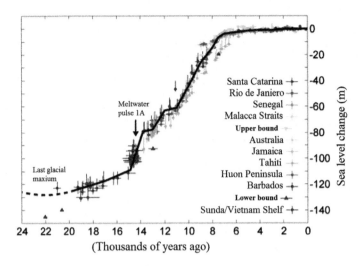

Fig. 6.1 Sea level changes after the last glacial maximum. *Source* Created by Robert A. Rohde based on data from Fleming et al. (1998), Fleming (2000), and Milne et al. (2005). Courtesy of Global Warming Art

Fig. 6.1.[9] For example, global sea levels were about 120 m lower around 18,000 years ago and rose until 8,000 years ago when they reached current level. The lowest point of sea level during the last glaciation is not well constrained by observations (shown as a dashed curve in Fig. 6.1), but is generally argued to be approximately 130 ± 10 m below present sea level and to have occurred at approximately 22 ± 3 thousand years ago.

The global floods could have resulted from a rise in sea levels after the Ice Age. In North America, for example, the deluge myth may be based on a sudden rise in sea levels caused by the rapid draining of prehistoric Lake Agassiz at the end of the last Ice Age, about 8,400 years ago (Seger 1934, p. 135). There is also evidence promoting the hypothesis that global flood stories were inspired by ancient observations of seashells and fish fossils in inland and mountain areas. The ancient Greeks, Egyptians, and Romans all documented the discovery of such remains in these locations; the Greeks hypothesized that Earth had been covered by water on several occasions, citing the seashells and fish fossils found on mountain tops as evidence of this history (Mayor 2011).

---

[9]Note that the black curve in Fig. 6.1 is based on minimizing the sum of squares error weighted distance between this curve and the plotted data. It was constructed by adjusting a number of specified tie points, typically placed every 1 kyr but at times adjusted for sparse or rapidly varying data. A small number of extreme outliers were dropped.

6.2 Rivers and Cyclical Floods

The worldwide flood myths may refer to the flood stories that occurred at different periods of time. Excavations in Iraq have revealed evidence of localized flooding at Shuruppak (modern Tell Fara, Iraq) and various other ancient Sumerian cities. A layer of riverine sediments, radiocarbon dated to about 2900 BC, interrupts the continuity of settlement, extending as far north as the city of Kish, which took over hegemony after the flood. Polychrome pottery from the Jemdet Nasr Period (3000–2900 BC) was discovered immediately below the Shuruppak flood stratum. Other culture sites, such as Ur, Uruk, Kish, Lagash, and Nineveh, also present evidence of flooding at ancient times (Bandstra 2009, p. 61).

The earliest signs of transition from the nomadic to a permanent lifestyle can be seen in the Levant (an area in the Eastern Mediterranean) from 12,500 BC, till the Natufian culture became sedentary and evolved gradually into an agricultural society by around 10,000 BC.[10] The earliest proto-urban settlements with several thousand inhabitants emerged in the Neolithic Age. However, human civilizations did not begin to rise until the end of global floods about 8,000 years ago when the global sea levels reached current level (shown in Fig. 6.1). By the thirty-first century BC, the first large cities to house several tens of thousands were Ur and Uruk in Mesopotamia.

Global floods did not cease during the civilizational era, neither did the Great Flood myths. In China, for example, the flood myth was about how Yu the Great put the flood under control and that how the establishment of China's first dynasty—the Xia—was largely the result of his contribution to the flood control. It earned Yu renown throughout Chinese history (Guo 2018, Chap. 5). For a long time in the past, it had been a subject of argument that if the story about Yu the Great was real. However, recent research and excavations have proved that the legendary Xia dynasty did exist in history. They have also provided evidence that supports the hypothesis that a long-lasting, disastrous flood did occur 4000–4200 years ago, and that the flooding areas covered not only China but also many other places in the Northern Hemisphere.[11]

In addition, it is interesting to note that in ancient Egypt, from 2250 BC to 1950 BC, the low inundations of the Nile caused the drying out of Lake Moeris, leading to the end of the Old Kingdom (Butzer 1976, p. 28). Given that precipitation is a major component of the Earth's water cycle and that in a place the average amount of rainfall is constant for a period of time, one place's drought must imply a heavier rainfall in the rest of the world. In other words, if the unusual drought in ancient Egypt was real, then, ceteris paribus, an unusual flooding must have occurred somewhere in the rest of the world (including China) at that time.

---

[10]Data source: http://www.columbia.edu/itc/anthropology/v1007/baryo.pdf. Accessed 2016-10-2.

[11]See, for example, Weiss et al. (1993); Xia-Shang-Zhou Chronology Project Expert Group (2000, pp. 1–56); and Wu and Ge (2005).

The valley of the Yellow River is the cradle of Chinese civilization. The river has played a crucial role in China's civilizational development. During the past thousands of years, the management of the Yellow River has consumed large amount of physical and human capitals and, consequently, generated various technologies and tools, all of which have become important elements of the Chinese culture. Attempts at controlling the Yellow River, according to existing historical records, began in as early as the twenty-second century BC. An engineer named Yu the Great was appointed to take preventive measures after a disastrous flood, who came up with the idea of dredging the river to encouraging the water to flow in its proper channel. Yu later was made the king of China's first dynasty, the Xia, for his contribution to the control of terrific flooding of the Yellow River. The Yellow River had bore the test of almost all kinds of upheavals and difficulties, and finally created the Chinese civilization. And again, to some extent, the Yellow River also is the symbol of the spirit of the Chinese people: grittiness, industriousness, and assiduity. However, one of the most serious weaknesses of the Chinese civilization was its geographical isolation from the other, earlier civilizations during ancient times. The Himalayas between China and India and the Pamirs in central Asia had been the major geographical obstacles for China to receive cultural influences from India and Mesopotamia during the pre-modern times.

In China, the story of the Great Flood plays a dramatic role in mythology. Flood narratives in Chinese mythology share certain common features despite being somewhat lacking in internal consistency as well as incorporating various magical transformations and divine or semidivine interventions. For example, the flood usually results from natural causes rather than "universal punishment for human sin" (Christie 1968, p. 83). Another distinct motif of the myth of the Great Flood of China is an emphasis on the heroic and praiseworthy efforts to mitigate the disaster (Yang et al. 2008, p. 117); flooding is alleviated by constructing dikes and dams, digging canals, widening or deepening existing channels, and teaching these skills to others. In the course of coping with the disaster of the deluge, humans have also achieved the development of more complicated civilization.

Hundreds of thousands of years ago, when one or more groups of modern humans left the African continent, other groups who still remained there might have the first laugh. Yes, nature selected the latter as they were more suited to the environment of the African continent. However, after generations of struggles against the nature and between themselves, the successors of those who were not selected by nature and had to migrate out of Africa have been living quite well in the rest of the world—at least not worse than their counterparts, or the successors of the earlier winners, in Africa. However, after taking into account the Paleo-Indian migration from Eurasia to the Americas that occurred tens of thousands of years ago, we can only but have a different scenario: For a long period of time prior to the European colonization starting in the sixteenth century, the Americas as a whole had lagged far behind Eurasia—technologically, economically, and culturally. If all the humans living in the African, Eurasian, and American continents have the same ancestor and are still not different from each other in gene, then why have there been so technological, economical, and cultural differences throughout the world?

Why did cultural complexity first occur in hydraulic-related areas? Historically, almost all of the earliest indigenous civilizations found in both the Eastern and the Western Hemispheres grew up in river valleys. Plentiful water, and the enrichment of the soil due to annual flooding, made it possible to grow excess crops beyond what was needed to sustain an agricultural village. This allowed for some members of the community to engage in non-agricultural activities such as construction of buildings and cities, metalworking, trade, and social organization (Mountjoy 2005, p. 15). Most of the world's great ancient civilizations are centered in river valleys. The Sumerians were located along the Euphrates and the Tigris and their tributaries, and the Egyptians around the Nile. Roots of the ancient Harappan (Indus) civilization originate along the Indus and the Ghaggar-Hakra rivers and their tributaries; and the earliest Chinese dynasties centered their culture on the banks of the Yellow River. Not only were rivers used for irrigating crops and daily water needs (such as washing, cooking, and bathing), but societies also relied on the rivers for communication and transportation. Rivers were the major highways in these areas. In addition, advantages of locating human communities near a river include good hunting and fishing.[12]

For thousands of years, Egyptians referred to its annual flooding as the "Gift of the Nile." In each summer, like clockwork, the river would take possession of a strip of land on either side of its bank. When the water receded, a very thin, evenly spread layer of black mud was left behind. Farmers would immediately plant their crops—never needing fertilizers because the flood soil itself was so rich. Farming in Egypt was dependent on the cycle of the Nile. As the Nile was such an important factor in Egyptian life, the ancient calendar was even based on the three cycles of the Nile. The Egyptians recognized three seasons at ancient times: inundation, planting and growing, and harvesting. Each of these seasons consists of four months—each of which lasts thirty days. The flooding season is the time of the year when the Nile flooded, leaving several layers of fertile soil behind, aiding in agricultural growth in the following, planting and growing season. The last season is the harvest season (see next section for a more detailed description of the Egyptian calendar).

The flooding of the Nile has been an important natural cycle in Egypt since ancient times. This cycle was so consistent that the Egyptians timed its onset using the heliacal rising of Sirius, the key event used to set their calendar. It is celebrated by Egyptians as an annual holiday for two weeks starting August 15, known as Wafaa El-Nil (meaning "flooding of the Nile" in Coptic—the descendant of Demotic, an ancient Egyptian language used in the Nile Delta). The first indications of the rise of the river may be seen at the first of the cataracts of the Nile (at Aswan) as early as at the beginning of June, and a steady increase goes on until the middle of July, when the increase of water becomes very great. The Nile continues to rise until the beginning of September, when the level remains stationary for a period of about three weeks. In October, it rises again and reaches its highest level. From this period it begins to subside, and though it rises yet once more and reaches occasionally its

---

[12]For more detailed analyses of some ancient hydraulic civilizations, see, among others, Butzer (1976) and Clayton and Dent (1973).

former highest point, it sinks steadily until the month of June when it is again at its lowest level.[13]

The flooding season lasted from June to September, depositing on the river's banks a layer of mineral-rich silt ideal for growing crops. After the floodwaters had receded, the growing season lasted from October to February. Farmers plowed and planted seeds in the fields, which were irrigated with ditches and canals. Egypt received little rainfall, so farmers relied on the Nile to water their crops. From March to May, ancient Egyptians used sickles to harvest their crops. Flax plants, uprooted before they started flowering, were grown for the fibers of their stems. These fibers were split along their length and spun into thread, which was used to weave sheets of linen and to make clothing. Papyrus growing on the banks of the Nile was used to make paper. Vegetables and fruits were grown in garden plots, close to habitations and on higher ground, and had to be watered by hand.[14]

A number of assumptions have served to preset the narratives of prehistory. Among them are that early humans were subject to environmental pressures, climate change, and geography, and that resource supply to humans was only fully achieved with the invention of agriculture. In summary, reasons why rivers were important to civilizations are as follows:

- River water is diverted for agricultural irrigation, industry, hygiene, and related uses.
- Rivers connect major cities; navigable waters carry trade by ship and barge.
- Some communities depend on the fish that live in or travel along rivers.
- Some rivers carry dissolved minerals and organic compounds.
- Alluvial deposits can form fertile deltas where a river flows into a lake or ocean.

The hydrological characteristics of rivers heavily influenced ancient riparian civilizations. Large workforces were needed to divert water for irrigation and to build protective work to minimize flood damage. This led to increasing sedentism, high population density, and the need for a centralized administration along rivers. The cost of hydraulic construction and its subsequent maintenance required a political and social structure capable of forceful extraction of labor. Furthermore, with regard to the utilization and management of water resources in river valleys, upstream communities usually have geographical advantages over downstream residents. As a result, social stratification and armed military forces emerged alongside large-scale water control. These were very important processes in the development of ancient civilizations.

---

[13] Flooding reached Aswan about a week earlier than Cairo, and Luxor 5–6 days earlier than Cairo. Typical heights of flood were 45 feet (13.7 m) at Aswan, 38 feet (11.6 m) at Luxor (and Thebes), and 25 feet (7.6 m) at Cairo (Budge 1895, pp. 45–49).

[14] See Nicholson (2000, pp. 514, 577 and 630) for a more detailed account.

In addition, it is reasonable to suppose that the deltas of most, if not all, rivers giving birth to ancient civilizations were characterized as wetlands and not suitable for agriculture during ancient times.[15] This might be the reason why the ancient Egyptian, the Indus/Harappan, and the Chinese civilizations did not originate in the deltas of the Nile, the Indus, and the Yellow rivers, respectively. However, all these were only necessary conditions for a civilization to emerge. They were not sufficient conditions. Still, there were not any powerful indigenous civilizations in many large river valleys of the world, which include, among others, the Amazon, Yangtze, Mississippi, Volga, and Rhine. Then, what was the most important factor contributing to the emergence of ancient civilizations in river valleys?

6.3 Cyclical Challenges and Civilization

Far before the historic period, men had left their footprints on every continent of the world. However, in the Eastern Hemisphere, the greatest ancient civilizations—Sumerian, Egyptian, Harappan (or Indus), and Chinese—were found only in northern Africa, the Middle East, Southwest Asia, and East Asia, but not elsewhere. Why have other places of the Eastern Hemisphere not given birth to any independent, indigenous civilizations as powerful as the above ancient civilizations? In addition, there were two early, primary civilizations—called the Norte Chico and the Olmec—in north-central Peru and Mesoamerica, respectively. However, the indigenous civilizations of the New World (or called Western Hemisphere) had neither sustained longer nor become more powerful than those of the Old World (or called Eastern Hemisphere) do?

Obviously, the environment must have played an important role in the birth of (or lack of) an indigenous civilization at a specific place. However, the environmental factors that have been classified as either "good" or "bad" ones in Chap. 4 are only the necessary conditions under which a civilization might (or might not) be created. They are not the sufficient conditions. Before answering what are the sufficient conditions under which a civilization can be created, let us first look at the geographical locations of all the earliest civilizations. In brief, the approximate latitudes of the above six civilizations from earth's equator are as the following:

- Sumer (Mesopotamia): 30° north
- Ancient Egypt (the Nile Valley): 30° north
- Harappa (the Indus–Ghaggar-Hakra river valleys): 30° north
- Xia/Shang China (the Yellow River Valley): 35° north
- Olmec (Mesoamerica): 17° north
- Norte Chico (Andean Peru): 10° south.

[15]Even today, we can still find wetlands at the deltas of the Indus, the Euphrates, the Tigris, and the Yellow rivers.

The above information shows that the two indigenous civilizations of the New World have been based at places of 10–17° from earth's equator, while all the four indigenous civilizations of the Old World have been around 30–35° from earth's equator. What do these geographical facts mean? Have they decided the different fates of the civilizations on both sides of the earth? Convincing answers have not yet been given in the usual text of world history. Archaeologists have recognized that in some cases, simple societies for one reason or the other morph into more complex societies, and in the process some societies become civilizations eventually. Even though there have not been any standard criteria for the creation of a new culture or civilization, the characteristics of complexity recognized in ancient civilizations are pretty much agreed upon as the following:

- increasing sedentism and high population density
- social stratification and ranking
- numbering and writing system
- time and calendar
- centralized rule and/or armed military force
- control of food as in agriculture or pastoralism
- craft specialization and metallurgy
- luxury and exotic goods
- trade or exchange networks
- architecture and monumental buildings.

Not all of these characteristics necessarily have to be present for a particular cultural group to be considered a civilization, but all of them are considered evidence of relatively complex societies. As many more individuals of each tribe are born than can possibly survive, especially in areas with serious natural disasters and threats and, consequently, there is a frequently recurring struggle for existence, it follows that any being, if it varies, however slightly, in any manner profitable to itself, under the complex and sometimes changing conditions of life, will have a better chance of surviving, and thus will naturally outlive others.

The root of the word "disaster" comes from the Latin "aster" meaning "of the stars." "dis" means "bad or misfortune." At ancient times, stars were assumed to predict impeding events including bad events. So what they combinedly imply is that when the stars are in a bad position a bad event will happen. A natural disaster is an event caused by natural forces that often pose a significant danger to human life or have a significant effect on the property of human beings. Typically, after the disaster, the human populations either are displaced (left homeless) or killed. The resulting loss depends on the capacity of the human population to circumvent or resist the disaster. Although natural hazards have been around ever since the earth came into existence, they will hence never result in damages to human beings in areas without vulnerability (e.g., strong earthquakes in uninhabited areas).[16]

---

[16]The term "natural" has consequently been disputed because the events simply are not hazards or disasters without human involvement.

Natural disasters often have economic and emotional effects on people and property. Environmentally, natural disasters can also be important to local ecosystems. The tragic consequences of natural disasters include death, injuries, loss of clean water, and so on. Having a better understanding of these natural disasters and their influences on human beings can help to better prepare against and perhaps minimize or prevent damages resulting from these disasters. Furthermore, the ability to predict and to combat or prevent natural disasters that threaten human beings is crucial to the formation of human civilizations. As a result, predicting the changes of seasons was particularly important in preventing any forthcoming natural (usually flood-related) disasters that would threat the people concerned.

The creation of "calendar," one of the most important components considered as signs of the birth of a civilization, was closely related to the regularity of "river flooding." In ancient Egypt, the 15th day of June, or the start of flooding season of the Nile, was selected as the first day of a new year. The Egyptians may have used a lunisolar calendar during the reign of First Dynasty King Djer (c. 3000 BC), with the intercalation of an extra month regulated either by the heliacal rising of Sothis or by the inundation of the fields by the Nile. According to the calendar, the first inundation was observed in Egypt's first capital, Memphis, at the same time as the heliacal rising of Sirius (Parker 1950, pp. 13–32). As the Nile was such an important factor in the Egyptian life, a new year in the ancient calendar even began with the inundation of the Nile. However, the seasons of ancient Egypt have been either falsely presented in the ancient Egyptian literature or misinterpreted by modern historians. Not likely? Let us first look at three Egyptian terms and their respective hieroglyphs (here I define them as Version I), as follows:[17]

Version I:

(1) Akhet (hieroglyphs: 𓈗𓂝𓇳): inundation season

(2) Peret (hieroglyphs: 𓉐𓂋𓇳): planting and growing season

(3) Shemu (hieroglyphs: 𓈒𓇳): harvesting season.

It is very likely that the hieroglyphs for Akhet and Shemu were reversely used by the ancient Egyptians, and that the terms Peret and Shemu are incorrectly defined by later historians—if not by the ancient Egyptians themselves—in Version I. Finally, the original Egyptian seasons (defined as Version II) are as follows:[18]

Version II:

(1) Akhet (hieroglyphs: 𓈒𓇳): inundation season

(2) Shemu (hieroglyphs: 𓈗𓂝𓇳): planting and growing season

(3) Peret (hieroglyphs: 𓉐𓂋𓇳): harvesting and storage season.

All the other ancient civilizations in the Eastern Hemisphere also adopted a lunisolar calendar even though none of these calendars is as precise as the modern Gregorian

---

[17]Note that there are slightly different versions of hieroglyphs for each season.

[18]Obviously, in the old, 360-year calendar, the hieroglyphs for all the seasons in Version II will become those in Version I after a period of approximately 22.9 ($\approx 120 \div [365.24 - 360]$) years. See Guo (2018, Chap. 3) for a more detailed analysis.

calendar we are using now. However, it is these challenges from the nature as well as the disagreements and challenges of humans themselves at both ancient and modern times that have promoted human civilizations to advance. (Section 7.3 in Chap. 7 for a more detailed analysis).

In Mesoamerica, the Mayans seem to have a different civilization from those in the Eastern Hemisphere. For example, in Mesoamerica, prior to the arrival of Europeans, the Mayans used a so-called Long Count calendar ignoring seasonal changes within each year. It is still not clear why they did not apply the lunar- or solar-based calendars that have been adopted by other civilizations in the Eastern Hemisphere. Nevertheless, the Maya civilization must have been influenced by the natural and environmental conditions there. To this, it is reasonable to guess that the dates that may distinguish seasonable changes were not required in the Maya society. In other words, there were no serious climate changes or that those changes did not seriously affect Maya's social and economic activities.

It must be noted that the so-called Long Count calendar adopted by the Mayan people is much simpler than those that have been applied worldwide. In riverine civilizations, especially in the four earliest civilizations in the Eastern Hemisphere, unruly rivers have long driven a hard bargain. In exchange for rich soil, irrigated land, and convenient transportation, they toiled the floodplain dwellers to deal with an occasional washout. A level of sediment consistent with a flood has been found in many parts of Mesopotamia and in some other parts of the world.[19] In addition, since the natural disasters and threats could be regularly found in river valleys (instead of other geographical places), people living there had more crying need to develop various scientific methods and technological tools in order to survive than those living in the other places did. While it is still not quite clear why the Mayan people invented and applied the "Long Count calendar," the inventions of "lunar" and lunisolar calendars (including the Gregorian calendar which is the de facto international standard) were a much more complicated and challengeable taskforce, which, ceteris paribus, have induced people to develop more wisdom for their own.

Hydraulically, when water flows through a river with uneven topographies, it will make a curve movement by which to produce a centrifugal force. Under the influence of the force, the flow of surface water tends to be meandering in a concave bank, and at the bottom of the river, water under pressure will flow from the concave course to a convex one, thus forming a bend circulation. Influenced by the bend circulation, deposition occurs on the convex bank. In contrast, both lateral erosion and undercutting occur on the cut bank or concave bank (i.e., the bank with the greatest centrifugal force). Continuous deposition on the convex bank, on the one hand, and erosion of the concave bank of a meandering river, on the other hand, cause the formation of a very pronounced meander with two concave banks getting closer. The narrow neck of land between the two neighboring concave banks is finally cut through, either by lateral erosion of the two concave banks or by the strong currents of a flood. When this happens, a new straighter river channel is created and an abandoned meander loop, called a cutoff, is formed. When deposition finally seals

[19]Literature in this regard would include Worsher (1985), Gelles (2000), and Scarborough (2003).

off the cutoff from the river channel, an oxbow lake is formed. The oxbow lake usually is a U-shaped body of water that forms when a wide meander from the main stem of a river is cut off, creating a freestanding body of water. This landform is so named for its distinctive curved shape, resembling the bow pin of an oxbow. This process can occur over a timescale from a few years to several decades or even longer.

Of course, the river's course now looks straighter than the old one. But as long as the topography is uneven, the new river as a whole still is a curved one and thus the regular or cyclical changes of its course are inevitable later on. In some places, especially in a low-lying plain where the river banks are easy to be eroded, the above-mentioned changes of watercourses could have become disasters to the riverine people living there. At least since the last glacial episode, the frequent changes of many, if not all of the world's river courses have been decided by this mechanism, which have also influenced the evolution and development of civilizations during the past thousands of years or so. For example, a popular Chinese proverb says that "Thirty years on the east, and thirty years in the west of the river" (30 nian hedong, 30 nian hexi). Its extended meaning is that many things are too hard to predict, but it is almost certain that in the long run they will have experienced a period of boom at first, which is followed by a period of decline at last (or vice versa).

During the past thousands of years, the management of the changing watercourses of rivers has been at the cost of large amount of physical and human capitals. It has, consequently, generated various technologies and tools and created a particular political culture (collectivism and authoritarianism). Above all, periodic or regularly repeating events, including river floods, are natural phenomena that have clocklike behaviors like the rising and setting of the Sun. Their predictability makes it possible for humans to enhance their long-term capacity-building.

More than 2,000 years ago, during the Warring States period (475–221 BC) of China, the Min River—the longest tributary of the Yangtze River—flowed quickly down from the mountains in southeastern China. As it ran across the Chengdu plain, it frequently flooded the agricultural area where local farmers who lived along the banks of the Min River were plagued by annual flooding in summer (May to October). At that time, Li Bing (c. 250–200 BC) served as the Qin's governor to Sichuan. Li Bing discovered that the river was swelled by fast flowing spring meltwater from the local mountains that burst the banks when it reached the slow moving and heavily silted stretch below. One solution would have been to build a dam; the waterway should kept open for military vessels to supply troops on the frontier. So instead Li Bing decided to construct an artificial levee to redirect a portion of the river's flow and then to cut a channel through Mt. Yulei to discharge the excess water upon the dry Chengdu plain beyond. The levee was constructed from long sausage-shaped baskets of woven bamboo filled with stones known as Zhulong held in place by wooden tripods known as Macha. Cutting the channel proved to be a far greater challenge at the time. Prior to the invention of gunpowder, people were unable to penetrate the hard rock of the mountain; so Li Bing used a combination of fire and water to heat and cool the rocks until they cracked and could be removed.

Li Bing's Irrigation System consists of three main constructions that work in harmony with one another to ensure against flooding and keep the fields well supplied with water. The irrigation made Sichuan the most productive agricultural place in China. Unlike contemporary dams where the water is blocked with a huge wall, the Dujiangyan still lets water go through naturally. Modern dams do not let fish go through very well, since each dam is a wall and the water levels are different. By eliminating disaster and ensuring a regular and bountiful harvest, the construction of the Dujiangyan has been highly credited. In 2000, the Dujiangyan became a UNESCO World Heritage Site. On May 12, 2008, a massive earthquake struck the Dujiangyan area. Even though the Yuzui Levee was cracked by the quake, the Dujiangyan Irrigation System as a whole was not damaged. It has been working well since then.

6.4   Let Floods Come More Violent!

Almost all existing earliest civilizations have been found in river valleys (see Table 6.1 for a brief summary). Specifically, the Eastern Hemisphere is the home to four civilizations (Mesopotamian or Sumerian, ancient Egyptian, Indus or Harappan, and ancient Chinese), while in the Western Hemisphere there are two civilizations—they are the Norte Chico in Peru and the Olmec in Mesoamerica. Except the Norte Chico civilization, whose birthplace is found in the Southern Hemisphere, all the other five civilizations are found to be located in the Northern Hemisphere. To be more precise, of the five "northern" civilizations, four (Mesopotamian or Sumerian, ancient Egyptian, Indus or Harappan, and ancient Chinese) civilizations are located in or near the north temperate zone.[20]

Like the civilizations that originated independently or indigenously in the Eastern Hemisphere, the Norte Chico was a typical riverine civilization. It, in fact, depended on even more complicated river systems than the other civilizations in the Old World (see Table 6.1). There is still a bigger question: why did Norte Chico give birth to the first civilization in the Americas? Perhaps this is a question similar to why Mesopotamia had the first civilization in the Eastern Hemisphere. Of course, both of them are riverine civilizations. Moreover, most of the world's earliest civilizations emerged in dry climate; and this might not be done by chance. The rivers played a key role in the emergence of ancient China along the Yellow River, of the Harappan civilization within the Indus–Ghaggar-Hakra valleys, of the Sumerian civilization in Mesopotamia (an area covering the Tigris and the Euphrates), and of the ancient Egyptian civilization along the Nile.

In South America, the Norte Chico civilization—the oldest civilization in the Americas—has been found to be located within the valleys of four independent river systems, an area that is much more hydraulically complicated than elsewhere.

---

[20]Specifically, the north temperate zone extends from the Tropic of Cancer (approximately 23.5° north latitude) to the Arctic Circle (approximately 66.5° north latitude); and the south temperate zone extends from the Tropic of Capricorn (approximately 23.5° south latitude) to the Antarctic Circle (at approximately 66.5° south latitude).

Table 6.1 Rivers and the earliest civilizations

River	Length (km)	Average discharge (m^3/s)	Drainage area (km^2)	Civilization
Nile	6,650	5,100	3,254,555	Ancient Egypt
Yellow	5,464	2,110	745,000	Ancient China
Indus	3,180	7,160	960,000	Indus (Harappa)
Ghaggar-Hakra	(a)	(a)	(a)	
Tigris	1,950	1,014	375,000	Mesopotamia (Sumer)
Euphrates	2,800	356	500,000	
Coatzacoalcos	325	1,163	17,563	Mesoamerica (Olmec)
Balsas (Mezcala)	770	15–850	105,900	
Fortaleza	<100	NA	1,800	Norte Chico
Pativilca	<100	NA		
Supe	<100	NA		
Huaura	<100	NA		

Notes (a) The Ghaggar-Hakra River, which flowed actively in parallel with the Indus in the third and fourth millennium BC, is now an intermittent river in India and Pakistan that flows only during the monsoon season

Sources Bilen (1994, p. 100), Kolars (1991, p. 47), IMEWRMPW (2006, p. 91), Isaev and Mikhailova (2009, p. 385), Haas et al. (2005), Barkin and King (1970, pp. 221–223), Salas (1991, p. 3), and Author

Unfortunately, all the rivers and the land through which these rivers flow are too small to sustain a larger civilization there. And civilizations developed within small geographical areas are always too fragile to survive—this has been particularly so when natural or environmental disasters or external threats suddenly occurred.

The world's climate change has ended a period of successful hunting and gathering by early humans, resulting in the global pattern of deserts and fertile areas we are familiar with today. The process was slow, and the people adapted, until they found themselves largely concentrated around dwindling resources, such as river valleys in dry regions. In those regions, because of the dwindling opportunities to gather and hunt food, the people had great need of concentrated sources of food, and this is the period of time in which people around the world, in similar circumstances, made the transition from gathering and hunting for food, to farming and husbandry. These new methods of food production allowed for more people to live in a small area than was possible without food production. As will be discussed in Sect. 7.1 in Chap. 7, almost all of the six major riverine civilizations first appeared in geographically and hydraulically disadvantageous places. Specifically, except the Indus/Harappa civilization, whose ancient river systems have not been completely clarified, the other five civilizations were usually based on the lower reaches or any other places that were disadvantageous to humans living there (see Table 6.2).

Table 6.2 A spatial and dynamic overview of the six major civilizations of the world

Civilization	Year (BC) in which a first culture/civilization emerged[a]	
	Lower reaches/land	Upper reaches/land
Mesopotamia	4000 (Uruk Period, Iraq)	3100 (Jemdet Nasr Period, Iraq)
Nile Valley	3100 (Early Dynastic Period, Egypt)	2500 (Kerma, northern Sudan)
Indus/Ghaggar-Hakra (Sarasvati) river valleys	2500 (Mohenjo Daro, Sindh, Pakistan); c.2650 BC (Dholavira, Gujarat, western India)	2600 (Harappa, Punjab, Pakistan); c. 2500 BC (Banawali, Haryana, northern India)
Yellow River Valley[b]	2070 (Xia, Henan, China)	1046 (Zhou, Shaanxi, China)
Mesoamerica	1500 (Olmec, southern Mexico and Guatemala)	700 (Zapotec, Oaxaca Valley, southern Mexico)
Andean Peru (Norte Chico)[c]	3100 (Caballete, Fortaleza River, Peru)	2000 (Shaura, Fortaleza River, Peru)

Notes (a) The table is created to compare the lower and upper reaches (lands) of each culture (civilization). An intercultural comparison may be inappropriate since the criteria for selecting the sites as civilizations may be different from case to case. (b) The pre-Xia cultures are not included. (c) The Norte Chico may not be defined as a civilization if compared with those of the Old World
Source Author based on Guo (2018)

Given their close geographical proximity, the Indus/Harappa culture may not be a truly indigenous civilization and was, to a greater or lesser extent, influenced by the Neolithic cultures in the Middle East. For example, about 200 km west of the Indus, Mehrgarh is a Neolithic site near the Bolan Pass on the Kacchi Plain of Balochistan, Pakistan. One of the earliest sites with evidence of farming and herding in South Asia, the Mehrgarh culture is believed to have influenced the Indus Valley and became part of the Indus/Harappa civilization later on (Parpola 2015, p. 17). As a matter of fact, the Mehrgarh had also been significantly influenced by the Neolithic cultures in the Near East from c. 7000 BC to 2500 BC (Gangal et al. 2014). As a result, cultural formation of the Mehrgarh might not be endogenously determined by the geographical and human features of its own.

The Tigris and the Euphrates in the Middle East, the lower Nile in Egypt, the Indus in South Asia, and the Yellow River in northern China are all famous for flooding. The Chinese have historically referred to the Yellow River as "China's sorrow" for its destructive power. But all of the floods magnified the agricultural advantage by enriching the soil annually, allowing for greater concentrations of population in river valleys than in other areas. This can be witnessed by what the ancient Greek historian Herodotus called Egypt the "gift of the Nile." People in these regions in the period of drier global climates and of increased local populations responded by inventing civilization. Each group did it independently, and each invention shared characteristics with the others.

While various natural and geographical challenges have largely determined the developments of ancient civilizations exist, not all natural disasters (threats) have contributed to the birth of civilizations. Although the unfriendly environment—as long as it could sustain humans—has incentivized humans to create the first and powerful civilizations, not all places of such kind of environment have become cradles of civilizations. To be sure, in the explanation of the rise and fall of civilizations, natural and geographical factors are the exogenous variable, and human behaviors should always be treated as an endogenous variable.

For example, with regard to the question why Mesopotamia has given birth to the earliest civilization in the Eastern Hemisphere, historians have suggested that fertile land and other favorable geographic factors along the Euphrates and the Tigris have helped Sumerians make a creative leap to the early civilization. However, this is not the real story, and many critical geographic factors (conditions) promoting the birth of various civilizations have not been presented at the usual text.

Indeed, it is a more difficult task for humans to understand the hydraulic characteristics in an X-potamia than they do in a single river valley. However, the more difficult the task, the more wisdom are invented by we humans—perhaps writing and understanding the above formulas may have also encompassed part (though minor) of the complex civilizations. According to the same logic, humans subject to more complicated river systems must have a more crying need to develop sophisticated techniques by which to deal with river floods and, as a result, to advance their civilizations.

6.5 Method: Calculating the Probability of Floods in X-potamia

The new term "X-potamia" is defined here as an area with a number of interactive river systems. Specifically, when $X = 1$, it refers to as a river valley; when $X = 2$, it refers to as "Mesopotamia"; when $X = 3$, it refers to as "Tripotamia"; and when $X > 3$, it refers to as "Multipotamia." Even though it is now quite difficult to clarify the spatial hydraulic features of rivers during ancient times, those that are located over hundreds-of-km away from each other (such as the Yangtze and Yellow rivers) are not likely to form an X-potamia. This assumption is simply based on the fact that, without any canals built between independent rivers that may support shipping, any prehistoric economic activity could not exceed a hundreds-of-km distance across those rivers.

There are a number of assumptions which are made to complete the analysis which determines the probability of river floods (Stedlinger 1993, pp. 18.1ff). First, the extreme events observed in each year must be independent from year to year. In other words, the maximum river flow rate from, for example, 2015 cannot be found to be significantly correlated with the observed flow rate in 2016. Similarly, the maximum river flow rate from 2016 cannot be correlated with that in 2017, and so forth. The second assumption is that the observed extreme events must come from the same probability distribution function. The third assumption is that the probability distribution relates to the largest storm (rainfall or river flow rate measurement) that occurs in any one year. The fourth assumption is that the probability distribution function is stationary, meaning that the mean (average), standard deviation, and max/min values are not increasing or decreasing over time.

A T-year flood is a flood event that has a $100/T\%$ probability of occurring in any given year. For river systems, the T-year flood is generally expressed as a flow rate. Based on the expected T-year flood flow rate, the flood water level can be mapped as an area of inundation. The resulting floodplain map is referred to as the T-year floodplain. Areas near the coast of an ocean or large lake also can be flooded by combinations of tide, storm surge, and waves. Maps of the T-year river floods had been always a difficult job of riveriners at ancient times and may still figure importantly in building permits, environmental regulations, flood insurance, and so on.

It is a common misunderstanding that a T-year flood is likely to occur only once in a T-year period. Specifically, the chance of one or more 100-year floods occurring in any 100-year period is not 100%; instead, it is only approximately 63.4%.[21] For example, on the Danube River at Passau, Germany, the actual intervals between 100-year floods during the period from 1501 to 2013 ranged from 37 to 192 years (Eychaner 2015). Mathematically, the probability for floods to occur in a single river valley during any period can be expressed, using the binomial distribution, as the following:

$$P = 1 - (1 - \frac{1}{T})^n$$

where T is the flood threshold period (e.g., 100-year, 50-year, 20-year, 10-year, etc.); and n is the number of years in the period. The probability of exceedance P is also described as the natural, inherent, or hydrologic risk of failure.

Now, let us extend the above analysis into in an area including X rivers—that is, an X-potamian system. The probability for one or more floods occurring in the X-potamia during any period, expressed by PX, can be expressed, using the binomial distribution, as the following:

$$P_X = \sum \left(1 - (1 - \frac{1}{T(X)})^{n(X)}\right)$$

[21] This figure is calculated as $1-(1 - \frac{1}{100})^{100}$.

where $\sum(\cdot)$ is the sum of $(\cdot)$. And the probability for floods to simultaneously occur in all rivers during any period, expressed by p_X, now becomes:

$$p_X = \Pi \left(1 - (1 - \frac{1}{T(X)})^{n(X)} \right)$$

where $\prod(\cdot)$ is the product of $(\cdot)$; $X=1, 2, 3\ldots$; $T(X)$ is the flood threshold period of the Xth river; and $n(X)$ is the number of years in the period of the Xth river.

Consider the simplest case: Assuming $T(1) = T(2) = T(3) =\ldots T(X) = T$ and $n(1) = n(2) = n(3) =\ldots n(X)=n$, then we have $P_X=X{\cdot}P$, where P is the probability for floods to occur in a single river valley during any period. Since $P > 0$ and $X > 1$, then we have $PX > P > 0$ and $P_1 < P_2 < P_3\ldots$ In other words, ceteris paribus, the probability for floods to occur in the X-potamia always grows with respect to the number (denoted by X) of rivers involved. On the other hand, $p_X=PX$. Since $P < 1$ and $X > 1$, then we have $p_X < P$ and $p_1 > p_2 > p_3\ldots$

References

Bandstra BL (2009) Reading the old testament: an introduction to the hebrew bible, 4th edn. Wadsworth/Cengage Learning, Belmont, CA

Barkin D, King T (1970) Regional economic development: the river basin approach in Mexico. Cambridge University Press, Cambridge

Bilen Ö (1994) Prospects for technical cooperation in the Euphrates-Tigris Basin. In: Biswas AK (ed) International waters of the middle east: from euphrates-tigris to Nile. Oxford University Press, Oxford, pp 95–116

Brooks N (2006) Cultural responses to aridity in the Middle Holocene and increased social complexity. Quatern Int 151:29–49

Bros P (2005) The case for the flood: Exposing the scientific myth of the ice age. In: Kenyon JD (2005, ed.). Forbidden history: prehistoric technologies, extraterrestrial intervention, and the suppressed origins of civilization, Rochester. Bear and Company, Vermont pp 44–52

Budge WEA (1895) The Nile: notes for travelers in Egypt (3rd Edition). Ithaca, NY: Cornell University LibraryButzer, Karl W. (1976). Early Hydraulic Civilization in Egypt: A Study in Cultural Ecology ('Prehistoric Archeology and Ecology' series). University of Chicago Press, Chicago, IL

Christie A (1968) Chinese mythology. Hamlyn Publishing Group, Feltham, UK

Clayton PA, Dent J (1973) The Ancient River Civilizations. Western man and the modern world series. amsterdam, Elsevier BV

Cohn N (1999) Noah's flood: the genesis story in western thought. Yale University Press, New Haven and London

Cotter DW (2003) Genesis. Liturgical Press, Collegeville, Minn

Eychaner JH (2015) Lessons from a 500-year record of flood elevations. Technical Report 7. Association of State Floodplain Managers, Madison, Wisconsin, USA. http://www.floods.org/ace-files/documentlibrary/publications/asfpmpubs-techrep7_2015.pdf. Accessed 6 Oct 2016

Fant CE, Reddish MG (2008) Lost treasures of the bible: understanding the bible through archaeological artifacts in world museums. Wm. B. Eerdmans Publishing, Cambridge

Fleming KM (2000) Glacial rebound and sea-level change constraints on the greenland ice sheet, PhD Thesis. Australian National University, Canberra

Fleming K, Johnston P, Zwartz D, Yokoyama Y, Lambeck K, Chappell J (1998) Refining the eustatic sea-level curve since the Last Glacial Maximum using far- and intermediate-field sites. Earth and Planet Sci Lett 163(1–4):327–342

Gangal K, Sarson GR, Shukurov A (2014) The near-eastern roots of the neolithic in South Asia. PLOS ONE. http://dx.doi.org/10.1371/journal.pone.0095714. Accessed 15 Oct 2016

Garcia-Mata C, Shaffner FI (1934) Solar and economic relationships: a preliminary report. Q J Econ 49(1):1–51

Gelles PH (2000) Water and power in highland Peru: the cultural politics of irrigation and development. Rutgers University Press, Fredericksburg, PA

Genesis (1978, 1984, 2011). Holy Bible—New International Version. Biblica, Inc., New York

Haas, J, Creamer W, Ruiz A (2005) Power and the emergence of complex polities in the Peruvian Preceramic. Archaeol Papers Am Anthropol Assoc 14(1):37–52

Guo R (2018) Civilizations revisited: the historians may be wrong, really. University Press, Hong Kong

Hole F (1991) The ecology of seasonal stress and the origins of agriculture in the Near East. Am Anthropol 93:46–69

IMEWRMPW (2006) Volume I: Overview of Present Conditions and Current Use of the Water in the Marshlands Area/Book 1: Water Resources. Iraqi Ministries of Environment, Water Resources and Municipalities and Public Works. New Eden Master Plan for Integrated Water Resources Management in the Marshlands Areas, New Eden Group

Isaev VA, Mikhailova MV (2009) The hydrology, evolution, and hydrological regime of the mouth area of the Shatt al-Arab river. Water Resour 36(4):380–395

Kolars JF, Mitchell W (1991) The euphrates river and the southeast anatolia development project. Carbondale and Edwardsville. Southern Illinois University Press, Illinois

Lambert WG, Millard AR (1970) Atrahasis: the babylonian story of the flood. Clarendon Press, reprint edition, Oxford

Lynch PA, Roberts J (2010) African Mythology A to Z (Second Edition). Mythology A to Z series. Chelsea House, New York

Mayor A (2011) The first fossil hunters: paleontology in greek and roman times. Princeton University Press, Princeton, NJ

Mencius (c. 300 BC) [1999] Analects of mencius (English-Chinese Edition). Foreign Languages Press, Beijing

Milne GA, Long AJ, Bassett SE (2005) Modeling holocene relative sea-level observations from the caribbean and south America. Quatern Sci Rev 24(10–11):1183–1202

Mountjoy S (2005) The indus river. Rivers in World History series. Chelsea House Publishers, New York

Nicholson PT (2000) Ancient Egyptian materials and technology. Cambridge University Press, Cambridge

Parker RA (1950) The calendars of ancient Egypt. Studies in ancient oriental civilization, 26. University of Chicago Press, Chicago

Parpola A (2015) The roots of hinduism. The early aryans and the indus civilization. Oxford University Press, Oxford

Roux G (2001) Did the Sumerians emerge from the sea? In: Bottéro J (ed.) and Antonia Nevill (trans.). Everyday Life in Ancient Mesopotamia. Johns Hopkins University Press, Baltimore, MD pp 3–23

Salas GP (1991) Economic geology, Mexico. Geological Society of America, Boulder, Colorado

Scarborough VL (2003) The flow of power: ancient water systems and landscapes. SAR Press, Santa Fe, NM

Seger JH (1934; 2007) Early days among the cheyanne and arapahoe Indians (Second Edition). University of Oklahoma Press, Norman, Oklahoma

Sima Q (91 BC) [1997] Shiji (Records of the Grand Historian) (in Chinese). Taihai Press, Beijing

Speiser EA (1969) The epic of gilgamesh. In: Pritchard JB (ed) Ancient Near Eastern Texts Relating to the Old Testament, 3rd edn. Princeton University Press, Princeton, N.J., pp 72–98

Weiss H, Courty M, Wetterstrom W, Guichard F, Senior L, Meadow R, Curnow A (1993) The genesis and collapse of third millennium North Mesopotamian civilization. Science 261(20):995–1004

Worsher D (1985) Rivers of empire: water, aridity, and growth of the American west. Pantheon Books, New York

Wu K-C (1982) The Chinese Heritage. Crown Publishers, New York

Wu WX, Ge QS (2005) The possibility of occurring of the extraordinary floods in the eve of establishment of the Xia dynasty and the historical truth of Dayu's successful regulating of floodwaters. Quat Sci 25(6):741–748

Xia-Shang-Zhou Chronology Project Expert Group (2000) Report on the Xia-Shang-Zhou Chronology Project, 1996–2000, Simplified edn. World Publishing Co. Ltd., Beijing

Yang L, An D, and Turner JA (2008). Handbook of Chinese Mythology (Handbooks of World Mythology). Oxford University Press, New York

Chapter 7
Studying Civilizations: Retrospect and Prospect

Abstract Why did the Middle East host the oldest civilization of the Old World? And why did Andean South America give birth to the oldest civilization in the Western Hemisphere? Civilizations cannot be created in places where there is extremely impoverished soil—a space suitable for living is the precondition for the reproduction of human beings. However, it is not the soil fertility that had eventually given birth to the earliest civilization in Mesopotamia. In Andean South America, since it had far less frequent intercultural influences than those in the Old World did, the exogenous factors contributing to the rise of cultures and civilizations can be minimized, if not totally ignored. As a result, the endogenous geographical and environmental factors contributing to the rise of cultures and civilizations can be more clearly identified accordingly.

Keywords Civilization · Cultural formation · Earth's cycle · River valley
Intercultural dynamics

7.1 In Search of Civilizations

Humans are newcomers to Earth, even though their achievements have been enormous. It is only at the end of or after the Pleistocene epoch that the development of agriculture occurred. Humans have spent most of their history—both before and after their migration out of southern Africa—as hunting and food-gathering beings. Only after their migration out of southern Africa in the past 10,000 years or so, did humans discover how to raise crops and tame animals. Such changes probably first took place in the hills to Mesopotamia—the cradle of civilization. Historically, all the earliest civilizations in the Eastern Hemisphere grew up in river valleys. People settled along riverbeds for access to fresh water, one of the most important requirements for sustaining a population. However, rivers still had more important roles in the rise and fall of civilizations.

Generally speaking, the world's earliest indigenous civilizations were found in the following six areas: Mesopotamia, Egypt, the Yellow River Valley, the Indus and the Ghaggar-Hakra valleys, South America, and Mesoamerica. In the USA and

Table 7.1 A comparison of the four riverine civilizations in the Eastern Hemisphere

Indicator	Sumerian	Ancient Egyptian	Indus or Harappan[a]	Chinese
Appearance of written language	3300 BC	3100 BC	NA	1300 BC
Creation of religion or law	2400 BC	2350 BC	2600–1900 BC	1044 BC
Invention of calendar or time measurement	3000 BC	3000 BC	2600–1900 BC	1766 BC
Date of birth of state(s)	3500 BC	3100 BC	NA	1988 BC

Source Guo (2018)
Note [a]Since the Harappan civilizations had become extinct before 1700 BC, some figures shown in this column may not be accurate

Canada, the Advanced Placement World History (also known as AP World History or APWH), in its "Course and Exam Description," effective of fall 2017, requires high-school students to be able to understand the following six core and foundational civilizations (APWH 2017, p. 28):

- Mesopotamia in the Tigris and Euphrates valleys
- Egypt in the Nile River Valley
- Mohenjo-daro and Harappa in the Indus Valley
- Shang in the Yellow River (or Huanghe) Valley
- Olmecs in Mesoamerica
- Chavín in Andean South America.

According to the common archaeological usage of naming a civilization after its first findspot, the term "Harappan civilization" remains the correct one. Nevertheless, the terms "Indus civilization" and "Harappan civilization" can be used interchangeably, though the latter will be used more frequently.

Like the Harappa, the Chavín is an extinct, prehistoric culture or civilization. It is named for Chavín de Huántar (located in the Andean highlands of the present-day Ancash Region in northern Peru), the principal archaeological site at which its artifacts have been found. The culture developed in the northern Andean highlands of Peru from 900 BC to 200 BC. It extended its influence to other civilizations along the coast. However, since the 1990s, scholars have defined the Norte Chico (also known as the Caral or Caral-Supe) in the coastal area of present-day Peru as the earliest independent site of civilization in the Americas. A 2001 paper in *Science*, providing a survey of the Caral research, and a 2004 article in *Nature*, describing fieldwork and radiocarbon dating across a wider area, revealed Norte Chico's full significance and led to widespread interests in the earliest civilization in the Western Hemisphere.[1]

---

[1]See Shady et al. (2001) and Haas et al. (2004) for more details about the archaeological evidence of this civilization.

The Shang dynasty (c. 1700–c. 1046 BC) is China's first dynasty that has been known to have a history with written records. In fact, in addition to the prehistoric Xia dynasty (c. 2100–c. 1700 BC) that has been recognized to exist in the Yellow River Valley, China had many prehistoric cultures, some of which might not be based in the Yellow River Valley. Examples include the Xinglongwa culture (c. 6200–c. 5400 BC) in the Inner Mongolia-Liaoning border area, the Hemudu culture (c. 5000–c. 3300 BC) in modern Yuyao city, Zhejiang, China, the Hongshan culture (c. 4700–c. 2900 BC) in Inner Mongolia, Liaoning, and Hebei, and the Liangzhu culture (c. 3400–c. 2250 BC) in modern Hangzhou city, Zhejiang, China.[2] However, the Yellow River and its tributaries still saw the earliest cultures of China that include, inter alia, the Nanzhuangtou culture (c. 8500–c. 7700 BC) in southern Hebei, the Dadiwan culture (c. 7800–c. 4800 BC) in Gansu and western Shaanxi, the Peiligang culture (c. 7000–c. 5000 BC) in Henan, and the Houli culture (c. 6500–c. 5500 BC) in Shandong.

The earliest culture of North America may date back to 5000 years ago, when inhabitants, collectively called Mound Builders, constructed various styles of earthen mounds in present-day Louisiana of the USA for religious and ceremonial, burial, and elite residential purposes. These sites include the pre-Columbian cultures of the Archaic period, the Woodland period (including the Adena and Hopewell cultures), and the Mississippian period, all dating back from roughly 3400 BC to the sixteenth century, and living in regions near the Great Lakes, the Ohio River, and the Mississippi River and its tributaries (Squier 2012, p. 1). Since all these cultures were not able to advance to the level of those in the Old World, they cannot be treated as separate New World civilizations.

More often than not, "civilization" has been defined as one bigger than "culture" because it is a complex aggregate of the society that dwells within a certain area, along with its forms of government, norms, and even culture. Thus, each civilization can contain not only one but several cultures. However, the terms "civilization" and "culture" sometimes are also used interchangeably. Even though other indigenous cultures also existed or even still exist, the world's major earliest indigenous civilizations are as the following[3]:

- Mesopotamia
- Ancient Egyptian civilization
- Indus (Harappan) civilization
- Chinese civilization
- Mesoamerica
- Andean South America

Even though much earlier cultures or, to a looser degree, civilizations can be found, the oldest civilization, dating back to about 3500 BC, was along the Tigris and the Euphrates in the Middle East. The name given to the place of that civilization,

---

[2]The Hemudu and Liangzhu cultures have been identified to be sources of modern Austronesian and Daic (including Thai and Lao) or, possibly, of modern Hmong-Mien (Miao-Yao) populations (Yan 2005, p. 36; and Li et al. 2007).

[3]See Guo (2018) for a more detailed description of these six civilizations that cannot be found in the usual text.

Mesopotamia, means "[land] between the rivers." The Nile Valley in Egypt had been home to agricultural settlements in 5500 BC or earlier, but the development of ancient Egypt as a civilization was slightly later than that of Mesopotamia. A third civilization, though lacking a writing system, is believed to emerge along the Indus and Ghaggar-Hakra rivers and their tributaries around 3300 BC, in parts of what are now in India and Pakistan. The fourth oldest riverine civilization grew up around 2000 BC near the banks of the Yellow River in China.

When dealing with such question as how civilizations were born, it has been quite common that historians simply reply that the cradle of civilization should be a fertile land with sufficient fresh water. For example, popularized by University of Chicago archaeologist James Henry Breasted, the Fertile Crescent is defined as a crescent-shaped region containing the comparatively moist and fertile land of otherwise arid and semiarid Western Asia, the Nile Valley and Nile Delta of northeast Africa. In current usage, the Fertile Crescent usually includes Mesopotamia and the land around the Tigris and Euphrates rivers. The modern-day countries with significant territory within the Fertile Crescent are Iraq, Kuwait, Syria, Lebanon, Jordan, Israel, Palestine, Cyprus, and Egypt, besides the southeastern fringe of Turkey and the western fringes of Iran.

Of course, civilizations cannot be created in places where there is extremely impoverished soil—a space suitable for living is the precondition for the reproduction of human beings. However, it is not the soil fertility that had eventually given birth to the earliest civilization in Mesopotamia. Why? Let us look at Andean South America: Since it had far less frequent intercultural influences than those in the Old World did, the exogenous factors contributing to the rise of cultures and civilizations can be minimized, if not totally ignored. As a result, the endogenous geographical and environmental factors contributing to the rise of cultures and civilizations can be more clearly identified accordingly.

Broadly speaking, rivers not only made the civilizations possible by making food plentiful but also made them necessary by giving the people living along river valleys new challenges that only "civilization" could solve. "Civilization," to anthropologists and archaeologists, may be simply defined as the art of collective behaviors of human beings living in close proximity to each other. It requires rules, rulers, boundaries, special skills, and economic concentration and specialization (that is, for every society, only a portion of people were needed to engage in agriculture, instead of everyone gathering and hunting in the pre-civilizational era). Each of the early riverine civilizations developed the following on its own: technologies for growing and storing food and for channeling water, a system of laws to keep peace and preserve property, socioeconomic classes, theistic cosmology, writing, cyclical, astronomically-based calendars, and other trappings of "civilization."

We have found that physical weakness may provide incentives (whereas physical advantages may provide disincentives) for humans to develop complex societies from previous simpler ones (see Sect. 2.3 in Chap. 2) and that the humans' physical output and mental output are negatively correlated (see Fig. 2.4 in Chap. 2). However, it is not appropriate to say that the growth of a culture or civilization is always negatively determined by the average physical capacity of and is always positively determined by the average mental capacity of the human population concerned. In other words, there exist more complicated patterns for the dynamic behaviors of civilizations (see model at the end of this chapter for a mathematical description of conditions under which a civilization exists).

Thousands of years ago, facing the insufficient supply of food from the nature, humans began to cultivate arid and semiarid lands. Whenever rain was little and flood was thus absent, the wadis received the only precious water and thus had the natural advantages in agricultural production over other, higher lands. On the other hand, whenever rain was heavy and flood was thus serious, people living in wadis suffered accordingly, and they, in order to survive, must invent various techniques (cultures) by which to conduct inundated waters out of the wadis. Then, why have cultures and civilizations been usually found in the wadis (lower lands) vis-à-vis higher lands? This was subject the frequencies of rainy and dry climates. *Only if the frequency of dry climate is higher than that of rainy climate, could the wadis have the higher chance to become the cradle of civilization.* This is why almost all of the world's first civilizations were based in desert or semidesert areas.

In desert or arid areas, in addition to wadi, another geographical feature—wahe—has also been of importance to humans. In the later attested Coptic language (the descendant of Demotic—an ancient Egyptian language used in the Nile Delta), the word for oasis is wahe or ouahe which means a "dwelling place."[4] It came into English and French directly from Late Latin oasis, from Greek oasis, which in turn is a borrowing from Demotic Egyptian. In Arabic, the term wahe is read wahat. Geographically, an oasis is an isolated area of vegetation in a desert, which is typically surrounded by a spring or connected to a pond or small lake. Oases have provided habitat for animals and humans as well.

The location of oases has been of critical importance for trade and transportation routes in desert areas. Even though wahes were important places at both ancient and modern times, it is the *wadis* and the seasonable and, sometimes, destructive river floods through them—not the *wahes* or any other geographical features, where are free of serious river floods—that had contributed to the growth of various civilizations.

Indeed, floods have created all of the world's first civilizations. And, over the course of the past thousands of years or longer, river floods and other various disasters and threats have made humans—either individuals or as collectives—become stronger and more powerful. However, it is only those cyclical disasters and threats especially annual or seasonable river floods—not the other irregular disasters and threats—that have enabled humans to be more prepared and intelligent and thus to possess brilliant civilizations of today!

All nations, large or small, and civilizations as a whole, have followed a similar logic: whenever they have faced challenges or external threats, they would have more incentives to struggle and innovate, and whenever they have reached the highest level of success, they would be too hesitated to change until latecomers overtook them. Believe it or not, this is the real story of human civilizations…

---

[4]Source: http://www.etymonline.com/index.php?search=oasis, accessed 2017-2-18.

7.2   Spatial and Intercultural Dynamics

An emphasis on inter-continental differences is an important angle of viewing inter-cultural differences throughout the world. And, unquestionably, natural and environmental influences on the structure and distribution of world civilizations did exist throughout history. However, it should be noted that human beings have always played, and will continue to play, the most important role in *their* cultural evolutions. Remember that all civilizations on Earth are also human civilizations. Without human beings, there would be no civilization. Therefore, in order to understand the driving forces behind the rise and fall of civilizations, one should first examine the inherent characteristics of humankind (including you and me) per se. Or, at the very least, humans and the environments in which humans have been living should be used as a joint proxy for the explanation of the whole history of civilizations.

In geography, temperate zones or tepid latitudes of Earth lie between the tropics and polar regions. Usually, the climate changes in the temperate zones between summer and winter are generally relatively moderate, rather than extreme hot (in the tropics) or cold (in the polar regions), providing more suitable living conditions for human beings. However, all the four Old World civilizations were located at desert or semidesert areas. Even though the Norte Chico is not located in the south temperature zone, it has been under the influences of the Humboldt Current which makes conditions there extremely arid, creating one of the driest deserts in the world. Since the Humboldt Current, also called the Peru Current, is a cold, low-salinity ocean current that flows north along the west coast of South America from the southern tip of Chile to northern Peru, the Norte Chico civilization might have meteorological or other environmental conditions similar to those of the other four civilizations in the Eastern Hemisphere.

In Southwest Asia, two rivers (Euphrates and Tigris) run in parallel to each other. The land between the Euphrates and the Tigris is known as Mesopotamia, which means "[land] between the rivers" in ancient Greek. Then, when serving as the cradle of civilization, how did Mesopotamia have any environmental or hydraulical differences from the Nile and the Yellow River Valleys?

Mesopotamia has remained as the center of many different civilizations and given natural resources to millions of inhabitants living there. Both the Tigris and the Euphrates have provided much of the water that supported the development of the ancient Mesopotamian culture. The Tigris–Euphrates Valley was the birthplace of the ancient Mesopotamian civilization. In northern Iraq, the Euphrates forms the western boundary of the area known as Al Jazirah. To the southeast, the alluvial lands between the two rivers were the site of the glorious Babylonian civilizations of ancient times. According to the historical data yielded by archaeological excavations on the banks of the Tigris and the Euphrates, irrigation made it possible for the locals to develop agriculture within the Euphrates–Tigris Valley (Kolars and Mitchell 1991, p. 23). This resulted in the development of great ancient civilizations within the Tigris–Euphrates Valley, where water played an important starting role.

In the Middle East, land is of mostly dry climate. But there is still an exception—a flat plain known as Mesopotamia lies between the Tigris and the Euphrates. Because of this region's shape and the richness of its soil, it is called the "Fertile Crescent." The rivers flooded at least once a year, leaving a thick bed of mud called silt. Probably attracted by the rich soil, Sumerians first settled in this region. However, this was not the main reason for the birth the Sumerian civilization in the Middle East. As a matter of fact, as stated in Chap. 4, it is the disadvantages and environmental challenges (such as flooding and dry summer months) of an area that helped people living there to develop a more complicated social organization (or called civilization) for their own. However, this still cannot explain why Mesopotamia had the world's earliest civilization.

The Euphrates has been an important river up through history, and the Tigris, too, has contributed greatly to the birth of ancient civilizations. Then, what was the main reason why Mesopotamia had the earliest human civilization?

The major contribution of the Tigris and the Euphrates to the civilizations was their suitability to irrigation, and, as a result, the earliest farmlands were developed within the Tigris–Euphrates Valley. To control these floods, the Iraqis have diverted water from the Tigris to the Euphrates, where the Euphrates has less alleviation than the Tigris. The Euphrates and the Tigris were turbulent, and many sections of them were unsuitable for traffic. At times, floodwaters would destroy large areas. Because of the irregularities of the tributaries' flows, the Tigris is widely known for its infamous floods. Furthermore, during the ancient times, the land between the Euphrates and the Tigris had remained as the center of human activities that were seriously influenced by the two parallel rivers via even more complicated ways than any other parts of the world. Consequently, the Mesopotamian people were required to form a more centralized rule and to invent more technical wisdom in order to deal with the cyclical floods occurring at *both* rivers. The final result is that Mesopotamia—an area with influences from two independent river systems—gave birth to an oldest civilization in the Eastern Hemisphere.

We can find more evidence that supports the hypothesis that the earliest civilizations were easily created in areas with complicated river systems. In the Western Hemisphere, an indigenous civilization—the Norte Chico civilization, also known as the Caral or Caral-Supe civilization—flourished between 3000 BC and 1800 BC. This civilization mainly comprised four valleys of the Supe, the Pativilca, the Fortaleza, and the Huaura rivers in the central-north coastal region of Peru, all of the latter sharing a common coastal plain (see Guo 2018, Chap. 7). As the oldest known civilization in the Americas and one of the six oldest sites where civilizations originated independently and indigenously in the ancient world, the Norte Chico civilization predated the Olmec civilization in Mesoamerica by more than one millennium and the Chavín civilization in Andean South America by more than two millennia. As early as in 3000 BC, there were already very advanced urban centers in the Norte Chico; perhaps the only other site with the similar degree of urban complexity was Sumer in Mesopotamia.

Like the Mesopotamians, who had been influenced by two independent river systems in parallel, people living in the Norte Chico must have learnt to manage challenges resulting from more complicated river systems. This is why one of the world's earliest civilizations emerged there. As a matter of fact, South America's population aggregation, an early sign of urbanization and civilization, can be more easily found in the Norte Chico than elsewhere. Generally, as long as land is available for the settlement of splinter communities, these villages undoubtedly split from time to time as they grow in population size. For instance,

> Village splitting among tribes can be more easily found in Amazonia than in the coastal valleys of Peru: in Amazonia, splitting often takes place at a village population level of less than 100, and village size seldom exceeds 200. In the coastal valleys of Peru, however, villages could not fission so readily, and thus grew to population levels which may have averaged over 300.[5]

In early agricultural times, human settlements seem to have been denser along the sea coast than in these river valleys in the coastal region of Peru, and subsistence appears to have been based more on fishing than on farming. However, once subsistence began to be based predominantly on agriculture, the settlement pattern changed, and communities were thenceforth concentrated more in the river valleys, where the only land of any size suitable for cultivation was located. As a matter of fact, in addition to the Norte Chico area in which the earliest American civilization was based, many other short and narrow river valleys in the coastal region of Peru are also found to have contributed to the development of later cultures or civilizations in South America.[6] However, none of these river valleys have given birth to an indigenous civilization as great as those in the Old World.

The world's civilizations have evolved through different phases, since they first emerged about 5000 years ago. Some regions witnessed two or three generations of affiliated cultures, with the demise of one culture and interregnum followed by the rise of another successor generation. A brief glance at the evolutions of human civilizations simply reveals that the interaction of civilizations has existed frequently in many places of the world. For example, with close proximity to Mesopotamia, the cradle of human civilization in the Eastern Hemisphere, two other earliest civilizations have been found in today's Egypt and India and Pakistan. And their socioeconomic relations with Mesopotamia were also very apparent.

The ancient Egyptians engaged in trade with their foreign neighbors to obtain rare, exotic goods not found in Egypt. In the pre-dynastic period, they established trade with Nubia to obtain gold and incense. They also established trade with Palestine, as evidenced by Palestinian-style oil jugs found in the burials of the First Dynasty (c. 3050–c. 2890 BC) pharaohs. By the Second Dynasty (c. 2890–c. 2686 BC), ancient Egypt's trade with Byblos yielded a critical source of quality timber not found in Egypt. By the Fifth Dynasty (c. 2494–c. 2345 BC), trade with Punt provided gold, aromatic resins, ebony, ivory, and wild animals such as monkeys and baboons (Shaw 2002, p. 72). Punt as an ancient kingdom was located to the southeast of Egypt, most likely in the coastal region of what is today's Somalia, Djibouti, Eritrea, northeast

---

[5]Cited from Lanning (1967, p. 64).

[6]For example, the total number of the short and narrow valleys that are found to have hosted agricultural villages is as many as 78 (Lanning 1967, pp. 57–59).

Ethiopia, and the Red Sea coast of Sudan. Since the ancient Egyptians called the land of Punt as Pwenet or Pwene, its original name may be "Pwan" or "Puwa" or any other word derived from the common ancestral word "wa" and has the meaning of "god's land" or "great land."

Then, why did the ancient Egyptians so adored the land of Punt? Obviously, this had stemmed from the latter's relatively more abundant natural resources as compared with those of the Nile Valley. However, it is the scarcity of natural resources that incentivized the ancient Egyptians and other ancients to eventually advance their cultures and civilizations (we have discussed this in Chap. 4). In order to overcome the disadvantage of some key natural resources, Egypt had to rely on trade with Anatolia (today's eastern part of Turkey) for essential quantities of tin as well as supplementary supplies of copper, both metals being necessary for the manufacture of bronze. The ancient Egyptians prized the blue stone lapis lazuli, which had to be imported, though not directly, from far-away Afghanistan. Egypt's Mediterranean trade partners also included Greece and Crete, which provided, among other goods, supplies of olive oil. In exchange for its luxury imports and raw materials, Egypt mainly exported grain, gold, linen, and papyrus, in addition to other finished goods including glass and stone objects.[7]

Around 5,000 years ago, an important civilization developed on the Indus floodplain. From about 2600 to 1700 BC, a vast number of settlements were built on the banks of the Indus and the surrounding areas. Indus civilization remnants have been discovered from as far south as Mumbai in India and as far north as the Himalayas and northern Afghanistan. The westernmost sites are on the coast of the Arabian Sea in Baluchistan, Pakistan, right next to the Iranian border. In the valleys of the Indus and Ghaggar-Hakra rivers, in what is today Pakistan and western India, it developed around 2500 BC into the Harappan civilization on the northern Indian subcontinent.[8] The people of the Harappan civilization achieved great mastery in measuring length, mass, and time. Engineers already followed the decimal division of measurement. In the coastal city of the Harappa civilization, remarkable docks were built after studying the effects of tides, waves, and currents (Coppa et al. 2006).

As recorded in some ancient Mesopotamian texts, there were prominent trading partners of Sumer—Magan and Meluhha—in the neighborhood during the Middle Bronze Age. This trade was mainly conducted in the third millennium BC, with real financial sophistication in amounts that could be used to import copper as well as other commodities that were not available in Mesopotamia. The location of Magan (also Makkan) is not known with certainty, but archaeologists suggest that it was part of what are now Oman, a region of Yemen, the south of Upper Egypt, Nubia or the Sudan, and others as part of today's Iran or Pakistan (Lawton 1983). Meluhha (or Melukhkha) was treated by the ancient Mesopotamians as a land of exotic commodities. A wide variety of objects produced in the Indus Valley have been found at various sites in

---

[7] See, for example, Harris (1990, p. 13).

[8] This phase is earlier than the Third Dynasty of Ur (c. 2047–1940 BC) in Mesopotamian and the First Intermediate Period (c. 2181–2055 BC) of Egypt.

Mesopotamia.[9] In addition, the major excavations in the Harappa sites have shown that the Harappan civilization had gradually spread from west to east. This might have been the result of intercultural trade with Mesopotamia in which there was the first major human civilization in the world.

Thanks to their geographical proximity to Mesopotamia, the Nile and the Indus valleys have been able to receive direct cultural influences from Mesopotamia and vice versa. This might be the primary reason for the Nile and the Indus valleys and, of course, Mesopotamia to have civilizations that were all older than that of the lonely Yellow River Valley in the Far East.[10]

7.3 Civilizations Come from Earth's Axial Tilt

Certain phenomena recur at regular intervals, often referred to as cycles. There are solar and lunar cycles in weather, earthquakes, and volcanic eruptions. Other phenomena also show cycles that match lunar and solar cycles in biological, physical, and socioeconomic phenomena.

Yes, we are living in a world of countless cycles. Every day, when the Sun rises from the horizon, we get up for breakfast and then go to work, which means that Earth has just run for a complete circle, or 24 h. The Moon completes its orbit around Earth in approximately 27.322 days, which is called a sidereal month. And it has been found that Earth circles the Sun completely once every 365 days 6 h 9 min 9.5 s.

In general, agriculturally based people historically divide a year into various seasons (see Fig. 7.1). These usually depend on if the surface of Earth directly faces the Sun. Due to Earth's axial tilt, the amount of sunlight reaching any given point on the surface varies over the course of the year (see Fig. 7.2). This causes the seasonal change in climate, with summer in the Northern Hemisphere occurring when the Tropic of Cancer is facing the Sun and winter taking place when the Tropic of Capricorn in the Southern Hemisphere faces the Sun. During the summer, the day lasts longer, and the Sun climbs higher in the sky. In winter, the climate becomes cooler and the days shorter. The four seasons are determined by the solstices—the points in the orbit of maximum axial tilt toward or away from the Sun—and the equinoxes, when the direction of the tilt and the direction to the Sun are perpendicular. In the Northern Hemisphere, winter solstice currently occurs around December 21; summer solstice is near June 21, spring equinox is around March 20, and autumnal equinox is about September 23. In the Southern Hemisphere, the situation is reversed, with the summer and winter solstices exchanged and the spring and autumnal equinox dates swapped.

In ancient times, especially at the early stage of human civilizations, it had been a much difficult task for our ancestors to precisely monitor these various cycles. However, human beings at the agricultural society had a crying need to develop a

---

[9]Cited from www.harappa.com/har/indus-saraswati.html. Accessed 2016-10-1.

[10]See Table 7.1 for a comparison of the four ancient civilizations in the Eastern Hemisphere.

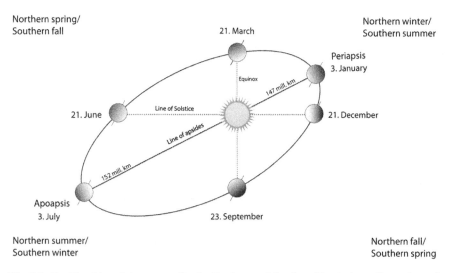

Northern spring/
Southern fall

21. March

Northern winter/
Southern summer

Periapsis
3. January

Equinox

147 mill. km

Line of Solstice

21. June

21. December

Line of apsides

152 mill. km

Apoapsis
3. July

23. September

Northern summer/
Southern winter

Northern fall/
Southern spring

Fig. 7.1 Earth's orbit and the seasons for the Northern and Southern Hemispheres *Source* https://commons.wikimedia.org/wiki/File:Seasons1.svg (under the Creative Commons Attribution-Share Alike 3.0 Unported license). *Note* The elliptical form is strongly exaggerated

precise calendar so as to have a better prediction of seasons and of seasons-related natural phenomena and disasters (including river flooding).

A calendar is a system of organizing days for social, religious, commercial, or administrative purposes. This is done by giving names to periods of time, typically days, weeks, months, and years. A date is the designation of a single, specific day within such a system. Periods in a calendar (such as years and months) are usually, though not necessarily, synchronized with the cycle of the Sun or the Moon. Many civilizations and societies have devised a calendar, usually derived from other calendars on which they model their systems, suited to their particular needs.

Except the "Long Count" and "Short Count" calendars used in the Mayan civilization, nearly all other calendar systems group consecutive days into "months" and also into "years." In a solar calendar, a year approximates Earth's tropical year (that is, the time it takes for a complete cycle of seasons), traditionally used to facilitate the planning of agricultural activities. In a lunar calendar, the month approximates the cycle of the Moon phase. Consecutive days may be grouped into other periods such as the week.

Because the number of days in the tropical year is not a whole number, a solar calendar must have a different number of days in different years. This may be handled, for example, by adding an extra day in leap years. The same applies to months in a lunar calendar and also the number of months in a year in a lunisolar calendar. This is generally known as intercalation. Even if a calendar is solar, but not lunar, the year cannot be divided entirely into months that never vary in length.

In the Western Hemisphere, the Mayan people adopted the so-called Long Count and Short Count calendars for their own. In ancient times, there was a tradition

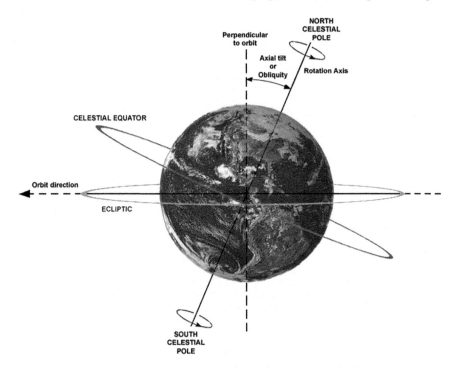

Fig. 7.2 Earth: Axial tilt, rotation axis, and celestial equator and ecliptic *Source* Made by Dna-webmaster based on the earth-image from NASA (under the Creative Commons Attribution-Share Alike 3.0 Unported license). *Note* Earth is shown as viewed from the Sun; and the orbit direction is counter-clockwise (to the left)

of practicing astronomy in Mesoamerica, studying the Moon, stars, and night sky movements. The Mayans prepared almanacs recording past and recent solar and lunar eclipses, the phases of the Moon, the periods of Venus and Mars, the movements of various other planets, and conjunctions of celestial bodies. These almanacs also made future predictions concerning celestial events. All of these are remarkably accurate, given the technology available, and indicate a significant level of knowledge among Mayan astronomers (Carmack et al. 2006, p. 55).

These seasons of the year were, and still are, important as they indicate seasonal changes that directly impact the lives of agriculturalists. However, the Mayan people did not closely observe and duly record the seasonal markers. For example, the "Long Count" calendar is not a cyclical, lunar- or solar-based, calendar. If it is defined as solar calendar, a tun, which includes 18 uinals, with each uinal including 20 days, equals only 360 days, which are still at least five years shorter than those of a year. This means that the calendar cannot be used for keeping track of the seasons.

Neither the "Short Count" calendar is accurate enough to be able to govern agricultural activities in Mesoamerica. The "Short Count" calendar, consisting of twenty 13-day months, is believed to be associated with religious holidays, as well as to mark the movements of celestial bodies and to be used for divination. The names given to the days, months, and years in the calendar came, for the most part, from animals, flowers, heavenly bodies, and cultural concepts that held symbolic significance in Mesoamerican culture. This calendar together with the "Long Count" calendar was used throughout the history of ancient Mesoamerica by nearly every culture.[11] However, the calendar cannot be used for the prediction of the agricultural seasons.

Due to the limited influences from any seasonable or cyclic natural disasters in Mesoamerica, the Mayan people used a "Long Count calendar." In the Eastern Hemisphere, since the earliest riverine civilizations were highly dependent on the cyclical changes of meteorological and other environmental conditions, we define them as "nonlinear civilizations." Research on cycles and cycle-like phenomena has never stopped since ancient times, and it has become the most dynamic part of nonlinear civilization. In general, the most significant research progress was achieved during two major periods. The first period started at the early stage of civilizations, in which human beings had a crying need to develop a calendar. The second period lasted from the late nineteenth century till the end of the Cold War, with the interwar period being the most productive years of research. In this stage, scientists set out to discover, understand, and explain the true nature and origin of cycles, to solve the mystery of recurrent rhythms observed in natural and the social sciences and to instruct others in the application of this new knowledge.

It has still not been clear why the Mayans used the *unusual* calendar systems that ignore seasonal changes. But it is reasonable to guess that the lunar/lunisolar calendar that may distinguish seasonable changes were not required in the Mayan society. In other words, there were much less serious climate changes in Mesoamerica than in other places where great civilizations were born (see, for example, Fig. 7.3).

It has been for a long history a challengeable but crucial task for people in the Eastern Hemisphere to produce a precise calendar by which to predict seasonable climates and natural disasters (mainly river flooding). According to the "Canon of Yao" (*yaodian*) in the "Book of History" (*Shujing*), ancient Chinese had a crying need for a more accurate calendar in order to divide seasons of a year as well as to predict floods. At the beginning of his reign, around 2200 BC, legendary Emperor Yao was supposed to have appointed four ministerial officials (two sets of two brothers) to make the necessary astronomical observations for a reformed calendar. Each of these individuals was sent to the limits of the royal territory, one in each of the cardinal directions, where they were supposed to observe certain stars at sunset on each of the solstices and equinoxes, so the results could then be compared, and the calendar accordingly adjusted.[12]

In ancient Mesopotamia, Sumerians had the first attempt to associate current events with certain positions of the planets and stars. The Babylonian astronomers were very adept at mathematics and could predict eclipses and

---

[11]Even today, several Maya groups in Guatemala, including the K'iche', Q'eqchi' and Kaqchikel, and the Mixe people of Oaxaca, continue using modernized forms of the Mesoamerican calendar.

[12]See Wu (1982, pp. 66–67 and 467) for a more detailed account.

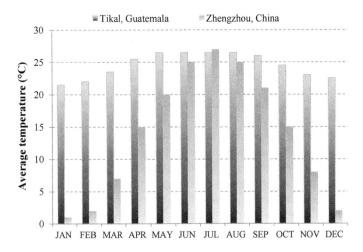

Fig. 7.3 Tikal (Guatemala) and Zhengzhou (China): Average monthly temperatures *Source* Created by author

solstices. Mesopotamian astronomers worked out a 12-month calendar based on the cycles of the Moon. They divided the year into two seasons: summer and winter. The origins of astronomy as well as astrology date from this time. During the eighth and seventh centuries BC, Babylonian astronomers developed a new approach to astronomy. They began studying philosophy dealing with the ideal nature of the early universe and began employing an internal logic within their predictive planetary systems. This was an important contribution to astronomy and the philosophy of science, and some scholars have thus referred to this new approach as the "first scientific revolution" (Brown 2000, p. 1). Babylonian astronomy served as the basis for much of Greek, classical Indian, Sassanian, Byzantine, Syrian, medieval Islamic, Central Asian, and Western European astronomy (Pingree 1998, pp. 125–137).

At ancient times, the lunar calendar, which is one in which days are numbered within each lunar phase cycle, was widely applied. Because the length of the lunar month is not an even fraction of the length of the tropical year, a purely lunar calendar quickly drifts against the seasons, which do not vary much near the equator.[13] Most calendars referred to as "lunar" calendars are in fact lunisolar calendars. That is, months reflect the lunar cycle, but then intercalary months (e.g. "second Adar" in the Hebrew calendar) are added to bring the calendar year into synchronization with the solar year. Some examples are the Chinese and Hindu calendars. In some lunisolar calendars, such as the Chinese calendar, the first day of a month is the day when an astronomical new moon occurs in a particular time zone. In others, such as some Hindu calendars, each month begins on the day after the full moon or the new moon.

---

[13]It does, however, stay constant with respect to other phenomena, notably tides, which are vital to people living in coastal areas.

Others were based in the past on the first sighting of a lunar crescent, such as the Hebrew calendar.

Widely applied by agriculturalists in China and some of its neighboring countries, the "24 Solar Periods" is a Chinese traditional calendar that divides the climate of a whole year into twenty-four periods in order to govern agricultural arrangements. It is applied in parallel with the Chinese lunisolar calendar. During the Shang dynasty (c. 1700–1046 BC), only four periods (i.e., spring, summer, autumn, and winter) were used, and the Zhou dynasty (1046 BC–221 BC) used eight periods, but it was not until the Western Han dynasty (206 BC–AD 24) that the 24 terms were finally decided upon, as the following:

- 1st Period: Spring Begins (licun), usually on February 3, 4, or 5
- 2nd Period: Rain Water (yushui), usually on February 18, 19 or 20
- 3rd Period: Insects Awaken (jingzhe), usually on March 5, 6, or 7
- 4th Period: Vernal Equinox (cunfen), usually on March 20, 21 or 22
- 5th Period: Pure Brightness (qingming), usually on April 4, 5 or 6
- 6th Period: Grain Rain (guyu), usually on April 19, 20 or 21
- 7th Period: Summer Begins (lixia), usually on May 5, 6 or 7
- 8th Period: Grain Buds (xiaoman), usually on May 20, 21 or 22
- 9th Period: Grain in Beard (mangzhong), usually on June 5, 6 or 7
- 10th Period: Summer Solstice (xiazhi), usually on June 21 or 22
- 11th Period: Lesser Heat (xiaoshu), usually on July 6, 7 or 8
- 12th Period: Greater Heat (dashu), usually on July 22, 23 or 24
- 13th Period: Autumn Begins (liqiu), usually on August 7, 8 or 9
- 14th Period: End of Heat (chushu), usually on August 22, 23 or 24
- 15th Period: White Dews (bailu), usually on September 7, 8 or 9
- 16th Period: Autumn Equinox (qiufen), usually on September 22, 23 or 24
- 17th Period: Cold Dews (hanlu), usually on October 8 or 9
- 18th Period: Frost's Descent (shuangjiang), usually on October 23 or 24
- 19th Period: Winter Begins (lidong), usually on November 7 or 8
- 20th Period: Light Snow (xiaoxue), usually on November 22 or 23
- 21th Period: Greater Snow (daxue), usually on December 6, 7 or 8
- 22th Period: Winter Solstice (dongzhi), usually on December 21, 22 or 23
- 23th Period: Lesser Cold (xiaohan), usually on January 5, 6 or 7
- 24th Period: Greater Cold (dahan), usually on January 20 or 21

These 24 solar periods each suggest the position of the Sun every time it travels 15 degrees on the ecliptic longitude. In each month, there are two solar terms. Their dates are mirrored by the Gregorian calendar. These solar terms have meaningful titles. Some of them reflect the change of seasons such as the "Spring Begins," "Summer Begins," "Autumn Begins," and "Winter Begins"; some embody the specific phenomena of climate like "Insects Awaken" (jingzhe), "Pure Brightness" (qingming), "Grain Buds" (xiaoman) and "Grain in Beard" (mangzhong); and some indicate the changes of climate like "Rain Water" (yushui), "Grain Rain" (guyu), "Lesser Heat" (xiaoshu), "Greater Heat" (dashu), and so on.

The approximation of 365¼ days for the tropical year had been known for a long time but was not used directly since ancient calendars were not solar. However, the Egyptian calendar and Iranian calendar are two exceptions. The Julian calendar, introduced by Julius Caesar in 46 BC, was a reform of the Roman calendar. It took effect in 45 BC, shortly after the Roman conquest of Egypt. It was the predominant calendar in most of Europe, and in European settlements in the Americas and elsewhere, until it was refined and superseded by the Gregorian calendar (Urban and Seidelmann 2012, p. 595). However, there is still a 0.002% difference in the average length of the year between Julian (365.25 days) and a solar year (365.2425 days). This discrepancy was corrected by the reform conducted in 1582 under the instruction of Pope Gregory XIII.

Calendars in widespread use today include the Gregorian calendar, which is the de facto international standard, and is used almost everywhere in the world for civil purposes. The Gregorian calendar improves the approximation made by the Julian calendar by skipping three Julian leap days in every 400 years, giving an average year of 365.2425 mean solar days long. This approximation has an error of about one day per 3,300 years with respect to the mean tropical year. However, because of the precession of the equinoxes, the error with respect to the vernal equinox (which occurs, on average, 365.24237 days apart near 2000) is 1 day every 7,700 years. By any criterion, the Gregorian calendar is substantially more accurate than the 1 day in 128 years error of the Julian calendar (average year 365.25 days).[14]

Human research on cycles and cycle-like phenomena has lasted for a long period of time since the beginning of civilizations. But most of the interests were the creation of a precise calendar, in addition to a few of natural and astronomic phenomena. Unfortunately, due to the lack of the knowledge of natural sciences and of advanced techniques and devises, the early research did not produce significant achievements. Thanks to the Renaissance, the Protestant Reformation, the Enlightenment, and the Industrial Revolution from the fifteenth to the early nineteenth century, the cycles research entered the most productive stage from the late nineteenth century onwards.

William Stanley Jevons (1835–1882), a British economist, was the first person to recognize the phenomenon of business cycles. As the President for the British Association for the Advancement of Science in 1870 and a professor of logic and philosophy, Jevons wrote extensively on economic theory. He suggested in the 1870s that there is a relationship between sunspots and business cycle crises. He stipulated an 11-year cycle resembling the sunspot activity. Jevons also reasoned that sunspots affect Earth's weather, which, in turn, influences crops and, therefore, the economy as a whole (Garcia-Mata and Shaffner 1934).

Clément Juglar (1819–1905), a French doctor and statistician, was the first to develop an economic theory of business cycles. He identified the 7–11 year fixed investment cycle that is now associated with his name. Within the Juglar cycle, one can observe oscillations of investments into fixed capital and not just changes in the

---

[14]See Meeus and Savoie (1992) and Urban and Seidelmann (2012, p. 595).

level of employment of the fixed capital (and respective changes in inventories), as is observed with respect to Kitchin cycles.[15]

In economics, the term pork cycle, hog cycle, or cattle cycle is used to describe the phenomenon of cyclical fluctuations of supply and prices in livestock markets. It was first observed by Mordecai Ezekiel (1899–1974) in 1925 in pig markets in the USA and by the German scholar Arthur Hanau (1902–1985) in Europe in 1927.[16] After having analyzed American and British interest rates and other data, Joseph Kitchin (1861–1932), a British businessman and statistician, found evidence for a short business cycle of about 40 months (Kitchin 1923).

The Kitchin cycle is believed to be accounted for by time lags in information movements affecting the decision making of commercial firms. Firms react to the improvement of commercial situation through the increase in output through the full employment of the extent fixed capital assets. As a result, within a certain period of time (ranging between a few months and two years), the market gets "flooded" with commodities whose quantity becomes gradually excessive. The demand declines, prices drop, the produced commodities get accumulated in inventories, which informs entrepreneurs of the necessity to reduce output. However, this process takes some time. It takes some time for the information that the supply exceeds significantly the demand to get to the businessmen. Further, it takes entrepreneurs some time to check this information and to make the decision to reduce production, and some time is also necessary to materialize this decision (these are the time lags that generate the Kitchin cycles).

Later, Nicholas Kaldor (1908–1986), a Cambridge economist, proposed a model of fluctuations in agricultural markets. The model is based on a time lag between supply and demand decisions. Agricultural markets are a context where the model might apply, since there is a lag between planting and harvesting. Kaldor (1934) gives two agricultural examples: rubber and corn. Suppose, for example, that as a result of unexpectedly bad weather, farmers go to market with an unusually small crop of strawberries. This shortage results in high prices. If farmers expect these high price conditions to continue, then in the following year, they will raise their production of strawberries relative to other crops. Therefore, when they go to market, the supply will be high, resulting in low prices. If they then expect low prices to continue, they will decrease their production of strawberries for the next year, resulting in high prices again. This procedure repeats itself cyclically.

The Kuznets swing is a claimed medium-range economic wave identified in 1930 by Simon Kuznets (1901–1985). Kuznets connected various business waves with demographic processes, in particular with immigrant inflows/outflows and the changes in construction intensity that they caused, that is why he denoted them as "demographic" or "building" cycles/swings. Kuznets swings have been also inter-

---

[15]Employing spectral analysis Korotayev and Tsirel (2010) confirmed the presence of the Juglar cycles in world GDP dynamics.

[16]See, for example, Rosen et al. (1994).

preted as infrastructural investment cycles.[17] The first major research project in which Kuznets was involved was the study of long series of economic dynamics in the USA undertaken in the mid-1920s. The collected data covered the period from 1865 to 1925, and for some indices achieved 1770. Applying for the analysis of time series, Kuznets identified medium-term extended cycles of economic activity, which lasted 15–25 years and had an intermediate position between the Kondratiev "long waves" and short business cycles. Aspiring to determine the nature of these cycles, Kuznets analyzed the dynamics of population, the construction industry performance, capital, national income data, and other variables. These movements became known among economists and economic historians as the "Kuznets Cycles," and alternatively as "long swings" in the economy's growth rate (Abramovitz 1961).

In economics, Kondratiev waves (also called supercycles, great surges, long waves, K-waves, or the long economic cycle) are supposedly cycle-like phenomena in the modern world economy. It is claimed that the period of the wave ranges from forty to sixty years, and the cycles consist of alternating intervals between high sectoral growth and intervals of relatively slow growth (Korotayev and Tsirel 2010). The Soviet economist Nikolai Kondratiev (1892–1938), also written as Kondratieff, was the first to bring these observations to international attention in his 1925 book *The Major Economic Cycles* (in Russian).[18] Kondratiev identified three phases in each cycle: expansion, stagnation, recession. Writing in the 1920s, Kondratiev proposed to apply the theory to the nineteenth century: 1790–1849 with a turning point in 1815; and 1850–1896 with a turning point in 1873. Kondratiev further supposed that, in 1896, a new cycle had started. Unfortunately, Kondratiev's ideas were not supported by the Soviet government. Subsequently, he was sent to the gulag and was executed in 1938.

Since the inception of Kondratiev's theory, various studies have expanded the range of possible cycles, finding longer or shorter cycles in the data. In 1939, Joseph Schumpeter (1883–1950), the Austrian-born economist who moved to America, published a two-volume work, "Business Cycles: A Theoretical, Historical and Statistical Analysis of the Capitalist Process." In this work, he argued that long waves stemmed from innovation. A modern example could be "Just in Time" which appears to have first been used in the car industry before spreading throughout manufacturing. Schumpeter constructed a model in which the four main cycles, Kondratiev (54 years), Kuznets (18 years), Juglar (9 years), and Kitchin (4 years) can be added together to form a composite waveform.[19] One of the most influential thinkers to argue that long cycles are caused by innovation, Schumpeter brought Kondratiev's ideas to the attention of English-speaking economists. In Schumpeter's view, technological innovation is at the cause of both cyclical instability and economic growth. Fluctuations in innovation cause fluctuation in investment and those cause cycles in

---

[17]See, for example, Kuznets (1930), Forrester (1977, pp. 107–121), and Korotayev and Tsirel (2010).

[18]The English version of this book, titled *Long Wave Cycle*, was published in 1984 (Kondratieff 1984).

[19]See Schumpeter (2005) and Keklik (2003).

economic growth. Schumpeter sees innovations as clustering around certain points in time periods that he refers to as "neighborhoods of equilibrium," when entrepreneurs perceive that risk and return warrant innovative commitments. These clusters lead to long cycles by generating periods of acceleration in aggregate growth.[20]

In the early 1970s, and based on System Dynamics—a technique based on conceptions in control theory, organization theory, and on the available techniques of computer simulation—developed by Jay W. Forrester, an MIT research team constructed a computer model to simulate likely future outcomes of the world economy. The most prominent feature of system dynamics is the use of feedback loops to explain behavior. It is a unique tool for dealing with questions about the way in which complex systems behave over time. The standard model run assumes no major change in the physical, economic, or social relationships that have historically governed the development of the world system. All variables included in the model follow historical values from 1900 to 1970. One end result of this ambitious study was originally published in 1972 under the title *The Limits to Growth* (Meadows et al. 1972), which was subsequently updated and revised in 1992 and 2004, respectively (Meadows et al. 1992; 2004). Three main conclusions were reached by this study. The first suggests that within a time span of less than 100 years, society will run out of the non-renewable resources on which the world's industrial base depends. Thus, according to this study, growth will eventually cease, one way or another. Still, the authors conclude that it is possible to avoid the collapse if we make the right choices now.

Modern social scientists from different fields have introduced cycle theories to predict cyclical patterns of civilizations. For example, Tainter (1988) suggests a civilizational life cycle, and, in more micro-studies that follow the work of Malthus, Lempert (1987 and 1996) presents models of population, economics, and political response, including violence, in cyclical forms. Unlike the short-term business cycle, the mechanism of long-wave process is very complicated, and, thus, long-wave theory has not accepted by many mainstream economists. Regardless of this, there was still considerable progress in numerous investigations of the relationship between technological innovation and economic cycles.[21]

Because people have fairly typical spending patterns through their life cycle, such as schooling, marriage, first car purchase, first home purchase, upgrade home purchase, maximum earnings period, maximum retirement savings and retirement, demographic anomalies such as baby booms and busts exert a rather predictable influence on the economy over a long time period (Tylecote 1991, pp. 7–35). Debt deflation is a theory of economic cycles, which holds that recessions and depressions are due to the overall level of debt shrinking (deflating): The credit cycle is the cause of the economic cycle.[22]

---

[20] See Rosenberg (1994, pp. 62–84).

[21] Some of the works involving long cycle research and technology include Marchetti (1986), Ayres (1989), and Tylecote (1991).

[22] This theory was developed by Irving Fisher following the Wall Street Crash of 1929 and the ensuing Great Depression. See, for example, Minsky (1992) and Keen (1995).

The technological view of change needs to demonstrate that changes in the rate of innovation govern changes in the rate of new investments and that the combined impact of innovation clusters takes the form of fluctuation in aggregate output or employment. The process of technological innovation involves extremely complex relations among a set of key variables: inventions, innovations, diffusion paths, and investment activities. The impact of technological innovation on aggregate output is mediated through a succession of relationships that have yet to be explored systematically in the context of long wave. New inventions are typically primitive, their performance is usually poorer than existing technologies, and the cost of their production is high. A production technology may not yet exist, as is often the case in major chemical inventions, pharmaceutical inventions. The speed with which inventions are transformed into innovations and diffused depends on actual and expected trajectory of performance improvement and cost reduction.[23]

7.4   In Cycles Civilizations Only Exist

The end of the Cold War saw a period of silence in the circle of cycles research. The 2008–09 Financial Crisis has increased an interest in the theories of long economic cycles as a potential explanation of its cause. For example, Korotayev and Tsirel (2010) employ spectral analysis and claim that it confirmed the presence of Kondratiev waves in the world GDP dynamics at an acceptable level of statistical significance.[24] They also detect shorter business cycles, dating the Kuznets to about 17 years and calling it the third harmonic of the Kondratiev, meaning that there are three Kuznets cycles per Kondratiev.

Might the financial crisis be the result of the coming end of the "wave of the information and telecommunications technological revolution"? Some authors have started to predict what the sixth wave might be. In 2010, for example, James Bradfield Moody and Bianca Nogrady even forecasted that the new wave will be driven by resource efficiency and clean technology (Moody and Nogrady 2010).

In 2011, a specific modification of the theory of Kondratieff cycles was developed by Daniel Šmihula who identified six long waves within modern society and the capitalist economy, each of which is described as a specific technological revolution and an application phase in which the number of revolutionary innovations falls and attention focuses on exploiting and extending existing innovations (Šmihula 2011). As soon as an innovation or a series of innovations become available, it becomes more efficient to invest in its adoption, extension, and use than in creating new innovations. Every wave of innovations lasts approximately until the profits from the new innovation or sector fall to the level of other, older, more traditional sectors. It is

---

[23] See Mansfield (1983).

[24] Spectral analysis is a technique that is used in the fields of electrical engineering for analyzing electrical circuits and radio waves to deconstruct a complex signal to determine the main frequencies and their relative contribution.

a situation when the new technology, which originally increased a capacity to utilize new sources from nature, reached its limits, and it is not possible to overcome this limit without an application of another new technology.

In fact, a new (or the third) wave of cycles research began even earlier. At the beginning of the twenty-first century, there was already considerable progress in historical economics and the history of technology, and numerous investigations of the relationship between technological innovation and economic cycles. In 2001 and 2002, for example, physicist and systems scientist Tessaleno C. Devezas and James T. Corredine advanced a causal model for the long-wave phenomenon based on a generation-learning model (Devezas and Corredine 2001) and a nonlinear dynamic behavior of information systems (Devezas and Corredine 2002). In their works, a complete theory is presented, which contain not only the explanation for the existence of a K-Wave but also, for the first time, the calculation for the width of the K-Wave (i.e., about 60 years or two generations).[25]

More recently, contributions to the development of the mathematical models of long-term socio-demographic cycles have been made. What is the most important is that Nefedov (2003 and 2004), Turchin (2003), Turchin and Korotayev (2006), and Korotayev et al. (2006) have managed to demonstrate that socio-demographic cycles were a basic feature of complex agrarian systems in ancient world. It has become possible to model these dynamics mathematically in a rather effective way. The basic logic of these models is as follows:

- After the population reaches the limit of the carrying capacity of land, the system began to experience the decline in the living standards of the common population, increasing the severity of famines, growing rebellions, etc.
- Most complex agrarian systems had considerable reserves for a period of stability; however, these reserves were usually exhausted later on, and, after that, the system began to experience a demographic collapse, when increasingly severe famines or internal warfare (or any other disasters) led to a considerable decline of population.
- As a result of this collapse, more resources became available, per capita production and consumption considerably increased, the population growth resumed, and a new socio-demographic cycle started.

Yes, demand decides supply. This is also the key to understanding the nonlinear behaviors of civilizations. In history, whenever similar crises and challenges occurred, there was a need for research on cycles—who were willing to *waste* a large amount of financial and human resources for an event that would not happen again? The contribution of cycles research to human civilizations has already been witnessed by our ancestors' early efforts on the creation of a precise calendar as well as by the dramatic academic achievements on cycles research during the interwar period.

The research on socioeconomic cycles still is a challengeable task—they are even more complicated than those natural and astronomical cycles. Like all other cultural

---

[25]Other, similar research includes Freeman and Louçã (2001) and Perez (2002). Perez (2002) places the phases on a logistic or *S* curve, with the following labels: beginning of a technological era as irruption, the ascent as frenzy, the rapid build out as synergy, and the completion as maturity.

phenomena, the cycles research also conforms to the "response-to-challenge" rule. However, as witnessed by the past experiences, successful civilizations have always been nonlinear or those that have paid enough attention to cycles and cycle-like phenomena.

Indeed, there is no end of the cycle of cycles research; this is also part of the nonlinearity of civilizations. Therefore, let us be prepared and promote more research on cycles before it is too late to take any actions.

7.5   Model: Mathematical Description of a Civilization

To explain the mechanism of civilizations, let us borrow Boserup's "demand determines supply" theory (see Sect. 4.1 in Chap. 4) and have the following conditions under which the human and Earth systems interact:

1. That the physical and mental capacities of a human population are negatively correlated.
2. That favorable environmental and external factors may become disincentives (whereas unfavorable environmental and external factors may become incentives) for humans to advance cultural developments.
3. That no civilization will be born, and existing civilization will stagnate in areas where the sum of physical and mental capacities of the human population exceeds the maximum level of challenges they face.
4. That it is cyclical natural disasters (or, more precisely, seasonable river floods)—not other natural factors or disasters—that gave birth to the earliest great civilizations.

Condition 3 may not precisely exist in the modern world (since human and cultural behaviors have been more complicated than they were in the prehistoric world). Sometimes, modern humans use their expectations of (non-existing) challenges as incentives for their dynamic behaviors.[26] However, when regarding the prehistoric era and, in most circumstances, the modern world, the following law exists: Physically stronger people have fewer incentives to create cultural complexity by which to survive, so do intelligently stronger people. They each have already been able to cope with various challenges. Only those who cannot *individually* overcome various challenges they face have incentives to *jointly* create cultures and civilizations. To summarize them, let us use the following model to illustrate the human and environmental conditions under which a new civilization emerges or an existing civilization keeps growing:

$$\begin{cases} W \sum f(p, m) + F(\Sigma p, \Sigma m) \\ m = g(p, c), \text{ with } \partial m / \partial p < 0 \text{ and } \partial m / \partial c > 0 \text{ (for all people)} \\ p + m < c \text{ (for the majority of people)} \end{cases}$$

---

[26]This is a topic that needs to be further discussed in a greater detail.

where W is the size or level of a civilization; p and m denote the physical and mental capacities (or outputs), respectively, of an individual people; c represents the level of challenge faced by the individual people; and ∂ is the sign of partial differential. Obviously, if the average level of human capacity exceeds that of challenge (as denoted by $p + m > c$)—either physically (as denoted by $p > c - m$) or mentally (as denoted by $m > c - p$)—for the majority of people in a society, then a new civilization will not emerge, or the existing civilization will begin to recede in there.

References

Abramovitz M (1961) The nature and significance of Kuznets cycles. Econ Dev Cult Change 6(3): 225–48

APWH (2017) AP world history: course and exam description effective fall 2017. Advanced Placement World History (APWH), Princeton, NJ

Ayres R (1989) Technological transformations and long waves. http://www.iiasa.ac.at/Admin/PUB/Documents/RR-89-001.pdf. Accessed 05 Jan 2015

Brown D (2000) Mesopotamian planetary astronomy-astrology ('Cuneiform Monographs' series, vol. 18). Leiden, Brill

Carmack RM, Gasco JL, Gossen GH (2006) The legacy of mesoamerica: history and culture of a Native American Civilization, 2nd edn. Prentice Hall, Upper Saddle River, NJ

Coppa A, Bondioli L, Cucina A, Frayer DW, Jarrige C (2006) Early neolithic tradition of dentistry: flint tips were surprisingly effective for drilling tooth enamel in a prehistoric population. Nature 440:755–756

Devezas Tessaleno C, Corredine James T (2001) The biological determinants of long-wave behavior in socioeconomic growth and development. Technol Forecast Soc Chang Int J 68(1):1–57

Devezas Tessaleno C, Corredine James T (2002) The nonlinear dynamics of technoeconomic systems—An informational interpretation. Technol Forecast Soc Chang Int J 69(4):317–357

Forrester JW (1977) New perspectives on economic growth. In: Meadows DL (ed) Alternatives to growth I—a search for sustainable futures. Ballinger, Cambridge, MA, pp 107–121

Freeman Chris, Louçã Francisco (2001) As time goes by: from the industrial revolutions to the information revolution. Oxford University Press, Oxford

Garcia-Mata C, Shaffner FI (1934) Solar and economic relationships: a preliminary report. Q J Econ 49(1):1–51

Guo R (2018) Civilizations revisited: the historians may be wrong, really. University Press, Hong Kong

Haas J, Creamer W, Ruiz A (2004) Dating the late archaic occupation of the Norte Chico region in Peru. Nature 432(7020):1020–1023

Harris James R (1990) The facsimiles of the book of Abraham, a study of the Joseph Smith Egyptian Papyri. Harris House Publishing, New York

Nicholas K (1934) A classificatory note on the determination of equilibrium. Rev Econ Stud 1:122–136

Keen Steve (1995) Finance and economic breakdown: modeling minsky's financial instability hypothesis. J Post Keynesian Econ 17(4):607–635

Keklik M (2003) Schumpeter, innovation and growth: long-cycle dynamics in the post-WWII american manufacturing industries ("Alternative Voices in Contemporary Economics" series). Ashgate Pub Ltd, London

Kitchin J (1923) Cycles and trends in economic factors. Rev Econ Stat 5(1):10–16

Kolars, JF and Mitchell W (1991) The Euphrates River and the Southeast Anatolia Development Project. Southern Illinois University Press, Carbondale and Edwardsville, Illinois

Kondratieff N (1984) Long wave cycle. In: Guy D (Trans) E. P. Dutton, Boston, MA

Korotayev AV, Tsirel SV (2010) A spectral analysis of world GDP dynamics: Kondratieff waves, Kuznets swings, Juglar and Kitchin cycles in global economic development, and the 2008–2009 economic crisis. Struct Dynam 4(1):3–57

Korotayev Andrey, Malkov Artemy, Khaltourina Daria (2006) Introduction to social macrodynamics: secular cycles and millennial trends. URSS, Moscow

Kuznets Simon (1930) Secular movements in production and prices: their nature and their bearing upon cyclical fluctuations. Houghton Mifflin, Boston

Lanning Edward P (1967) Peru before the Incas. Prentice-Hall, Englewood Cliffs, NJ

Lempert David H (1987) A demographic-economic explanation of political stability: Mauritius as a microcosm. East Afr Econ Rev 3(1):77–90

Lempert DH (1996) Daily life in a crumbling empire (Eastern European Monographs, Book 444). Columbia University Press, New York

Li H, Ying H, Mustavich LF, Zhang F, Tan JZ, Wang LE, Qian J, Gao MH, Jin L (2007) Y chromosomes of prehistoric people along the Yangtze river. Human Genet 122:383–8

Lawton J (1983) Oman - The lost land. Saudi Aramco World, (May/June 1983), 35: 18–19

Mansfield, Edwin (1983). Long waves and technological innovation. Am Econ Rev 73(2) (Papers and Proceedings of the Ninety-Fifth Annual Meeting of the American Economic Association, May), 141–145

Marchetti Cesare (1986) Fifty-year pulsation in human affairs, analysis of some physical indicators. Futures 17(3):376–388

Meadows D, Meadows DL, Randers J (1972) Limits to growth: a report of the club of rome's project on the predicament of mankind. The Club of Rome, Rome

Meadows D, Meadows DL, Randers Jorgen (1992) Beyond the limits: confronting global collapse, envisioning a sustainable future. Chelsea Green Publishing Company, White River Junction, VT

Meadows D, Randers Jorgen, Meadows Dennis L (2004) Limits to Growth: The 30-Year Update, 3rd edn. Chelsea Green Publishing Company, White River Junction, VT

Meeus J, Savoie D (1992) The history of the tropical year. J Br Astron Assoc 102(1):40–42

Minsky H (1992) The financial instability hypothesis. Jerome Levy Economics Institute Working Paper No. 74. Social Science Research Network (SSRN) 161024

Moody JB, Nogrady B (2010) The sixth wave: how to succeed in a resource-limited world. Random House, Sydney

Nefedov SA (2003) A theory of demographic cycles and the social evolution of ancient and medieval oriental societies. Oriens 3:5–22

Nefedov Sergey A (2004) A model of demographic cycles in traditional societies: the case of ancient China. Social Evol Hist 3(1):69–80

Perez Carlota (2002) Technological revolutions and financial capital: the dynamics of bubbles and golden ages. Edward Elgar Publishing, Cheltenham, UK

Pingree David (1998) Legacies in astronomy and celestial omens. In: Dalley Stephanie (ed) The legacy of mesopotamia. Oxford University Press, Oxford, pp 125–137

Rosen S, Murphy K, Scheinkman J (1994) Cattle cycles. J Polit Econ 102(3):468–492

Rosenberg N (1994) Exploring the black box: technology, economics, and history. Cambridge University Press, Cambridge

Schumpeter JA (2005 [1939]). Business cycles: a theoretical, historical, and statistical analysis of the capitalist process (A 2-vol set). Martino Publishing, Eastford, CT

Shady RM, Haas J, Creamer W (2001) Dating Caral, a Preceramic site in the Supe valley on the central coast of Peru. Science 292 (5517, 27):723–726

Shaw I (2002) The oxford history of ancient Egypt. Oxford University Press, Oxford

Šmihula D (2011) Long waves of technological innovations. Studia politica Slovaca (Bratislava) (2):50–69

Squier EG (2012) Ancient monuments of the mississippi valley. Gale Sabin Americana, Farmington Hills, Michigan

Tainter JA (1988) The collapse of complex civilizations (new studies in archaeology). Cambridge University Press, Cambridge

Turchin P (2003) Historical dynamics: why states rise and fall (Princeton Studies in Complexity). Princeton University Press, Princeton, NJ

Turchin P, Korotayev A (2006) Population Dynamics and Internal Warfare: A Reconsideration. Social Evol Hist 5(2):112–147

Tylecote Andrew (1991) The long wave in the world economy. Routledge, London

Urban SE, Kenneth Seidelman P (2012) (eds) Explanatory supplement to the astronomical almanac (3rd ed). University Science Books, Mill Valley, CA

Wu KC (1982) The Chinese heritage. Crown Publishers, New York

Yan W (2005) The beginning of farming. In: Kwang-Chih C, Pingfang X, Sarah A, Liancheng L (eds) The formation of chinese civilization: an archaeological perspective. Yale University Press, New Heaven, MA, pp 27–42

Epilogue

My childhood was spent in central China's Henan (meaning "south of the river" in Chinese) Province; more precisely, my hometown is only a few miles away from the Yellow River. In history, Henan was a place that suffered frequent floods resulting from the unruly Yellow River. I still remember that during my childhood, my mother repeatedly told me the tragic stories about how her prosperous family was suffering the deadly flood of the Yellow River in 1938, in which her father and two sisters were killed; and that, thereafter, the remaining family members, including herself, became homeless.

I was very weak when I was born; even unluckier was that I had a serious illness when I was two years old. The village doctor, having not diagnosed any vital signs of mine, suggested that my mother should immediately move my body outside the door—a traditional habit that had adopted for many years in rural China. Upon hearing this news, all my siblings cried. And my mother, who was reluctant to follow the doctor's instruction, held me within her arms during the whole day and night, waiting for a miracle to occur…

I have a big family. My mother gave birth to nine children (including two daughters in the late 1940s—all died before the age of ten, three daughters and one son in the 1950s, and two sons and one daughter in the 1960s). Given the difficult situations during the 1950s and 1960s, it was not easy to keep every child alive in China, especially in some poor, rural areas. Of course, I was the lucky child—I eventually survived from that deadly disease. Even luckier was that, from the early 1970s to the 1980s, I smoothly completed all school educations in China—though some of which might not be of the world class.

Different from the Anglo-Saxon culture, Chinese society adheres to collectivism. For example, there is a Chinese character "zan," usually meaning "the two of us." It is used to include both the speaker and the person to whom she or he spoke (but excluding those who is (are) treated as a third partner). In my family, when referring to each other's real properties or other valuable belongings, it was very seldom to use the terms "yours" and "mine"; instead, the term "zan de" (meaning "the one of both of us") was more commonly applied. This kind of phenomenon reflected to

© Springer Nature Singapore Pte Ltd. 2019
R. Guo, *Human-Earth System Dynamics*,
https://doi.org/10.1007/978-981-13-0547-4

some extent close interpersonal relations, which can also be found in many other Chinese families, especially in rural areas.

One day, in Summer 2003, I was called by my younger brother from my hometown to participate in a family meeting. The subject under discussion was to persuade my elder brother to change his decision concerning the construction of a luxurious apartment in downtown Zhengzhou—capital of Henan Province. At that time, my brothers ran a real-estate firm—it had long been treated as the most money-making venture in China. However, my elder brother hired a Feng-Shui expert as the adviser to his company and, as a result, the underground sewer system of the 11-floor apartment was unusually designed to run through all corners of the building. According to this adviser, or, more precisely, according to the Feng-Shui situation as he had monitored, there was a lack of waters in the land near the building and that the special design could overcome that weakness.

Feng Shui (two Chinese characters in Pinyin, meaning "wind" and "water," respectively) is an ancient Chinese metaphysics of keeping a balance of forces in the land or surroundings. Historically, Feng Shui was widely used to orient buildings—often spiritually significant structures such as dwellings, tombs—in an auspicious manner. Depending on the particular style of Feng Shui being used, an auspicious site could be determined by reference to local features such as bodies of water, stars, or a compass. In Feng Shui, the land is regarded as living and as reflecting the pattern of heaven, and any development must be in harmony with this pattern. But the overuse of the Feng-Shui concept may not be helpful. With regard to the design of the long-winded underground sewer system, not only it was meaningless, but it could even become a heavy burden to the daily operations and management of that apartment.

I failed to persuade my elder brother to change his mind—actually, for a long time nobody in our family could have challenged him. During his childhood, my parents had had as many as five daughters but only one son. According to traditional Chinese culture, men are treated as superior to women. As a result, my elder brother had been pampered during his childhood. And this had naturally become a special culture in our family. (I still remember that in the late 1960s, my mother had to prepare different meals for us, and my elder brother always picked up the most delicious one.) However, his strong sense of superiority, together with his early success of business career, had resulted in a strange style of thinking and doing things. His real-estate firm eventually went bankrupt several years later. By way of contrast, my younger brother, who was believed to be of inferiority in terms of intellect and ability during his childhood, has been much more successful in doing business (at least being so when this draft was in preparation).

On my way back to Beijing, I was thinking about why the above ridiculous things could have happened in my family. Only when the train ran cross the Yellow River, did I suddenly realize that my hometown is so near to the river. I began to recall my daily lives in my childhood: They were closely related to rivers and waters. However, the proximity to the Yellow River has had mixed effects. On the one hand, it helped by bringing freshwater and soils with rich nutrients to sustain food production; on the other hand, however, it could generate terrific floods and result in disasters for all riverine people concerned. For instance, before 1938, my mother had had a wealthy family; after the deadly Yellow River flood, her family immediately became homeless. In the course of the past thousands of years, haven't numerous Chinese families, even the Chinese nation as a whole, been influenced— both positively and negatively—by the hydraulic complexity of the Yellow River?

Hydraulically, when water flows through a river with uneven topographies, it will make a curve movement by which to produce a centrifugal force. Under the influence of the force, the flow of surface water tends to be meandering in a concave bank, and at the bottom of the river, water under pressure will flow from the concave course to a convex one, thus forming a bend circulation. Influenced by the bend circulation, deposition occurs on the convex bank. In contrast, both lateral erosion and undercutting occur on the cut bank or concave bank (i.e., the bank with the greatest centrifugal force). Continuous deposition on the convex bank and erosion of the concave bank of a meandering river cause the formation of a very pronounced meander with two concave banks getting closer. The narrow neck of land between the two neighboring concave banks is finally cut through, either by lateral erosion of the two concave banks or by the strong currents of a flood. When this happens, a new straighter river channel is formed. This process can occur over a timescale from a few years to several decades. As a result, the location of the area encompassing the convex bank has now been reversed from one side of the river to the opposite side of it.

Of course, the river course now looks straighter than the old one. But as long as the topography is uneven, the new river as a whole still is a curved one and thus the regular of or cyclical changes of its course are inevitable later on. In some places, especially in a low-lying plain where the river banks are easy to be eroded, the above-mentioned changes of watercourses could have become disasters to the riverine people living there. At least since the last glacial episode, the frequent changes of many, if not all, of the world's river courses have been decided by this mechanism, which have also influenced the evolution and development of civilizations during the past thousands of years or so. For example, a popular Chinese proverb says that "Thirty years on the east, and thirty years in the west of the river" (30 nian hedong, 30 nian hexi). Its extended meaning is that many things are too hard to predict, but it is almost certain that in the long run they will have experienced a period of boom at first, which is followed by a period of decline at last (or vice versa). Have the experiences of individuals and even of nations just followed this kind of cyclical mojo?

Several years ago, when I was invited to revise the Guo family tree book, I noted that my ancestor, before his settlement in Henan Province, came from Fenyang, Shanxi Province, at the end of the Ming Dynasty (AD 1368–1644). Formally Prince Zhongwu of Fenyang, Guo Ziyi (AD 697–781) was a general who ended the Anshi Rebellion, characterizing him as the man who single-handedly saved the Tang Dynasty (AD 619–907). Guo Ziyi is reputedly one of the greatest generals in Chinese history and was revered as the most powerful general during the middle term of the Tang Dynasty. He also successfully participated in the expeditions against the Uyghur Khaganate and the Tibetan Empire. Future members of Guo's family would also go to become famous generals, among them Guo Baoyu, a general greatly used by Genghis Khan (1162–1227), and Guo Kan (1217–1277), Guo Baoyu's grandson and one of the best generals of the Mongol Empire. Guo Kan was the prototype of the leading character Guo Jing in the well-received Chinese martial arts novel titled "Legend of the Eagles Shooting Hero" (shediao xingxiong zhuan), or also called "Legend of the Desert Hero," which was written by Jin Yong in 1957 and was produced as the popular Chinese TV drama serial of the same title in 1983 and 1994, respectively.

However, not all of Guo Ziyi's later generations have been successful. For example, one of his grandsons, after having spent all the inherited property, became a beggar eventually. Below is a story about his begging experiences.

> One day, when the grandson begged in a village called Hexi (west side of river), he remembered that his wet nurse also lived there. When he arrived at her home, he was shocked by the riches there. But he did not quite understand why his former wet nurse's son was still busy in doing physical work by himself in the farmland. In response to his query, the son said: "A family's property, no matter how big it is, will be eaten empty. When my mother was alive, she had led us to work hard, so we just have this property. It is full of fun for us to be working hard and thrifty!" Guo's grandson was ashamed to hear this. In order to help him to survive, the son offered Guo's grandson for a job as cashier. However, after finding that Guo's grandson could do nothing about bookkeeping, the son could not help but sigh with emotion: "Oh, my! He has spent thirty years of luxury life in Hedong (west of river), but now he has to rely on other people for a living in Hexi (west of river) for another thirty years."

A Chinese proverb says "A family has three treasures: an ugly wife, a piece of infertile land, and tattered cotton-padded jackets" [Chinese: "jiayou 3 bao: chouqi, baodi, puomianao"]? Is that queer? Yes, even many Chinese, not to mention Westerners, cannot now understand what this old saying means. Before explaining its broad implications for the dynamic behaviors of civilizations and nations, let us look at a story relating to the Chinese proverb:

> A long time ago, there was a family of two brothers in the place of Dongming—now a county located at the southern bank of the Yellow river, between Shandong and Henan provinces. While the old brother was a farmer and doing some small businesses, the younger brother was still at school and thus did not provide any financial contribution to their family. As time went longer, the elder brother's wife began to show impatience: "All of us should contribute to our family by working and earning money!" As a result, the younger brother dropped out of school. One day, the elder brother took 100 silver and said to his younger brother: "You may use this money to go outside to do some business."
>
> The younger brother was a scholar. How could he conduct any business? So, after he left home, he went mindlessly before a river appeared in the front of him. There was a Taoist temple near the river and the day became dark, so he decided to approach it in order spend the night there. He was warmly received by a Taoist priest; and after knowing his story, the priest cooked food for him. After dinner, and seeing that the temple was very old, the younger brother decided to donate his only 100 silver, saying: "This temple is too shabby, let us fix it." One year later, the temple was fixed, looking much better than before. But when the younger brother was asked about how he would do in the future, he shed sad tears. Upon seeing this, the priest said to him: "After you go back, your brother must divide up family property and live apart with you. And when that day comes, please do not ask for

anything except your family's saline-alkali land and the tattered cotton-padded jacket which has not been worn by anyone for a long time. And, by the way, there will be a girl who is waiting for you on your way to home. Please do not mind her bad-looking and marry her."

Upon seeing his younger brother who brought back nothing but an ugly wife, the elder brother decided to divide up family property with him. Since the younger brother followed the priest's instruction, they quickly reached an agreement. On the next day, the new couple set up a new home—barely one with nothing but their only tattered cotton-padded jacket— on the saline-alkali land. Soon, after several serious floods, great changes occurred. The younger brother's land, though infertile and not suitable for agriculture, began growing a thick layer of white salt. In ancient times, salt was a big asset. Then, the couple started to do salt business. Two years later, they built a new house, and hired laborers. And his ugly wife was good at doing housework—they had a very happy family. In contrast, all other families were affected by the serious floods and thus could not survive. Then, the couple decided to provide relief to the people living in the nearby villages. Quite surprisingly, their elder brother family members were among the list of those waiting to receive relief.

In general, the three treasures (an ugly wife, a piece of infertile land, and tattered cotton-padded jackets) are used in this proverb to express the initial conditions of a traditional Chinese family. And, obviously, all these unfavorable conditions can still serve as incentives for the family to get rid of instability and poverty. Of course, it is difficult now to clarify whether or not the above story was real. Then, why has this queerish Chinese proverb been widely circulated among the people in China, especially in the northern, poor area?

Yes, as the German philosopher Georg Wilhelm Friedrich Hegel (1770–1831) said,

The real is the rational and the rational is the real.

Annex

A.1 Human and Geo-economic Indicators of the Old World by Country

Country/region	IQ	Average female height (cm)[a]	Distance from Ethiopia (km)	GNI per capita ($)
Afghanistan	84	164	4,607	700
Albania	90	162	4,804	4,960
Algeria	83	162	4,783	5,530
Andorra	98	163	5,873	19,000
Angola	68	162	2,625	1,840
Armenia	94	158	4,423	3,230
Austria	100	166	5,678	28,910
Azerbaijan	87	165	4,497	3,010
Bahrain	83	157	3,092	16,190
Bangladesh	82	151	6,150	1,720
Belarus	97	164	5,858	5,500
Belgium	99	168	6,367	28,130
Benin	70	159	4,067	1,060
Bhutan	80	152	6,315	1,969
Bosnia and Herzegovina	90	171	5,206	5,800
Botswana	70	159	2,976	7,740
Bulgaria	93	163	4,806	7,030
Burkina Faso	68	162	4,556	1,090
Burundi	69	159	1,426	630
Cambodia	91	152	7,495	1,970

(continued)

© Springer Nature Singapore Pte Ltd. 2019
R. Guo, *Human-Earth System Dynamics*,
https://doi.org/10.1007/978-981-13-0547-4

(continued)

Country/region	IQ	Average female height (cm)[a]	Distance from Ethiopia (km)	GNI per capita ($)
Cameroon	64	162	2,884	1,910
Central African Republic	64	159	2,000	1,170
Chad	68	163	2,604	1,010
China	105	156	7,867	4,520
Congo, DR of	64	158	2,034	700
Congo, Republic of	65	159	2,234	630
Côte d'Ivoire (Ivory Coast)	69	159	4,882	1,450
Croatia	90	167	5,386	10,000
Cyprus	91	165	3,817	18,650
Czech Republic	98	167	5,836	14,920
Denmark	98	169	6,614	30,600
Djibouti	68	158	1,303	2,040
Egypt	81	159	3,016	3,810
Equatorial Guinea	59	159	3,085	9,100
Eritrea	68	158	1,561	1,040
Estonia	99	165	6,536	11,630
Ethiopia	64	158	–	780
Finland	99	167	7,076	26,160
France	98	163	6,111	27,040
Gabon	64	158	2,928	5,530
Gambia	66	158	6,049	1,540
Georgia	94	165	4,594	2,270
Germany	99	168	6,178	26,980
Ghana	71	159	4,414	2,080
Greece	92	165	4,529	18,770
Guinea	67	159	5,486	2,060
Guinea-Bissau	67	159	5,972	680
Hong Kong	108	159	8,541	27,490
Hungary	98	164	5,406	13,070
Iceland	101	168	8,386	29,240
India	82	152	5,014	2,650
Iran	84	157	3,790	6,690
Iraq	87	156	3,614	1,027
Ireland	92	163	7,164	8,500
Israel	95	166	3,410	19,000
Italy	102	163	5,284	26,170
Japan	105	158	11,004	27,380
Jordan	84	158	3,344	4,180

(continued)

(continued)

Country/region	IQ	Average female height (cm)[a]	Distance from Ethiopia (km)	GNI per capita ($)
Kazakhstan	94	160	5,970	5,630
Kenya	72	158	905	1,010
Kuwait	86	156	3,334	17,780
Kyrgyzstan	90	158	5,833	1,560
Laos	89	152	7,548	1,660
Latvia	98	165	6,336	9,190
Lebanon	82	165	3,659	4,600
Lesotho	67	158	3,547	2,970
Liberia	67	157	5,305	1,000
Libya	83	159	3,744	7,570
Lithuania	91	164	6,184	10,190
Luxembourg	100	165	6,206	53,230
Macedonia	91	171	4,808	6,420
Madagascar	82	154	2,534	730
Malawi	69	155	1,672	570
Mali	69	160	4,760	840
Malta	97	160	4,582	17,710
Moldova	96	161	5,225	1,600
Mongolia	101	158	8,176	1,710
Morocco	84	159	5,755	2,000
Mozambique	64	156	2,166	990
Myanmar	87	159	6,667	930
Namibia	70	161	3,426	6,880
Nepal	78	151	5,737	1,370
Netherlands	100	170	6,440	28,350
Niger	69	160	3,689	800
Nigeria	69	160	3,465	800
Norway	100	168	7,179	36,690
Oman	83	156	3,034	13,000
Pakistan	84	159	4,673	3,730
Poland	99	165	5,916	10,450
Portugal	95	164	6,343	17,820
Qatar	78	161	3,074	19,844
Romania	94	157	5,164	6,490
Russia	97	164	8,402	8,080
Rwanda	70	158	950	1,260
Saudi Arabia	84	156	2,773	15,800
Senegal	66	163	5,934	1,660
Sierra Leone	64	159	5,575	500

(continued)

(continued)

Country/region	IQ	Average female height (cm)[a]	Distance from Ethiopia (km)	GNI per capita ($)
Singapore	108	160	7,317	23,730
Slovakia	96	166	5,590	12,590
Somalia	68	158	1,241	500
South Africa	72	159	3,856	9,810
South Korea	106	157	9,924	16,960
Spain	98	166	6,064	21,910
Sri Lanka	79	154	4,801	3,510
Sudan	71	158	1,885	1,740
Swaziland	68	159	3,137	4,730
Sweden	99	167	7,054	25,820
Switzerland	101	164	5,883	31,840
Syria	83	156	3,782	5,348
Taiwan	105	160	9,254	23,400
Tajikistan	87	158	5,394	1,640
Tanzania	72	157	847	580
Thailand	91	159	7,092	6,890
Togo	70	159	4,176	1,450
Tunisia	83	160	4,751	6,440
Turkey	90	156	4,238	6,300
Turkmenistan	87	158	4,837	4,780
Uganda	73	159	612	1,360
Ukraine	97	165	5,370	4,800
United Arab Emirates	84	156	3,093	24,030
UK	100	162	7,105	26,580
Uzbekistan	87	160	5,211	1,640
Vietnam	94	152	7,827	2,300
Yemen	85	159	1,921	800
Zambia	71	160	2,001	800

Sources (1) Lynn and Vanhanen (2006) for the data on IQ from 2002 to 2006 and PPP-GNI in 2002; (2) http://www.averageheight.co/average-female-height-by-country (accessed 2017-12-18) and miscellaneous news clippings for the data on average female height in the 2010s; and (3) calculation by author based on https://www.distance.to for the data on distance from Ethiopia.
Notes [a]Adult populations only. For countries whose data are not available, figures of neighboring or culturally similar countries are used. IQ = intelligent quotient; GNI = gross national income in purchasing power parity.

A.2 Data on Body Mass Index (in kg/m^2) by Country

Country/region	1980	2010
Afghanistan	20.95	21.15
Albania	25.18	25.95
Algeria	22.96	25.90
Andorra	NA	27.30
Angola	20.56	23.60
Antigua and Barbuda	23.75	27.85
Argentina	24.59	27.25
Armenia	24.85	26.30
Australia	24.25	26.95
Austria	24.36	25.25
Azerbaijan	25.37	26.75
Bahamas	24.97	28.35
Bahrain	24.56	27.90
Bangladesh	19.51	20.60
Barbados	25.47	28.15
Belarus	25.56	26.40
Belgium	25.04	25.45
Belize	25.10	28.45
Benin	20.86	23.10
Bermuda	26.23	NA
Bhutan	21.00	23.35
Bolivia	23.28	25.50
Bosnia	25.12	25.95
Botswana	21.42	24.35
Brazil	23.36	25.60
British Virgin Islands	24.22	NA
Brunei	23.08	26.00
Bulgaria	25.40	25.80
Burkina Faso	19.67	21.85
Burundi	20.12	20.70
Cabo Verde	NA	24.30
Cambodia	19.72	21.55
Cameroon	21.63	24.15
Canada	24.67	27.00
Cape Verde	20.69	NA
Central African Rep.	20.42	22.15
Chad	19.72	22.05
Chile	24.20	27.45
China	21.76	23.45

(continued)

(continued)

Country/region	1980	2010
Colombia	22.72	25.60
Comoros	20.88	23.75
Congo (DR)	20.26	21.95
Congo (R)	20.25	22.95
Cook Islands	NA	32.05
Costa Rica	23.54	26.55
Côte d'Ivoire	NA	23.40
Croatia	25.20	25.35
Cuba	23.24	25.70
Cyprus	24.55	26.80
Czech Republic	NA	26.85
Denmark	23.96	25.15
Djibouti	21.61	23.15
Dominica	23.61	26.55
Dominican Rep.	22.77	26.20
Ecuador	24.23	26.65
Egypt	24.83	28.75
El Salvador	23.71	27.00
Equatorial Guinea	20.62	25.15
Eritrea	19.29	20.50
Estonia	25.32	25.50
Ethiopia	19.12	20.35
Fiji	22.96	27.10
Finland	25.21	25.90
France	24.44	25.20
French Polynesia	25.88	NA
Gabon	22.16	25.10
Gambia	19.96	23.50
Georgia	25.23	26.75
Germany	25.08	26.15
Ghana	20.94	23.85
Greece	24.45	27.25
Greenland	25.18	NA
Grenada	23.62	26.45
Guatemala	23.04	26.15
Guinea	20.80	22.50
Guinea-Bissau	20.54	22.75
Guyana	23.18	25.85
Haiti	21.72	23.65
Honduras	23.05	26.05

(continued)

(continued)

Country/region	1980	2010
Hong Kong	21.64	NA
Hungary	25.17	26.25
Iceland	24.45	25.85
India	20.81	21.60
Indonesia	19.98	22.45
Iran	23.30	25.90
Iraq	25.58	27.55
Ireland	NA	27.25
Israel	24.54	26.05
Italy	25.30	25.90
Ivory Coast	21.17	NA
Jamaica	23.50	26.85
Japan	21.70	22.65
Jordan	26.08	28.65
Kazakhstan	25.00	26.95
Kenya	20.52	22.65
Kiribati	25.72	29.45
Korea (N)	21.86	21.80
Korea (S)	21.70	23.55
Kuwait	26.80	29.70
Kyrgyzstan	24.78	25.80
Lao	19.59	22.10
Latvia	25.32	25.75
Lebanon	24.07	27.25
Lesotho	22.85	24.60
Liberia	21.25	23.70
Libya	25.58	28.00
Lithuania	NA	26.50
Luxembourg	24.59	26.35
Macau	23.17	NA
Macedonia, FYR	25.37	25.65
Madagascar	20.50	20.95
Malawi	20.69	22.45
Malaysia	21.86	24.95
Maldives	21.09	24.80
Mali	19.66	22.45
Malta	NA	27.05
Marshall Islands	25.05	29.15
Mauritania	21.65	24.50
Mauritius	22.59	25.30

(continued)

(continued)

Country/region	1980	2010
Mexico	24.50	27.75
Micronesia	25.13	29.20
Moldova	25.81	26.50
Mongolia	23.94	25.35
Montenegro	25.73	25.85
Morocco	23.40	25.20
Mozambique	20.49	22.05
Myanmar	19.68	22.25
Namibia	22.05	23.90
Nauru	NA	32.60
Nepal	19.87	21.70
Netherlands	24.06	25.30
Netherlands Antilles	25.53	NA
New Zealand	24.70	27.60
Nicaragua	24.19	26.55
Niger	20.23	21.50
Nigeria	21.49	23.05
Niue	NA	32.00
Norway	24.16	25.85
Oman	23.98	26.55
Pakistan	21.65	23.50
Palau	25.91	29.35
Panama	23.74	26.60
Papua New Guinea	21.32	25.05
Paraguay	23.42	25.45
Peru	24.05	25.90
Philippines	21.20	22.85
Poland	25.49	26.20
Portugal	24.90	26.10
Puerto Rico	25.37	NA
Qatar	26.09	28.95
Romania	25.01	25.15
Russian Federation	25.86	26.20
Rwanda	21.02	21.70
Samoa	NA	31.40
Sao Tome and Principe	21.36	24.40
Saudi Arabia	25.67	28.10
Senegal	20.76	22.70
Serbia	25.87	25.70
Seychelles	23.40	26.45

(continued)

(continued)

Country/region	1980	2010
Sierra Leone	21.32	22.55
Singapore	23.04	23.60
Slovakia	25.82	26.30
Slovenia	NA	26.70
Solomon Islands	23.92	25.40
Somalia	20.89	21.75
South Africa	25.02	26.85
South Sudan	NA	24.85
Spain	25.22	26.60
Sri Lanka	20.63	22.50
St. Kitts and Nevis	25.82	29.15
St. Lucia	23.38	28.75
St. Vincent and the Grenadines	23.50	26.75
Sudan	20.77	24.85
Suriname	23.99	26.85
Swaziland	23.69	26.10
Sweden	24.54	25.60
Switzerland	24.45	25.15
Syrian Arab Republic	25.06	27.70
Taiwan	22.38	NA
Tajikistan	24.24	24.95
Tanzania	21.07	22.75
Thailand	20.86	23.80
Timor-Leste	19.68	20.90
Togo	20.60	22.90
Tonga	NA	31.80
Trinidad and Tobago	25.47	28.00
Tunisia	23.36	26.30
Turkey	24.88	27.45
Turkmenistan	24.25	25.80
Tuvalu	NA	29.10
Uganda	24.44	21.70
Ukraine	25.62	25.95
United Arab Emirates	26.06	28.85
UK	NA[a]	27.05
USA	25.23	28.50
Uruguay	23.71	26.45
Uzbekistan	24.41	25.55
Vanuatu	23.10	26.05
Venezuela	24.64	27.00

(continued)

(continued)

Country/region	1980	2010
Vietnam	18.79	21.10
West Bank	24.70	NA
Yemen	23.19	25.50
Zambia	20.52	22.35
Zimbabwe	23.45	23.25

Source Calculations by author based on (1) http://chartsbin.com/view/577 (for 1980's data by female and male); and (2) http://apps.who.int/gho/data/view.main.12461?lang=en (for 2010's data by female and male)—all accessed 2016-3-3.

Notes (1) Body mass index (BMI) is defined as a person's weight in kilograms divided by the square of his height in meters (kg/m^2). (2) All data are age-standardized estimates. (3) NA = not available. [a]denotes that the figure might be incorrect, which is therefore excluded from my analyses.

A.3 Racial and Geographic Features by Country

Country/region	White	Yellow	Black	SSA	AOI
Afghanistan	1	0	0	0	0
Albania	1	0	0	0	0
Algeria	1	0	0	0	0
Andorra	1	0	0	0	0
Angola	0	0	1	1	0
Antigua and Barbuda	0	0	1	0	1
Argentina	1	0	0	0	1
Armenia	1	0	0	0	0
Australia	1	0	0	0	1
Austria	1	0	0	0	0
Azerbaijan	1	0	0	0	0
Bahamas	0	0	1	0	1
Bahrain	1	0	0	0	0
Bangladesh	1	0	0	0	0
Barbados	0	0	1	0	1
Belarus	1	0	0	0	0
Belgium	1	0	0	0	0
Belize	1	0	0	0	1
Benin	0	0	1	1	0
Bermuda	0	0	1	0	1
Bhutan	0	1	0	0	0
Bolivia	0	0	0	0	1
Bosnia	1	0	0	0	0
Botswana	0	0	1	1	0

(continued)

(continued)

Country/region	White	Yellow	Black	SSA	AOI
Brazil	1	0	0	0	1
British Virgin Islands	0	0	1	0	1
Cabo Verde	0	0	1	0	0
Bulgaria	1	0	0	1	0
Burkina Faso	0	0	1	1	0
Burundi	0	0	1	0	1
Cambodia	0	1	0	0	0
Cameroon	0	0	1	1	0
Canada	1	0	0	0	1
Central African Rep.	0	0	1	1	0
Chad	0	0	1	1	0
Chile	1	0	0	0	1
China	0	1	0	0	0
Colombia	1	0	0	0	1
Comoros	0	0	1	1	0
Congo, Dem. Rep.	0	0	1	1	0
Congo, R.	0	0	1	1	0
Costa Rica	1	0	0	0	1
Côte d'Ivoire	0	0	1	1	0
Croatia	1	0	0	0	0
Cuba	1	0	0	0	1
Cyprus	1	0	0	0	0
Czech Republic	1	0	0	0	0
Denmark	1	0	0	0	0
Dominica	1	0	0	0	1
Dominican Republic	1	0	0	0	1
Ecuador	0	0	0	0	1
Egypt	1	0	0	0	0
El Salvador	0	0	0	0	1
Equatorial Guinea	0	0	1	1	0
Eritrea	0	0	1	1	0
Estonia	1	0	0	0	0
Ethiopia	0	0	1	1	0
Fiji	0	0	0	0	1
Finland	1	0	0	0	0
France	1	0	0	0	0
French Polynesia	0	0	0	0	1
Gabon	0	0	1	1	0
Gambia	0	0	1	1	0
Georgia	1	0	0	0	0

(continued)

(continued)

Country/region	White	Yellow	Black	SSA	AOI
Germany	1	0	0	0	0
Ghana	0	0	1	1	0
Greece	1	0	0	0	0
Greenland	1	0	0	0	1
Grenada	0	0	1	0	1
Guatemala	0	0	0	0	1
Guinea	0	0	1	1	0
Guinea-Bissau	0	0	1	1	0
Guyana	0	0	0	0	1
Haiti	0	0	1	0	1
Honduras	0	0	0	0	1
Hong Kong	0	1	0	0	0
Hungary	1	0	0	0	0
Iceland	1	0	0	0	0
India	1	0	0	0	0
Indonesia	0	0	0	0	1
Iran	1	0	0	0	0
Iraq	1	0	0	0	0
Ireland	1	0	0	0	0
Israel	1	0	0	0	0
Italy	1	0	0	0	0
Jamaica	0	0	1	0	1
Japan	0	1	0	0	0
Jordan	1	0	0	0	0
Kazakhstan	1	0	0	0	0
Kenya	0	0	1	1	0
Kiribati	0	0	0	0	1
Korea (South)	0	1	0	0	0
Kuwait	1	0	0	0	0
Kyrgyzstan	1	0	0	0	0
Laos	0	1	0	0	0
Latvia	1	0	0	0	0
Lebanon	1	0	0	0	0
Lesotho	0	0	1	1	0
Liberia	0	0	1	1	0
Libya	1	0	0	0	0
Lithuania	1	0	0	0	0
Luxembourg	1	0	0	0	0
Macau	0	1	0	0	0
Macedonia	1	0	0	0	0

(continued)

(continued)

Country/region	White	Yellow	Black	SSA	AOI
Madagascar	0	0	1	1	0
Malawi	0	0	1	1	0
Malaysia	0	1	0	0	1
Mali	0	0	1	1	0
Malta	0	0	0	0	1
Marshall Islands	0	0	0	0	1
Mauritania	0	0	1	1	0
Mauritius	1	0	0	1	0
Mexico	1	0	0	0	1
Micronesia	0	0	0	0	1
Moldova	1	0	0	0	0
Mongolia	0	1	0	0	0
Montenegro	1	0	0	0	0
Morocco	1	0	0	0	0
Mozambique	0	0	1	1	0
Myanmar	0	1	0	0	0
Namibia	0	0	1	1	0
Nepal	1	0	0	0	0
Netherlands	1	0	0	0	0
New Zealand	1	0	0	0	1
Nicaragua	0	0	0	0	1
Niger	0	0	1	1	0
Nigeria	0	0	1	0	0
Norway	1	0	0	0	0
Oman	1	0	0	0	0
Pakistan	1	0	0	0	0
Panama	0	0	0	0	1
Papua New Guinea	0	0	0	0	1
Paraguay	0	0	0	0	1
Peru	0	0	0	0	1
Philippines	0	0	0	0	1
Poland	1	0	0	0	0
Portugal	1	0	0	0	0
Puerto Rico	1	0	0	0	1
Qatar	1	0	0	0	0
Romania	1	0	0	0	0
Russia	1	0	0	0	0
Rwanda	0	0	1	1	0
Samoa	0	0	0	0	0
Sao Tome and Principe	0	0	0	1	0

(continued)

(continued)

Country/region	White	Yellow	Black	SSA	AOI
Saudi Arabia	1	0	0	0	0
Senegal	0	0	1	1	0
Serbia	1	0	0	0	0
Seychelles	0	0	0	1	0
Sierra Leone	0	0	1	1	0
Singapore	1	0	0	0	0
Slovakia	1	0	0	0	0
Slovenia	1	0	0	0	0
Somalia	0	0	1	1	0
South Africa	0	0	1	1	0
South Sudan	0	0	1	1	0
Spain	1	0	0	0	0
Sri Lanka	1	0	0	0	0
St. Kitts and Nevis	0	0	1	0	1
St. Vincent and the Grenadines	0	0	1	0	1
Sudan	0	0	1	1	0
Suriname	0	0	1	0	1
Swaziland	0	0	1	1	0
Sweden	1	0	0	0	0
Switzerland	1	0	0	0	0
Syria	1	0	0	0	0
Taiwan	0	1	0	0	0
Tajikistan	1	0	0	0	0
Tanzania	0	0	1	1	0
Thailand	0	1	0	0	0
Timor-Leste	0	0	0	0	1
Togo	0	0	1	1	0
Tonga	0	0	0	0	1
Trinidad and Tobago	0	0	0	0	1
Tunisia	1	0	0	0	0
Turkey	1	0	0	0	0
Turkmenistan	1	0	0	0	0
Tuvalu	0	0	0	0	1
Uganda	0	0	1	1	0
Ukraine	1	0	0	0	0
United Arab Emirates	1	0	0	0	0
UK	1	0	0	0	0
USA	1	0	0	0	1
Uruguay	1	0	0	1	0
Uzbekistan	0	1	0	0	0

(continued)

(continued)

Country/region	White	Yellow	Black	SSA	AOI
Vanuatu	0	0	0	0	1
Venezuela	0	0	0	0	1
Vietnam	0	1	0	0	0
West Bank	1	0	0	0	0
Yemen	1	0	0	0	0
Zambia	0	0	1	1	0
Zimbabwe	0	0	1	1	0

Source Author's calculations.

Notes (1) White, Yellow, and Black denote that if the countries are dominated by Caucasoid, Mongoloid, and Negroid, respectively ("1" denotes "Yes" and "0" denotes "No"). (2) SSA denotes that if the countries are in sub-Saharan Africa ("1" denotes "Yes" and "0" denotes "No"). (3) AOI denotes that if the countries are in the Americas, Oceania, or any islands that had been isolated from the Eurasian civilizations during the pre-Columbian era ("1" denotes "Yes" and "0" denotes "No").

A.4 Domestic Instability and External Threat Scores by Country

Country/region	Domestic instability (DI)	DI threshold (DI*)[a]	External threat (ET)
Afghanistan	7.8	1.7	1.1
Albania	6.2	5.4	1.8
Algeria	6.6	6.4	2.5
Angola	7.6	10.3	2.9
Armenia	5.8	3.5	2.9
Australia	3.6	3.2	1.6
Austria	3.6	8.5	1.3
Azerbaijan	5.2	9.1	3.7
Bahrain	5.5	11.6	2.3
Bangladesh	7.5	2.7	1.5
Belarus	4.8	8.9	1.6
Belgium	4.0	12.7	1.1
Belize	6.2	9.7	1.5
Benin	5.9	4.0	2.3
Bhutan	5.3	7.1	0.7
Bolivia	7.7	6.9	1.8
Bosnia and Herzegovina	7.5	5.1	2.0
Botswana	4.7	6.4	2.0

(continued)

(continued)

Country/region	Domestic instability (DI)	DI threshold (DI*)[a]	External threat (ET)
Brazil	5.4	1.8	2.5
Bulgaria	6.0	9.0	1.5
Burkina Faso	6.9	3.2	1.2
Burundi	6.9	1.5	3.5
Cambodia	8.0	9.0	1.8
Cameroon	6.9	2.9	3.0
Canada	2.8	4.9	1.9
Central African Republic	7.8	2.0	1.5
Chad	8.5	6.1	5.0
Chile	5.1	6.4	2.5
China	4.8	4.4	4.9
Colombia	7.0	2.7	3.8
Congo, Dem. Rep.	8.2	7.3	2.6
Congo, Rep.	6.3	14.2	1.5
Costa Rica	3.5	6.4	0.7
Cote d'Ivoire	7.8	8.4	0.9
Croatia	6.1	6.3	2.2
Cuba	4.2	3.8	2.3
Cyprus	4.1	8.0	2.4
Czech Republic	3.7	11.0	1.1
Denmark	2.2	8.3	3.3
Dominican Republic	7.6	3.7	0.4
Ecuador	7.7	4.7	2.2
Egypt, Arab Rep.	5.4	3.6	1.6
El Salvador	5.2	4.3	1.5
Equatorial Guinea	6.1	15.8	1.5
Eritrea	6.7	0.8	1.1
Estonia	6.7	12.5	1.4
Ethiopia	5.1	NA	2.3
Finland	3.2	6.5	1.2
France	5.3	4.3	3.0
Gabon	5.1	9.6	0.9
The Gambia	6.7	4.0	0.3
Georgia	6.3	5.8	2.7
Germany	3.8	7.1	1.6
Ghana	5.9	4.9	0.6
Greece	6.3	3.7	2.4
Guatemala	6.6	4.3	1.1

(continued)

(continued)

Country/region	Domestic instability (DI)	DI threshold (DI*)[a]	External threat (ET)
Guinea	7.5	4.7	0.7
Guinea-Bissau	7.5	3.3	1.6
Guyana	6.7	8.6	2.1
Haiti	7.8	2.6	0.7
Honduras	6.8	7.6	2.7
Hong Kong SAR, China	4.0	36.6	0.0
Hungary	6.1	13.7	1.4
Iceland	5.3	9.0	0.9
India	4.5	3.7	3.2
Indonesia	6.8	4.1	0.8
Iran, Islamic Rep.	6.2	4.2	4.6
Iraq	7.9	6.6	2.8
Ireland	4.6	17.2	1.2
Israel	5.5	5.8	5.3
Italy	5.0	4.2	1.4
Jamaica	6.0	5.2	0.5
Japan	3.8	2.5	1.8
Jordan	5.4	8.0	3.4
Kazakhstan	4.8	7.4	3.9
Kenya	7.5	3.5	1.8
Korea, Rep.	5.1	8.2	2.7
Kuwait	5.5	11.1	2.6
Kyrgyz Republic	7.1	8.6	3.9
Lao PDR	5.1	5.9	0.5
Latvia	6.7	9.0	1.5
Lebanon	7.0	6.1	3.3
Lesotho	7.0	7.4	1.9
Liberia	7.4	7.3	0.8
Libya	4.3	10.9	1.5
Lithuania	6.1	10.9	3.0
Luxembourg	3.6	29.8	0.3
Macedonia, FYR	6.6	6.6	1.6
Madagascar	7.1	4.2	0.8
Malawi	5.7	4.9	1.4
Malaysia	6.5	14.5	3.8
Mali	7.0	3.6	0.9
Malta	4.7	14.7	0.4
Mauritania	6.9	8.5	0.3

(continued)

(continued)

Country/region	Domestic instability (DI)	DI threshold $(DI*)^a$	External threat (ET)
Mauritius	3.5	8.8	1.4
Mexico	6.1	5.0	0.8
Moldova	7.5	6.5	0.6
Mongolia	6.1	7.8	0.5
Morocco	5.6	5.4	2.8
Mozambique	5.7	5.0	0.6
Namibia	5.8	8.0	2.9
Nepal	7.5	1.6	1.8
Netherlands	4.0	12.0	2.0
New Zealand	3.6	5.1	0.8
Nicaragua	5.9	6.4	1.5
Niger	7.5	3.7	1.9
Nigeria	7.0	4.2	1.5
Norway	1.2	6.6	1.3
Oman	3.9	9.5	6.1
Pakistan	7.8	2.3	2.4
Panama	7.1	11.8	0.3
Papua New Guinea	6.9	NA	0.3
Paraguay	6.4	9.2	1.5
Peru	7.0	4.4	2.0
Philippines	6.8	5.8	3.2
Poland	4.5	6.7	1.0
Portugal	4.8	5.0	1.6
Qatar	4.1	10.4	1.3
Romania	6.4	5.4	1.5
Russian Federation	6.5	4.9	7.3
Rwanda	4.9	2.0	2.0
Sao Tome and Principe	4.3	NA	0.3
Saudi Arabia	6.1	8.3	5.8
Senegal	7.5	4.2	0.9
Serbia	6.4	5.5	2.1
Seychelles	4.1	15.6	1.2
Sierra Leone	7.2	2.8	1.0
Singapore	4.7	33.2	2.4
Slovak Republic	5.5	12.8	1.2
Slovenia	3.8	10.7	1.8
South Africa	7.0	4.8	1.5
Spain	5.5	4.3	1.4
Sri Lanka	7.3	3.3	1.6

(continued)

(continued)

Country/region	Domestic instability (DI)	DI threshold (DI*)[a]	External threat (ET)
Sudan	8.0	3.3	1.5
Swaziland	4.7	9.8	2.1
Sweden	3.2	7.7	0.7
Switzerland	3.4	10.7	0.4
Taiwan	4.3	6.7	NA
Tajikistan	7.1	2.6	3.5
Tanzania	5.9	3.1	2.2
Thailand	7.0	11.0	2.1
Timor-Leste	7.3	1.6	2.0
Togo	5.3	6.7	1.9
Trinidad and Tobago	4.7	9.6	0.4
Tunisia	4.6	8.4	0.8
Turkey	6.8	3.5	2.6
Turkmenistan	6.2	13.0	2.8
Uganda	6.5	2.9	3.1
Ukraine	7.6	8.5	2.8
United Arab Emirates	4.1	13.1	4.8
UK	4.6	4.8	3.9
USA	5.3	2.1	4.8
Uruguay	5.2	4.4	2.0
Uzbekistan	6.3	5.3	2.0
Venezuela, RB	7.3	4.8	2.6
Vietnam	4.3	12.0	4.3
Yemen, Rep.	6.1	NA	3.6
Zambia	7.8	6.2	2.9
Zimbabwe	8.8	6.1	0.6

Sources (1) The DI scores are from EIU (available at http://viewswire.eiu.com/index.asp?layout= VWArticleVW3&article_id=874361472, accessed 2015-12-30); and (2) The ET scores are calculated by author. (3) The threshold (DI*) scores are calculated by author according to Eq. (5.3) in Sect. 5.4 in Chap. 5 and the World Bank Database.

Notes [a]If a country's actual DI score is smaller than its threshold, then the ET implies a positive contribution to its economic prosperity; and if a country's actual DI score is larger than its threshold, then the ET implies a negative contribution to its economic prosperity. "NA" denotes that the threshold is not available since the country is not included in the regression.

Printed by Printforce, the Netherlands